THE ART OF THE START
2.0

THE ART OF THE START 2.0

The Time-Tested, Battle-Hardened Guide for Anyone Starting Anything

Guy Kawasaki

PORTFOLIO / PENGUIN

PORTFOLIO / PENGUIN
Published by the Penguin Group
Penguin Group (USA) LLC
375 Hudson Street
New York, New York 10014

USA | Canada | UK | Ireland | Australia | New Zealand | India | South Africa | China
penguin.com
A Penguin Random House Company
This edition published by Portfolio / Penguin, a member of Penguin Group (USA) LLC, 2015

This is a revised and expanded edition of *The Art of the Start* (Portfolio, 2004).

Illustrations credits

Art 01_01: McDonald's Corporation; 01_03: Derek Sivers; 02_02: AP Photo/Paul Sakuma; 02_05: © Beech-Nut
Nutrition Company 2014; 02_06: Stephen Brashear; 04_01: Courtesy of Herman Miller, Inc.; 05_01: IndieGogo;
06_02: U.S. Air Force; 06_03: Courtesy of Guy Kawasaki; 08_02: Google Inc; 08_03: Adam Lee, AirAsia; 08_04:
Courtesy of Guy Kawasaki; 08_05: Courtesy of SCOTTeVEST; 08_06: Courtesy of Guy Kawasaki; 09_01:
Cadbury profile on Google+; 09_02: Peggy Fitzpatrick; 12_01: Courtesy of Guy Kawasaki; 12_02: Jayme Burrows/
Stocksy; Art_Afterword: Photo by Jason Roberts, used by permission of Lewis Pugh; "What Do Entrepreneurs
Do?": Lindsey Filby, Illustrator, ©2015 Guy Kawasaki; BM_01: Courtesy of Guy Kawasaki

ISBN 978-1-59184-784-7

Printed in the United States of America

3   5   7   9   10   8   6   4   2

Set in Sabon MT Std

Designed by Alissa Rose Theodor

To my children: Nic, Noah, Nohemi, and Gustavo.

Children are the ultimate startup, and I have four.

Many years ago Rudyard Kipling gave an address at McGill University in Montreal. He said one striking thing which deserves to be remembered. Warning the students against an over-concern for money, or position, or glory, he said: "Some day you will meet a man who cares for none of these things. Then you will know how poor you are."

—Halford E. Luccock

Acknowledgments

In giving advice, seek to help, not please, your friend.

—Solon

VERSION 2.0

My thanks to the readers of my drafts. They suggested hundreds of changes that made the book more relevant and useful. Ankit Agarwal, Biji Anchery, Christopher Batts, Mark Bavisotto, Stephen Brand, Dr. Julie Connor, Gergely Csapó, David Eyes, David Giacomini, Oskar Glauser, Allan Isfan, David F. Leopold, Eligio Merino, David Newberger, Greta Newborn, Mike Sax, Derek Sivers, Dale Sizemore, Eleanor Starr, Steven Stralser, Leslie Tiongco, Julius Vincze, and Maruf Yusupov.

Special thanks to these folks, who went above and beyond the call of duty: Raymond Camden, Mark Coopersmith, Andy Dahlen, Peg Fitzpatrick, Michael Hall, Chelsea Hunersen, Mohanjit Jolly, Bill Joos, Doug Leone, Bill Reichert, Beryl Reid, Peter Relan, Mike Scanlin, Ian Sobieski, Stacy Teet, and Hung Tran.

My gratitude to the Portfolio team: Rick Kot, Will Weisser, Adrian Zackheim, Diego Núñez, Stefanie Rosenblum, Victoria Miller, and Tara Gilbride. It's good to work with the A Team again. It's good to be working with you guys again. I hope I didn't drive you too crazy. And finally thank you Sloan "Hitman" Harris. I'm glad you are on my side.

Contents

Write what you know.
That should leave you with a lot of free time.

—Howard Nemerov

Obligation

Read Me First

I have never thought of writing for reputation and honor.
What I have in my heart must come out;
that is the reason why I compose.

—Ludwig van Beethoven

"If I knew then what I know now." Most experienced entrepreneurs say this at some point. My goal is that you won't have to because you read this book.

I've started three companies, invested in ten, and advised organizations as small as two people and as large as Google. I've worked for Apple twice, and I'm the chief evangelist of a startup called Canva. Hundreds of entrepreneurs have pitched me—until my right ear won't stop ringing.

When it comes to startups, I've been there and done that several times over. Now I'm doing what techies call a "core dump," or recording what's in my memory. My knowledge comes from my scars—in other words, you will benefit from my hindsight.

My goal is simple and pure: I want to make entrepreneurship easier for you. When I die, I want people to say, "Guy empowered me." I want *lots of* people to say this, so this book is for a broad population:

1. Guys and gals in garages, dorms, and offices creating the next big thing

2. Brave souls in established companies bringing new products to market

3. Social entrepreneurs in nonprofits making the world a better place

Great companies. Great divisions. Great schools. Great churches. Great nonprofits. Great entrepreneurs. That's the plan. A few details before we start:

- My original intent was to merely update the book. However, I kept adding, altering, and deleting. Thus, this isn't a "1.1" kind of revision. This is a "2.0," whole-integer, real-man revision. When my editor at Penguin told me to turn on Track Changes in Word, so that copyediting would be easy, I LOLed. Version 2.0 is 64 percent longer than version 1.0.

- For brevity, and because entrepreneurs are more similar than different, I use the word "startup" to refer to any new venture—profit or not-for-profit—and the word "product" to refer to any new product, service, or idea. You can apply the lessons of this book to start almost anything, so don't get hung up on semantics.

- If you're reading the paper version of this book, you'll see text that is underlined and italicized. This text is hyperlinked in the e-book version. You don't need to buy the e-book, but I guarantee that you will gain more than the cost of the e-book in additional knowledge if you did.

- For every recommendation, there is an exception, and I could also be wrong. Learning by anecdote is risky, but waiting for scientific proof is too. Remember, few things are right or wrong in entrepreneurship—there's only what works and what doesn't work.

I assume that your goal is to change the world—not study it. Entrepreneurship is about doing, not learning to do. If your attitude is "Cut the crap—let's get going," you're reading the right book by the right author. Onward . . .

Guy Kawasaki
Silicon Valley, California
GuyKawasaki@gmail.com

CONCEPTION

CHAPTER 1

The Art of Starting Up

The most exciting phrase to hear in science, the one that heralds new discoveries, is not "Eureka!" (I found it!) but "That's funny . . ."

—Isaac Asimov

GIST (Great Ideas for Starting Things)

It's much easier to do things right from the start than to fix them later. At this stage, you are forming the DNA of your startup, and this genetic code is permanent. By paying attention to a few important issues, you can build the right foundation and free yourself to concentrate on the big challenges. This chapter explains how to start a startup.

Answer Simple Questions

There is a myth that successful companies begin with grandiose ambitions. The implication is that entrepreneurs should start with megalomaniacal goals in order to succeed. To the contrary, my observation is that great companies began by asking simple questions:

- **THEREFORE, WHAT?*** This question arises when you spot or predict a trend and wonder about its consequences. It works like this: "Everyone will have a smartphone with a camera and Internet

---

* Inspired by *The Art of Profitability* by Adrian Slywotzsky.

access." Therefore, what? "They will be able to take pictures and share them." Therefore, what? "We should create an app that lets people upload their photos, rate the photos of others, and post comments." And, voila, there's <u>Instagram</u>.

- **ISN'T THIS INTERESTING?** Intellectual curiosity and accidental discovery power this method. Spencer Silver was trying to make glue but created a substance that barely holds paper together. This oddity led to <u>Post-it Notes</u>. Ray Kroc was an appliance salesman who noticed that a small restaurant in the middle of nowhere ordered eight mixers. He visited the restaurant out of curiosity, and it impressed him with its success. He pitched the idea of similar restaurants to Dick and Mac McDonald, and the rest is history.

- **IS THERE A BETTER WAY?** Frustration with the current state of the art is the hallmark of this path. Ferdinand Porsche once said, "In the beginning I looked around and, not finding the automobile of my dreams, decided to build it myself."* Steve Wozniak built the

---

* *Forbes FYI* (Winter 2003): 21.

Apple I because he believed there was a better way to access computers than having to work for the government, a university, or a large company. Larry Page and Sergey Brin thought measuring inbound links was a better way to prioritize search results and started Google.

- **WHY DOESN'T OUR COMPANY DO THIS?** Frustration with your current employer is the catalyzing force in this case. You're familiar with the customers in a market and their needs. You tell your management that the company should create a product because customers need it, but management doesn't listen to you. Finally, you give up and do it yourself.

- **IT'S POSSIBLE, SO WHY DON'T WE MAKE IT?** Markets for big innovations are seldom proven in advance, so a what-the-hell attitude characterizes this path. For example, back in the 1970s a portable phone was incomprehensible to most people when Motorola invented it. At the time, phones were linked to places, not people. However, <u>Martin Cooper</u> and the engineers at Motorola went ahead and made it, and the rest is history. Don't let anyone tell you that the "If we build it, they will come" theory doesn't work.

"The genesis of great companies is answering simple questions that change the world, not the desire to become rich."

- **WHERE IS THE MARKET LEADER WEAK?** Three conditions make a market leader vulnerable: First, when the leader is committed to a way of doing business. For example, IBM distributed computers through resellers, so Dell could innovate by selling direct. Second, when the customers of the leader are dissatisfied. For example, the necessity to drive to Blockbuster stores to pick up and return videos opened the door for Netflix. Third, when the market leader is milking a cash cow and stops innovating. This is what made Microsoft Office susceptible to Google Docs.

"How can we make a boatload of money?" is not one of the questions. Call me idealistic, but the genesis of great companies is answering simple questions that change the world, not the desire to become rich.

EXERCISE

Complete this sentence: If your startup never existed, the world would be worse off because _____.

Find Your Sweet Spot

If you have the answer to a simple question, the next step is to find a viable sweet spot in the market. Mark Coopersmith, coauthor of _The Other "F" Word: Failure—Wise Lessons for Breakthrough Innovation and Growth_, and senior fellow at the Haas School of Business, helps entrepreneurs do this by using a Venn diagram with three factors:

- **EXPERTISE**. This is the sum total of what you and your founders can do. Though you won't yet have a complete team, you must have a core of fundamental knowledge and ability to create something in order for a startup to start up.

- **OPPORTUNITY**. There are two kinds of opportunities: an existing market and a potential one. Either is okay, but do a reality check of the size of the market in the next few years. There's a reason people rob banks, not thrift stores. There are times, however, when there's no way to prove that an opportunity exists and you just have to believe.

- **PASSION**. This one is tricky because it's not clear whether passion causes success or success causes passion. Everyone assumes the former is true, but let's be honest: it's easy to get excited about a business that takes off, so the latter may be true too. Still, success may take a long time, so you'd better at least not hate what you're doing.

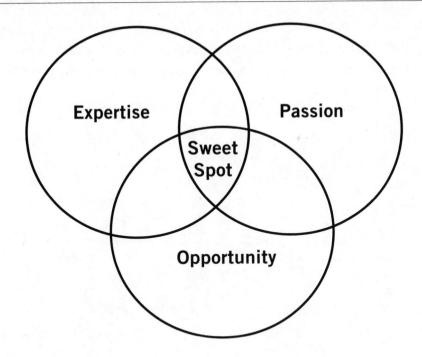

Don't get the impression that all three factors are necessary or even obvious at the start. If you have at least two of the factors, you can often develop the third if you try hard enough.

Find Soul Mates

The next step is to find some soul mates to <u>go on your adventure</u>—think Bilbo Baggins in *The Fellowship of the Ring*. However, people love the notion of the sole innovator: Thomas Edison (lightbulb), Steve Jobs (Macintosh), Henry Ford (Model T), Anita Roddick (The Body Shop), and Richard Branson (Virgin Airlines). It's wrong.

Successful companies are usually started, and become successful, with the contributions of at least two soul mates. After the fact, people may recognize one founder as the innovator, but it takes a team to make a new venture work.

"The first follower is what transforms the lone nut into a leader."

To illustrate this concept, Derek Sivers, the founder of <u>CD Baby</u>, showed <u>a video at the TED2010 conference</u> that starts with one person dancing alone in a field. A second person joins in, and then a third, and the crowd "tips" into a full-scale dance festival.

According to Sivers, the first follower plays an important role because he brings credibility to the leader. Subsequent followers emulate the first follower, not only the leader. In his words, "The first follower is what transforms the lone nut into a leader," and in a startup, that first follower is usually a cofounder.

Cofounding soul mates need to have both similarities and differences. The key desirable similarities are:

- **VISION**. Although this has become an overused word uttered by wannabe visionaries, in the context of soul mates, it means that founders share a similar intuition for how the startup and market will evolve. For example, if one founder believes that computers will remain a business tool for large organizations, and the other believes the future is small, cheap, and easy-to-use personal computers for everyone, they aren't a good match.

- **SIZE**. Not everyone wants to build an empire. Not everyone wants a lifestyle business. There aren't right and wrong expectations; there are only expectations that match or don't match. This doesn't mean founders can know what they want at the start, but it's nice if they're at least on the same page.

- **COMMITMENT**. Founders should share the same level of commitment. Does the startup, family, or a balanced life come first? It's hard to make a startup work when the founders have different priorities. One founder wanting to work for two years and flipping the startup for a quick sale and the other wanting to create a company that will endure for decades will create problems. Ideally, founders agree that they're in it for at least ten years.

The differences that are desirable include:

- **EXPERTISE**. At a minimum, a startup needs at least one person to make the product (Steve Wozniak) and one person to sell it (Steve Jobs). Founders need to complement each other to build a great organization.

- **ORIENTATION**. Some people like to sweat the details. Others like to ignore the details and worry about the big issues. A successful startup needs both types of founders to succeed.

- **PERSPECTIVE**. The more perspectives, the merrier. These can include young versus old, rich versus poor, male versus female, urban versus country, engineering versus sales, techie versus touchy, Muslim versus Christian, and straight versus gay.

Finally, a few words of wisdom about cofounders:

- **DO NOT RUSH**. Founders may have to work together for decades, so add them like you would pick a spouse—assuming you're not a serial divorcee. It's better to have too few founders than too many. Breaking up with founders, like spouses, is hard to do.

- **DO NOT ADD FOUNDERS TO ENHANCE FUNDABILITY.** The reason to bring in additional founders—and any other employee but especially founders—is to make your startup stronger and more likely to succeed. Ask yourself, "Would I hire this guy if we didn't need funding?" If your answer is no, you'd be insane to hire him.

- **ASSUME THE BEST, BUT PLAN FOR THE WORST.** Founding teams blow up all the time. Your startup may be the exception, but just in case, make everyone (including yourself) vest his stock over time to prevent people who leave in less than four years from owning large amounts of equity.

Make Meaning

Now take your answer to the simple question, sweet spot, and soul mates and assume that you do succeed. Then subject yourself to one more test: Does your startup make meaning? Meaning is not money, power, or prestige. Meaning is not creating a cool place to work with free food, Ping-Pong, volleyball, and dogs. Meaning is making the world a better place.

"If you make meaning, you'll probably also make money."

This is a difficult question to answer when you're two guys/gals in a garage who are writing software or hand-making gizmos, but it's also difficult to comprehend how an acorn can grow into an oak tree. If, in your wildest dreams, you cannot imagine that your startup will make the world a better place, then maybe you're not starting a tilt-the-earth company.

This is okay; there aren't many companies that tilt the earth. And there are even fewer in that category that set out to do so. But WTF, I want you to dream *big*. When today's humongous companies were only one year old, few people predicted their ultimate success or the meaning they would make. Trust me, if you make meaning, you'll probably also make money.

Make Mantra

The next step is to create a three- to four-word mantra that explains the meaning that your startup is seeking to make. For startups, the definition of "mantra" from the *American Heritage Dictionary of the English Language* is perfect:

> *A sacred verbal formula repeated in prayer, meditation, or incantation, such as an invocation of a god, a magic spell, or a syllable or portion of scripture containing mystical potentialities.*

Here are five examples (some hypothetical) that illustrate the power of a good mantra to communicate the meaning of organizations:

- Authentic athletic performance (Nike)[*]

- Fun family entertainment (Disney)[†]

- Rewarding everyday moments (Starbucks)[‡]

- Democratize commerce (eBay)

- Empower craftspeople (Etsy)

These examples illustrate the three most important characteristics of a mantra:

- **BREVITY.** Mantras are short, sweet, and memorable. (The shortest mantra is the single Hindi word "Om.") Mission statements are long, dull, and forgettable. From the CEO to the receptionist, everyone must know it. Compare the effectiveness of Starbucks's mantra, "Rewarding everyday moments," to its mission statement, "Establish Starbucks as the premier purveyor of the finest

---

[*] Scott Bedbury, *A New Brand World: Eight Principles for Achieving Brand Leadership in the Twenty-First Century* (New York: Viking, 2002), 51.
[†] Ibid., 52.
[‡] Ibid., 53.

coffee in the world while maintaining our uncompromising principles while we grow." I rest my case.

> "'Authentic athletic performance' is much better than 'Sell lots of shoes made in China.'"

- **POSITIVITY.** Mantras are uplifting and explain how your startup does good things that make the world a better place. "Authentic athletic performance" is much better than "Sell lots of shoes made in China."

- **OUTWARD FOCUS.** Mantras express what you do for customers and society. They are not selfish and self-serving. "Get rich" is the antithesis of a mantra. Customers want you to "democratize commerce," but they don't care about making you and your shareholders rich.

EXERCISE

Write your startup's mantra in this space: _____

EXERCISE

Think about how you serve your customers. What kind of meaning does your startup make?

EXERCISE

If someone asks your parents or your receptionist what your startup does, what would they say?

Pick a Business Model

You're likely to change your business model several times, so you don't have to make the right decision at the beginning. However, starting a discussion of this topic is important because it puts everyone in a moneymaking mind-set. All employees should understand that a startup either makes money or dies.

A good business model forces you to answer two questions:

- Who has your money in their pockets?

- How are you going to get it into *your* pocket?

These questions may lack subtlety, but making money isn't a subtle process. More elegantly stated, the first question involves identifying your customer and the need that she feels. The second question creates a sales mechanism to ensure that your revenues exceed your costs.

The best list of business models that I've found is in a book called *The Art of Profitability* by Adrian Slywotzky. Here are my favorites from his book:

- **INDIVIDUALIZED SOLUTION**. This involves a deep dive into customers' problems and doing what it takes to make them happy. Over time a startup can add deep relationships with other entities to reach significant total sales, but each new customer involves hand-to-hand combat. (Slywotzsky calls this the customer solution.)

- **MULTICOMPONENT**. Coca-Cola embodies this model, according to Slywotzsky. Coca-Cola sells in supermarkets, convenience stores, restaurants, and vending machines. The same product is sold in different business settings and at different prices per ounce.

- **MARKET LEADER**. Apple embodies the market-leader business model. A market leader creates the most innovative and coolest products. Attaining this position enables a startup to charge a premium for its products, but it must work brutally hard to achieve and then maintain this position.

"My daughter once bought $2,000 worth of 'treasures' for an iPhone game, so I know this can work."

- **VALUABLE COMPONENT.** Intel and Dolby don't sell products directly to consumers, but their products are valuable components in the devices they use. Intel supplies the computer chip for many hardware companies; Dolby provides audio-compression and noise-reduction technology for many audio and video manufacturers.

- **SWITCHBOARD.** Slywotzsky applies this term to describe an organization like De Beers, when it controlled the supply of diamonds. This business model involves several challenges: achieving control of supply and convincing people that that control is desirable and not subject to antitrust issues.

- **PRINTER AND TONER.** This business model involves selling a product that needs refilling. Whether it's an HP printer, a <u>Keurig</u> coffee maker, or a <u>SodaStream</u> soda maker, a sale is not an event but a stream of revenue for the course of the product's life. This can also apply to a startup that sells software and then charges for upgrades, service, and support. Slywotzsky calls this the after-sale model.

There are a few other business models that are attractive too:

- **FREEMIUM.** The freemium model involves giving away services, up to a point: when customers want more features or capacity or to remove advertising, then they have to pay. For example, <u>Evernote</u> enables people to store information in the cloud for free. However, if they want more storage space and more functionality, the fee is forty-five dollars a year.

- **EYEBALLS.** The eyeballs business model involves providing a platform to create or share content that attracts viewers. The concept here is that certain brands would like to reach these same eyeballs, so companies can sell advertising and sponsorships on the platform. <u>Facebook</u> and <u>Huffington Post</u> are examples of this business model.

- **VIRTUAL GOODS.** Imagine selling digital codes for items that had near zero cost of goods and inventory holding costs—stuff like virtual flowers, swords, and badges for members of a community. That's the digital-goods business. My daughter once bought $2,000 worth of "treasures" for an iPhone game, so I know this can work.

- **CRAFTSMAN**. Thomas Moser furniture is an example of the craftsman business model. This is the kind of startup that places the highest priority on quality and craftsmanship. It may never get large, but it's the finest in its sector . . . although with a marketplace like Etsy, you never know.

You'll tweak your business model constantly—in fact, it's scary if you don't change your model or do some major tweaking along the way. Here are some additional tips to help you during the process:

- **TARGET A SPECIFIC NICHE**. The more precisely you can describe your customer, the better. Many entrepreneurs are afraid of too narrow and specific a focus because it won't lead to worldwide dominance. However, most successful companies started off targeting a market or two and growing (often unexpectedly) to a large size by addressing other markets.

- **KEEP IT SIMPLE**. If you can't describe your business model in ten words or fewer, you don't have a business model. Avoid whatever business jargon is hip (strategic, mission-critical, world-class, synergistic, first-mover, scalable, enterprise-class, etc.).* Business language does not make a business model. Think of eBay's business model: charge a listing fee plus a commission. End of discussion.

- **COPY OTHERS**. Commerce has been around a long time, so by now people have pretty much invented every possible business model. You can innovate in technology, marketing, and distribution, but attempting to come up with a new business model is a lousy bet. Try to relate your business model to one that's already successful and understood. You have plenty of other battles to fight.

---

* Inspired by Michael Shermer, *Why People Believe Weird Things* (New York: A.W.H. Freeman, 2002), 49.

- **EXPANSIVE**. Business models involving creating a bigger pie rather than grabbing more of the same pie work better for startups. This is because customers expect to discover products that are innovative and cool and are less interested in me-too, better sameness from startups.

EXERCISE

STEP 1: Calculate the monthly costs of operating your organization.

STEP 2: Calculate the gross profit of each unit of your product.

STEP 3: Divide the results of step 1 by the results of step 2.

Weave a MATT (Milestones, Assumptions, Tests, Tasks)

A mat is "a heavy woven net of rope or wire cable placed over a blasting site to keep debris from scattering," according to the *American Heritage Dictionary of the English Language*. Preventing scattering is what's necessary for startups because entrepreneurs need to do many things at once. To stay in control, you need to weave a MATT, which stands for milestones, assumptions, tests, and tasks.*

- **MILESTONES**. Accomplishing a large number of goals is a necessary objective for every startup. However, some goals stand above the others because they mark significant progress along the road to success. The five most important milestones are:

  - Working prototype

  - Initial capital

  - Field-testable version

  - Paying customer

  - Cash-flow breakeven

---

* Inspired by Rita Gunther McGrath and Ian C. MacMillan, "Discovery-Driven Planning," *Harvard Business Review* (July–August 1995).

There are other factors that affect the survival of the organization, but none are as important as these milestones. Their timing will drive the timing of just about everything else, so you should spend 80 percent of your effort on them.

• **ASSUMPTIONS.** This is a list of the typical major assumptions that you might make about your business:

- Market size

- Gross margin

- Sales calls per salesperson

- Cost of customer acquisition

- Conversion rate of prospects to customers

- Length of sales cycle

- Return on investment for the customer

- Technical support calls per unit shipped

- Payment cycle for receivables and payables

Discussing and documenting these assumptions at an early stage is important because they are a reality check on the viability of a startup. For example, assuming that the length of the sales cycle is four weeks and finding out that it's a year will cause cash-flow problems.

• **TESTS.** You can come up with a solid list of assumptions, but everything is theoretical until you start testing them:

- Does the customer-acquisition cost permit profitable operation?

- Will people use your product?

- Can you afford to support them?

- Can the product withstand real-world use?

• **TASKS**. Finally, there are tasks that are necessary to reach milestones and test assumptions. Any activities that don't contribute to achieving them are not crucial and are low priority. Essential tasks include:

- Recruiting employees

- Finding vendors

- Setting up accounting and payroll systems

- Filing legal documents

The point of the list of tasks is to understand and appreciate the totality of what your startup has to accomplish and prevent important items from slipping through the cracks in the early, often euphoric, days.

Once you have your MATT, the next steps are to communicate it to the entire company, make revisions, begin implementation, and monitor results. Of all things, your MATT is not something to create and never refer to again. It is the epitome of a document to put to work and to alter.

Keep Things Clean and Simple

You will face hundreds of decisions during the startup process, and there's often a temptation to optimize each one of them—sometimes by breaking new ground. However, it's best to focus your energy and attention on milestone issues. For everything else, go with the flow and stick to your MATT by keeping things clean and simple. My experience and expertise is with U.S. companies, but these are generally accepted entrepreneurial practices:

> **"In the United States, if your goal is to create the next Google, you want to form a Delaware C corporation."**

• **CORPORATE STRUCTURE**. Every country has different commercial entities, such as corporations, partnerships, limited-liability corporations, and cooperatives. You want a corporate structure with three characteristics: one that is familiar, if not comfortable, for investors; sellable to other companies or on the public stock market; and capable of offering financial incentives to employees.

In the United States, if your goal is to create the next Google, you want to form a Delaware C corporation. This is a separate tax-paying entity that can accept outside investment and can issue multiple classes of stock. Owners are not personally responsible for debts and liabilities, and losses are not passed through to owners.

If your goal is to create a small business that isn't going to seek venture capital and you don't aspire to go public, then consider an S corporation, limited-liability corporation, or sole proprietorship.

• **INTELLECTUAL PROPERTY**. A startup should unequivocally own or unequivocally have licensed its intellectual property. This means that there are no lawsuits, or any risk of lawsuits, by former employers and no charges that the intellectual property infringes on someone's patents.

Also, the intellectual property and licenses should belong to the startup, not the founders. This is because you never want a situation where a disgruntled founder leaves the startup and takes the intellectual property with him—crippling the startup.

• **CAPITAL STRUCTURE**. This refers to the ownership of the startup. There are four warning signs; they all belong to the If-I-Knew-Then-What-I-Know-Now-Hall of Fame:

- A few founders own the vast majority of the startup, and they are not willing to extend ownership to other employees.

- A small group of investors that doesn't want dilution of ownership has dominant control of the company.

- Dozens of small investors make managing shareholders a burdensome and slow task.

- Overpriced previous rounds of financing make an investment unattractive to new investors.

- **EMPLOYEE BACKGROUND.** Areas of concern include executives who are married to each other and executives who are related to one another; unqualified friends in high-level positions; and high-level employees with criminal convictions. These issues may signal that the startup isn't a meritocracy.

- **REGULATORY COMPLIANCE.** This refers to issues with state or federal laws and regulations, nonpayment of taxes, and solicitations of unqualified investors. Typically issues with regulatory compliance indicate clueless or crooked management—both are unacceptable and will hinder progress.

Experts have written entire books about these five topics, so don't make decisions based on my brief explanation of such complex issues. These are areas where you only need to learn that you don't know what to do, so that you can find an expert who does.

Do Something Cringeworthy

If you are not embarrassed by the first version of your product, you've launched too late.

—Reid Hoffman

When I go back and read the first book I wrote, *The Macintosh Way*, I cringe at its crudeness. When I remember the first Macintosh, I cringe because it didn't have enough software, RAM, or storage, and it was slow. When you look back at the first version of your product, you might cringe too.

It's okay. It happens to everyone. The first version of a product is always flawed, but how it evolves is as important as how it begins. The fortunate startups are the ones who are still around because they eventually got the product and business model right, so give yourself a break.

Addenda

Minichapter: How to Separate Contenders from Pretenders

Once upon a time there were two engineering PhDs who were clueless about how to start a company. All they knew how to do was code. They were so desperate for money and adult supervision that when an experienced businessperson showed interest and offered to help raise money, they, in their own words, "followed him like dogs."

However, this adult didn't know much about tech startups and caused them to make many mistakes in legal and financial matters. They parted ways but only after much aggravation and the significant legal expense of reversing incorrect decisions.

> **"There are many experienced, successful, and savvy business executives who don't understand the particulars of startups and venture capital."**

This is not an unusual story, and it's an understandable one. First-time entrepreneurs are looking for any particle of positive feedback, reinforcement, and advice, so they jump at the first sign of interest. The demand for adult supervision in the form of advisers, board members, and investors far exceeds the supply, so you may need to take a chance with people who are untested in these roles. If no one will dance with you, the temptation is to dance with the first person who asks.

People who started their own company or worked at a company before an IPO can probably provide good advice. People who have not started a company or joined a company after it went public probably cannot. Experienced, successful, and savvy business executives at large companies don't necessarily understand the particulars of startups and venture capital.

For example, how much do you think a senior vice president of Microsoft who came from McKinsey knows about starting a company? Here is an EQ (entrepreneur's quotient) test to separate the contenders from the pretenders. These questions will help you identify good advisers, board members, and investors (if you have the luxury of choosing investors).

1. What kind of corporation should we form? Answer you're looking for: "C corporation," assuming the goal is to create the next Google.

2. In what state should we incorporate? Answer you're looking for: "Delaware."

3. Do our investors have to be accredited investors? Answer you're looking for: "Yes." Answer that should scare you: "No."

4. Should two founders split the company right down the middle? Answer you're looking for: "No, you should allocate 25 percent to future employees and 35 percent to the first two rounds of investments. That leaves 40 percent for the founders to split among themselves."

5. Should we sell common or preferred stock to investors? Answer you're looking for: "Preferred."

6. Should all employees, including founders, go through a vesting process? Answer you're looking for: "Yes, everyone should vest because you don't want a founder to leave with a significant percentage of the company after a few months."

7. Should we pay consultants with stock options? Answer you're looking for: "No, stock options are for long-term employees, not short-term consultants. If you can't afford consultants, do the work yourself."

8. Can we get a bank loan to start our business? Answer you're looking for: "No," assuming it's a tech business. Tech businesses don't have liquid assets to use as collateral.

9. Should we use an investment bank, broker, or finder to raise seed capital? Answer you're looking for: "No, angel and venture capital investors view early-stage entrepreneurs who use a banker, broker, or finder as clueless."

10. What do we need our revenue projections to look like in five years to attract investors? Answer you're looking for: "No investor will

believe them anyway, but they should be as good as the closest comparable successful company that has already gone public." Also, you don't want money from investors who do believe your projections, because they are clueless.

11. How long should our business plan be? Answer you're looking for: "You shouldn't write a business plan. You should get customers."

12. Is there someone else you would also recommend who could be a good adviser? Answer you're looking for: "Sure, my expertise is narrow, but let me come up with a list of other possibilities." Answer you're not looking for: "No, you don't need anyone else; I know everything you need to know."

13. Do you think we need a real CEO? Answer you're looking for: "Maybe, someday. But probably not right now. What you really need right now is a great product."

14. Should we use a headhunter to recruit people? Answer you're looking for: "No, at this stage, you don't have the money and can't afford to spend what little you have on headhunting fees."

15. What should we tell investors when they ask us for the valuation of the company? Answer you're looking for: "Find out what three or four investors think is fair, and then get more market traction to push it up." Wrong answers: "Price it high and negotiate down," "Price it low and negotiate up."

16. What do you think the KPIs are for our business? Answer you're looking for: dependent on your sector and type of business. Answer you're not looking for: "What's a KPI?"

17. How do I build buzz? Answer you're looking for: "Build something great and use social media."

18. How big should our advertising budget be? Answer you're looking for: "Zero dollars—use social media instead."

Again, these questions are relevant to U.S. companies with Google-esque ambitions, but the same kinds of questions apply in other circumstances. Run away from anyone who wants to advise you who can't answer most of these questions.

FAQ (Frequently Avoided Questions)

Q: I admit it: I'm scared. I can't afford to quit my current job. Is this a sign that I don't have what it takes to succeed?

A: It doesn't mean anything. You should be scared. If you aren't scared, something is wrong with you, and your fears are not a sign that you don't have the right stuff. In the beginning, every entrepreneur is scared. It's just that some deceive themselves about it, and others don't.

You can overcome these fears in two ways. First, the kamikaze method is to dive into the business and try to make a little progress every day. One day you'll wake up and you won't be afraid anymore—or at least you'll have a whole new set of fears.

Second, you could start by working on your product at night and on weekends and during vacations. Make as much progress as you can, try to get some proof of your concept, and then take the leap. Ask yourself what's the worst thing that could happen. It's probably not too bad.

Q: Should I share my secret ideas with anybody other than my dog?

A: The only thing worse than a paranoid entrepreneur is a paranoid entrepreneur who talks to his dog. There is much more to gain—feedback, connections, sales opportunities—by discussing your idea with many people than there is to lose.

Also, if discussing your idea makes it indefensible, you don't have much of an idea in the first place. Ideas are easy; implementation is hard. My hypothesis is that the more an entrepreneur insists on a nondisclosure agreement, the less viable the idea. After several decades of work with startups in Silicon Valley, I've never heard of a company stealing an idea and implementing it well.

Q: How far along should I be before I start talking to people about what I'm doing?

A: Start right away. By doing so you'll be constantly mulling over your idea—as both a foreground and background task. The more people you talk to, the richer your thoughts will be. If it's only you staring at your navel, all you'll see is lint building up.

Q: I think that I have a great idea, but I don't have a business background. What should I do now?

A: If all you've done is come up with a great idea—for example, "a new computer operating system that's fast, elegant, and bug free"—but you can't implement it, then you have nothing. This is why you need a cofounder—until you've convinced other people about your idea, you may be a nutcase.

Q: When should I worry about looking like a real business, with business cards, letterhead, and an office?

A: Your priorities are wrong. What you should worry about is a working prototype. A real business is one with something to sell—not one where people have business cards and letterhead.

Q: Do I need an MBA to start a company?

A: Not at all—and I have an MBA. You need an MBA to fulfill the expectations of an employer. In the case of a startup, you are the employer. It's better to spend two years in the trenches getting the shiitake kicked out of you than mastering business administration.

Recommended Reading

Berger, Warren. *A More Beautiful Question: The Power of Inquiry to Spark Breakthrough Ideas.* New York: Bloomsbury, 2014.

Hargadon, Andrew. *How Breakthroughs Happen: The Surprising Truth About How Companies Innovate.* Boston: Harvard Business School Press, 2003.

Livingston, Jessica. *Founders at Work: Stories of Startups' Early Days.* Berkeley, CA: Apress, 2008.

May, Matthew. *In Pursuit of Elegance: Why the Best Ideas Have Something Missing.* New York: Crown Business, 2009.

Shekerjian, Denise. *Uncommon Genius: How Great Ideas Are Born.* New York: Penguin Books, 1990.

Slywotzky, Adrian. *The Art of Profitability.* New York: Warner Books, 2002.

Ueland, Brenda. *If You Want to Write.* St. Paul, MN: Graywolf Press, 1987.

Utterback, James M. *Mastering the Dynamics of Innovation: How Companies Can Seize Opportunities in the Face of Technological Change.* Boston: Harvard Business School Press, 1994.

ACTIVATION

CHAPTER 2

The Art of Launching

The best brands never start out with the intent of building a great brand.
They focus on building a great—and profitable—product or service and
an organization that can sustain it.

—Scott Bedbury

GIST

Launching a product is exciting. The only events that exceed it are the birth of a child or completion of an adoption. I can remember the introduction of Macintosh in 1984 as if it were yesterday. You can <u>watch it here</u> if you weren't born yet.

No one ever succeeded by *planning* for gold, so don't test, test, test—that's a game for big companies. Don't wait for perfection. Good enough is good enough. There is time for refinement later. It's not how great you start—it's how great you end up. This chapter explains how to launch a product.

Jump Curves

In the late 1800s and early 1900s ice harvesting was a flourishing business in New England. This involved people, horses, and sleighs out on frozen lakes and ponds cutting blocks of ice. Call this Ice 1.0.

Thirty years later people froze water in ice factories, and icemen delivered ice in trucks. These entrepreneurs didn't have to wait for winter or live in a cold city. They could provide ice anytime and anywhere. Call this Ice 2.0.

Entrepreneurs created the refrigerator thirty years after that. Instead of buying ice from a factory, people had their own ice factory—the first PC (personal chiller). Call this Ice 3.0.

"Entrepreneurship is at its best when it alters the future, and it alters the future when it jumps curves."

None of the ice harvesters started ice factories, and none of the ice factories became refrigerator companies. They defined their business in terms of what they were *doing*—cutting blocks of ice out of frozen ponds, freezing water centrally, or manufacturing water-freezing gadgets—instead of what they *meant*—convenience and cleanliness. Had they taken this perspective, they might have jumped curves from harvesting to factory to refrigerator.

The concept of jumping curves is an excellent model for entrepreneurs. Entrepreneurship is at its best when it alters the future, and it alters the future when it jumps curves:

- Typewriter to daisywheel printer to laser printer to 3D printer

- Telegraph to telephone to mobile phone to smartphone

- Cassette player to Walkman to iPod

EXERCISE

Does your product offer "better sameness" or does it jump to the next curve?

A tactical framework is helpful to jump curves. I use the acronym DICEE for this purpose. It answers the fundamental question: What are the qualities of curve-jumping products?

- **DEEP.** Curve-jumping products provide features and functionality that customers might not appreciate or realize at first. Customers don't run out of power and outgrow curve-jumping products. Google is a deep company. It offers search, advertising, operating system, digital store, social media, analytics, apps, computers, tablets, phones, home delivery, online storage, hosting, Internet access, maps, and self-driving cars. You could use only Google products and have everything you need for computing.

- **INTELLIGENT.** A curve-jumping product shows people that the company who created it understood their pain or problem. Ford, for example, sells an option called the MyKey. Parents can program the top speed of the car and loudest volume of the stereo into the key for when their kids or valets drive it. That's an intelligent product.

- **COMPLETE**. Curve-jumping products are not isolated gizmos, online downloads, or web services. They include presales and aftersales support, documentation, enhancements, and complementary products. For example, Kindle Direct Publishing, the collection of services that Amazon provides self-published authors, has almost everything a writer needs. This includes distribution in e-book, print-on-demand, and audio-recording formats, production services, and marketing assistance.

- **EMPOWERING**. Curve-jumping products make people better by increasing their productivity and creativity. You don't fight great products—they become one with you. I have felt this way about Macintosh since 1983—it empowers me to write, speak, and advise. I would not be who I am without Macintosh.

- **ELEGANT**. Elegance is the combination of power and simplicity. Elegance is what is not there, not what is. It cuts through the noise, captures our attention, and engages our hearts. Companies that create curve-jumping products obsess about design and user interface. There's a high degree of craftsmanship and love that goes into curve-jumping products.

EXERCISE

Are you creating a product that is deep, intelligent, complete, empowering, and elegant?

Pick a Good Name

A good name for a startup and a product is like pornography: hard to define, but you know it when you see it. If you want a good example of what not to do, look at the names of Japanese products. For example, if your goal was to confuse your customers, you could not do a better job than naming your cameras the Nikon D4S, Df, D3x, D810, D7000, and D5100.

Here's how to pick a good name:

- **CHECK OTHER USAGE**. Two websites are your best friends in the naming process: the U.S. Patent and Trademark Office and the

Network Solutions WHOIS database. The former helps you determine if your name is already used. The latter helps you figure out if domain names are available. A third website to check is the Twitter <u>Advanced Search</u> page to see if the Twitter name is available. You should also perform these searches on Facebook, Google+, Pinterest, Instagram, and LinkedIn.

- **PICK A NAME WITH "VERB POTENTIAL."** In a perfect world your name enters the mainstream vernacular and becomes a verb. For example, people "google" words instead of "searching for them on the Internet." Names that work as verbs are short (no more than two or three syllables) and simple. I look forward to the day when people "canva" a graphic instead of "design" it.

EXERCISE

See if the names you're considering work in this sentence:
"_____ it."

- **RUN IT PAST PEOPLE FROM OTHER COUNTRIES.** Use online translation sites to check the meaning of your names in other languages. Even better, once you're sure you have the domain, ask your social media followers what the name means in their language. You're more likely to catch slang and negative connotations by using human assets in this manner.

- **PICK A WORD THAT BEGINS WITH A LETTER EARLY IN THE ALPHABET.** Someday your organization or product name will appear in an alphabetical list. When this happens, it's better to appear early in the list than later. Imagine, for example, the conference directory for an event with a thousand exhibitors. Where would you like your listing?

- **AVOID WORDS THAT BEGIN WITH NUMBERS OR *X* AND *Z*.** Numbers are a bad idea for names because people won't know whether to use numerals (123) or to spell out the number (One Two Three). *X* and *Z* yield names that are difficult to spell even after hearing them, and they are late in the alphabet.

- **PICK A NAME THAT SOUNDS DIFFERENT.** A name should not sound like anything else. For example: consider Clarins, Claritin, and Claria. Which name refers to online marketing versus cosmetics and antihistamines? Even if you did remember, it's likely that you would associate all three words with one category.

- **AVOID MULTIPLE-WORD NAMES UNLESS THE FIRST WORD HAS VERB POTENTIAL OR THE ACRONYM SPELLS OUT SOMETHING CLEVER.** For example, "Google Technology Corporation" would have been fine. The name Hawaiian Islands Ministries, a para-church organization that trains pastors and ministers, becomes "HIM"—a clever homonym with "hymn" and a play on "Him"—that is, God.

- **CAPITALIZE THE FIRST LETTER.** I made a mistake when naming a company I cofounded called garage.com. Lowercasing the *g* made it difficult to pick out the name in blocks of text. The visual cue that the word was a proper noun wasn't there—you'd think that someone named guy (*sic*) would know this.

Don't Worry, Be Crappy

The first step in launching a company is not to fire up Word, PowerPoint, or Excel. There's a time for using these applications, but it's not now. Instead, your next step is to build a prototype of your product and get it to customers.

I call this, "Don't worry, be crappy"—inspired by Bobby McFerrin's song "Don't Worry, Be Happy." Eric Ries, author of *The Lean Startup*, calls this the minimum viable product (MVP). Ries explains the MVP concept in this way:

It is not necessarily the smallest product imaginable, though; it is simply the fastest way to get through the Build-Measure-Learn feedback loop with the minimum amount of effort. . . . The goal of the MVP is to begin the process, not end it.

I'd add two words to MVP and transform it to MVVVP: minimum viable valuable validating product. First, the product can be *viable*—able to get through the feedback loop and make money—but that's not enough. It should also be *valuable* in that it jumps curves, makes meaning, and changes the world. Let's aim high!

Second, your product should also *validate* the vision of your startup. Otherwise, you may have a viable and valuable product (which is good) but not necessarily one that validates the big picture of what you're trying to achieve.

For example, the first iPod was not only a viable product (early to market and profitable); it was also *valuable* (the first way to legally and conveniently buy music for a handy device) and *validating* (people wanted elegant consumer devices and Apple could transcend selling only computers and peripherals).

NOTE WELL: this is not permission to ship a piece of crap. Here's a good test: Imagine your product is a new car. Would you let your kids ride in it? If you don't have kids, then your golden retriever.

Worry About Adoption, Not Scaling

In the early days of starting up, the ability to scale is overrated. "Scale," in case you haven't heard the term, refers to the concept that there are processes in place that are fast, cheap, and repeatable because there will soon be millions of customers who generate billions of dollars of revenue.

For example, if Pierre Omidyar had to test every used printer offered for sale, eBay couldn't scale. If Marc Benioff had to make every sales call, Salesforce.com couldn't scale. If Steve Wozniak had to manufacture every Apple I, Apple couldn't scale.

"I've never seen a startup die because it couldn't scale fast enough."

Holding yourself to a mass-scaling test in the early days is a mistake—putting the proverbial horse before the cart. This is akin to wondering if you should start a restaurant because it may be impossible to scale the perfectionism of an executive chef for multiple locations.

How about first ensuring that people within in a twenty-mile radius like the food before worrying about scaling the restaurant? That is, see if the business will work at all. For example, a company that I advise called Tutor Universe provides tutoring service via smartphones. Think of it as Uber for tutoring.

The long-term plan was that students could ask questions about any topic and receive help in under fifteen minutes. However, in the beginning, a critical mass of tutors for every subject didn't yet exist. Many startups face just such a chicken-or-egg challenge: If you had enough tutors, you'd attract enough students. If you had enough students, you'd attract enough tutors.

What do you do when you're faced with this kind of challenge? The answer is simple: you cheat! You use your own employees to answer questions, and hire tutors in the Philippines (highly educated, English speaking, and cheap) until you can reach a critical mass of a marketplace. Skeptics and inexperienced entrepreneurs might object, "You can't scale if you have to use employees or hire tutors, because they are too expensive."

This might be true, but it doesn't matter. What's important is that you establish three key points: you can get the word out, students are willing to install an app, and they will pay for help. Your priority, in short, is proving that people will use your product at all. If they won't, then it won't matter if you can't scale. If they will, then you will figure out a way to scale. I've never seen a startup die because it couldn't scale fast enough. I've seen hundreds of startups die because people simply refused to embrace their product.

Craft a Positioning

Allow me to introduce myself. My name is Wile E. Coyote, genius. I am not selling anything nor am I working my way through college.

So let's get down to cases: you are a rabbit, and I am going to eat you for supper.

Now, don't try to get away! I am more muscular, more cunning, faster, and larger than you are, and I am a genius. Why, you could hardly pass the entrance examinations to kindergarten.

—Operation: Rabbit

Most people consider positioning an unnatural act foisted upon them by marketing dweebs or highly paid and clueless consultants. In truth, positioning goes far beyond a marketing exercise, management offsite, or retention of consultants. When done properly, it manifests the heart and soul of a new organization by explaining:

- Why the founders started the organization

- Why customers should patronize it

- Why good people should work at it

Wile E. Coyote understands positioning better than most entrepreneurs: he's a coyote, and he eats rabbits for lunch. Startups should position themselves with comparable clarity by answering one simple question: What do you do?

Developing a good answer to this question involves seizing the high ground for your startup and establishing how it differs from the competition. Then you must communicate this message to the marketplace.

- **CREATE ONE MESSAGE.** While it's hard enough to create and communicate one message, many startups make the mistake of trying to establish more than one because they are afraid of being niched and want the entire market. "Our computer is for Fortune 500 MIS departments and for consumers to use at home." Volvos are safe and sexy. Toyotas are economical and lexurious (*sic*). Pick one message and stick with it for at least six months to see what happens.

"Do you describe your offering in a way that is opposite to that of your competition?"

- **AVOID JARGONESE.** If your branding uses extensive jargon, the odds are that (a) most people won't understand your branding, and (b) your branding won't last long. For example, "best MP3 decoder" presumes that people understand what "MP3" and "decoder" meant in 2004. What happens when MP3 is no longer the standard coding format?

- **TAKE THE OPPOSITE TEST.** Most companies use the same terms to describe their product. It's as if they all believe that their customers have never heard a product described as "high quality," "robust," "easy to use," "fast," or "safe." To see what I mean, apply the Opposite Test: Do you describe your offering in a way that is opposite to that of your competition? If you do, then you're saying something different. If you don't, then your positioning is useless.

- **CASCADE THE MESSAGE.** Marketing departments typically assume that once they've put out the press release or run the ad, the entire world will understand the message. If you've crafted what you believe is the perfect branding message, first cascade it up and down your own organization. Start with your board of directors and work down to Trixie and Biff at the front desk and ensure that every employee understands the branding.

- **EXAMINE THE BOUNCE BACK.** You know what messages you send, but you don't know what messages people receive. Here's a concept: ask them to bounce back the message that you sent so that you can learn how they interpret it. In the end, it's not so much what you say as much as what people hear.

- **FOCUS ON SOCIAL MEDIA, NOT ADVERTISING.** Many companies waste millions of dollars trying to establish a brand with advertising. Today brands are built on what people are saying about them on social media—not on what companies are saying about themselves.

- **FLOW WITH THE GO.** While you should not let the market position you, it's also true that you cannot ultimately control your positioning. You do the best you can to craft a good message and cascade it to your employees, customers, and partners. But then the market does a strange, powerful, sometimes frustrating, but often wonderful thing: it decides on its own. This can happen because unintended customers are using your product in unintended ways.

For example, moms bought Avon's <u>Skin So Soft</u> lotion as insect repellants for their kids, and Avon now sells it for that purpose too.

- When this happens to you, (a) don't freak out, and (b) listen to what the market is telling you. Perhaps it has done you a favor and found a natural positioning for you. Is it one you can live with? In the end, it's better to flow with what's going rather than to prop up something that's not credible.

EXERCISE

STEP 1: Write a one-paragraph description of your customer's experience when she's using your product.

STEP 2: Call up a customer and have her write a one-paragraph description of using your product.

STEP 3: Compare the two descriptions.

Cross the Chasm

In <u>*Crossing the Chasm*</u>, Geoffrey Moore explains a new-product adoption life cycle that includes five different kinds of psychographic profiles: innovators, early adopters, early majority, late majority, and laggards.

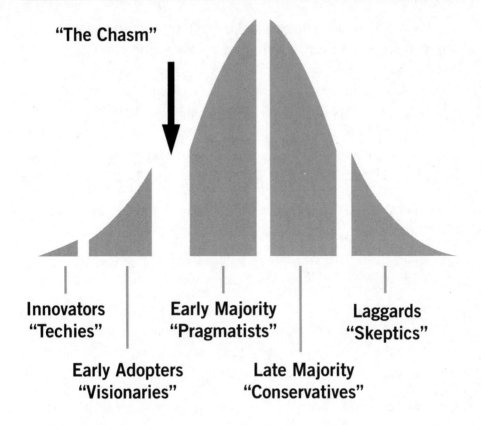

- **INNOVATORS**. These risk lovers seek out new products to try, so they are the people who have the latest and greatest before anyone else.

- **EARLY ADOPTERS**. They aren't the total geeks that innovators are, but they are confident they can put new products to good use.

- **EARLY MAJORITY**. Members of the early majority adopt a product when they see innovators and early adopters successfully use it.

- **LATE MAJORITY**. Late-majority customers are unsure they can handle new products. Thus, they wait until a product is well accepted by many people.

- **LAGGARDS**. These people resist new products and often buy them when they have no choice or the product is no longer "new."

The implication of these profiles is to direct your marketing efforts at innovators, then move on to early adopters, then early majority, and then late adopters ("crossing the chasm"). Eventually you sell to the laggards too. Each profile provides the reference base to succeed in the next profile—for example, innovators help persuade early adopters to take the leap.

There's no other way to put this: crossing the chasm requires sucking up, because innovators and early adopters are often bloggers, journalists, and other "experts." They expect you to curry favors. This is how to suck up:

- **BE REALISTIC.** It's much easier to help entrepreneurs if they have a great product. People want to be affiliated with products that are innovative, hip, and cool. The amount of sucking up you have to do is inversely related to product quality.

- **SHOW EMPATHY.** Who can resist a play on emotion? "Please help us. . . . We're just a little startup trying to make a go of it." Actually, I'll tell you who can resist this: buttheads who aren't worth sucking up to. The empathy approach usually works on me.

- **EMPHASIZE UTILITY.** The best suck-ups are mutually beneficial. You are not only getting something; you are also giving something. Or, if you're not in a position to give something right away, you promise to do so in the future.

- **PAY IT FORWARD.** According to social-psychology expert Robert Cialdini, if someone does something for you, you're obligated to do something in return. Therefore, one strategy is to do things indiscriminately for people and rack up points on the karmic scoreboard for later.

- **GO EASY ON THE FLATTERY.** You might think that this is the most important element in a suck-up, but most of the people you're sucking up to are frequently flattered (deservedly or not). Therefore, flattery isn't always effective. One sentence at the beginning of an e-mail is enough: "I learned a lot by reading *The Art of the Start*." Then focus on good reasons why the person should help you.

Plant Many Seeds

Just when you thought it was safe, there's an alternate approach to crossing the chasm. This one reflects the work of Emanuel Rosen and Itamar Simonson, which they explain in their book *Absolute Value: What Really Influences Customers in the Age of (Nearly) Perfect Information*.

Their idea is that the gradual-adoption, trickle-down approach that started when Moses went to see God is less applicable today because online information is getting fast, free, and perfect. For example, people can use websites like CNET and Amazon to read reviews hours after a product's introduction.

Innovators, early adopters, and early-majority users can express their opinions a few minutes after it ships—and with leaks, even before it ships. Information no longer trickles down; it disperses fast, free, and far. For example, in books, who waits to read a *New York Times* review before buying a book from Amazon?

The fast, free, and perfect nature of information can turn marketing upside down:

- **INFLUENTIALS MATTER LESS.** Many people can evaluate a product and spread their opinions immediately. Influentials still matter for reporting that something shipped but not necessarily for inspiring purchase or trial.

- **BRANDS ARE LESS IMPORTANT.** When information was incomplete and slow, people depended on a brand's imprimatur for quality assurance. In the book business, the average number of stars on Amazon and the first few comments that strangers have posted are more important and visible on Amazon than the publisher's name.

"Merit is the new marketing."

- **PAST EXPERIENCE AND LOYALTY ARE TRANSIENT.** In a perfect world the manufacturers of what you bought in the past produce great stuff in the future. In the real world, sometimes they do and sometimes they don't. For example, people may love the sharing features of Facebook but never use its e-mail service. I love my Macintoshes, but I use an Android phone; I don't use an iPhone just because it's from Apple.

All together this means that merit is the new marketing. Here's how to thrive in this world:

- **EMBRACE THE NOBODIES**. Lonelyboy15 and LATrixie are as likely to make your product a success as influential bloggers and traditional journalists. Anyone who gets your cause and wants to help is a friend to have. Nobodies are the new somebodies!

- **ABANDON THE ILLUSION OF CONTROL**. Omniscience and omnipotence are illusions. You can't know who can and will help you. Nor can you control people with your marketing and advertising. So blast your product out, and then flow with the go.

- **PLANT MANY SEEDS**. Plant fields of flowers, not flower boxes. This is a strategy of big numbers: the more seeds, the more flowers. You never know which seed will turn into a sunflower.

Which method should you use: Cross the chasm or perfect information? The answer is both. Some people you reach through influential, top-of-the-pyramid methods, and others you reach by blasting. As with other entrepreneurial topics, there isn't a right and wrong—there's only what works and what doesn't, and you can only find out what works by experimentation.

Tell a Story

I have watched dozens of product introductions by famous CEOs as well as by two guys/gals in a garage, and most of them follow the same script:

> Thank you for coming. We developed an innovative, patent-pending, curve-jumping, revolutionary, strategic new product after listening carefully to our customers.

This new product can slice and dice at a much lower price. Here's a list of vague features described with incomprehensible acronyms:

Blah
Blah
Blah

Now let me introduce Biff Smith, the product manager, who will demonstrate it since I don't know how to use it. We'll release the product sometime in the future at a price we haven't determined. We are announcing it today because we heard our competition is about to release a similar product.

This type of introduction (even a serious version of it) doesn't work because it focuses on information (and fails even to deliver that). People want more than information. They are up to their eyeballs in information. They want *faith*—faith in you, your product, your success, and in the story you tell. Faith, not facts, moves mountains.

Meaningful stories inspire faith in you and your product. Genuine influence goes deeper than getting people to do what you want them to do. It means people pick up where you stopped and go further because they have faith.

Here are four storylines from Lois Kelly, author of <u>Beyond Buzz: The Next Generation of Word-of-Mouth Marketing</u>, to help you inspire faith:

- **PERSONAL STORIES.** Epic is not necessary; illustrative is enough. For example, "My father owned a Cadillac, and he drove it 150,000 miles without major problems" versus "This car will last you a long time." Or, "I gave my teenage son an Android phone, and he told me he liked it better than his iPhone" versus "Android phones are good." Or, "My girlfriend wanted to sell her Pez dispensers online" versus "I wanted to create a perfect market." (This is the story that Pierre Omidyar uses to explain the genesis of eBay.)

- **GREAT ASPIRATIONS.** The hero wants to make the world a better place and knows that there must be a better way. Working nights and weekends and always believing in what he's doing, he creates a better gizmo that people love. To his surprise and delight, lots of people like what he creates. Example: Apple cofounder Steve Wozniak wanted to make it possible for everyone to use computers.

- **DAVID VERSUS GOLIATH.** Goliath has a head start, incredible resources, and a cast of thousands. There's no way that David can succeed against behemoth Goliath. But young David whips out his technological breakthrough—a slingshot—and succeeds despite the wisdom of the masses that there's no way he could. Examples: Southwest Airlines taking on the big airlines, Etsy taking on eBay, and Pinterest taking on Facebook.

- **PROFILES IN COURAGE.** Our hero suffers under major injustice. Despite these woes, he perseveres and accomplishes great things. When you learn what he has done, your reaction is "There's no way that I could have done that." Example: <u>Charlie Wedemeyer</u>, the high school football coach with ALS, and <u>Oskar</u> and <u>Emilie Schindler</u>, the couple who protected Jews during World War II.

A great launch is more than a press-release data dump, one-sided assertions, and boring sales pitches. It tells a story of innovation, change, and empowerment that catalyzes faith in what you're doing.

Provide a Safe, Easy First Step

You're probably making a big ask because innovation requires a change in behavior and defiance of the status quo. Thus, the path to adopting your product must have a slippery slope because of the size of the hill. This compels you to remove any speed bumps that you can. Here are the desired characteristics of a first step:

- **EASY TO START.** Companies often establish procedures that make it hard to do business—it's almost as if they are purposely trying to frustrate potential customers. The best example is <u>CAPTCHA</u> screens—the forms that people have to fill out in order to get an account on many websites. They are too difficult to read: upper versus lower case, I versus 1, and 0 versus O. I swear that this technology is called CAPTCHA because it captures folks in an endless loop of trying to prove to a machine that you're a human.

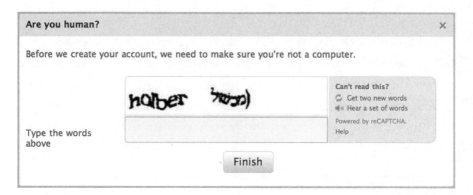

- **EASY TO CONVERT.** Ideally the slope to adopt your product is slippery and gradual so that the transition is easy. In tech businesses this means accepting your competition's data format as well as industry standards. In nontech businesses this means that your product uses the same plugs, packages, coupons, and practices so that people have to change their behavior as little as possible.

- **EASY TO USE.** Once you have people started and converted, the next step is to ensure that they can use and even master your product. This requires design sensibility, empathy for preventing frustration, and the ability to put yourself in the shoes of your customers. It means delivering an elegant, transparent user interface, clear and accurate documentation, and outstanding customer support.

"If you have a great product, getting in the door may be the hardest part of the battle."

- **EASY TO SHARE.** It's hard to make a product that's so compelling that people want to share it. If you do, it's a shame if there's not an easy way for people to share the good news about it. The next time you're visiting a website, look for buttons that say "Share this" or "E-mail this to a friend" and implement similar function-ality. AddThis and ShareThis are two services that you can use for this.

A positive example of providing a safe, easy first step is how a solar-panel company called Sungevity provides estimates. Whereas the first step for working with most home improvement companies is setting up an ap-pointment, Sungevity asks for your address and then uses a satellite photo to make an estimate of the size, power, and cost of solar panels for your house.

Get out of the Office

Buddha got out of the palaces where he would have lived if the decision had been up to his father. He saw how people living in the real world influenced his religious concepts. If getting out was good for Buddha, it's good for you too.

For example, Beech-Nut made a dramatic statement when it created a 100 percent natural line of baby food that contained no additives. This project started when Beech-Nut employees visited ten homes to watch how moms made food for their babies.

They learned that moms wanted total control of what went into the food and didn't trust manufacturers. Because of this research, when you see a jar of Beech-Nut baby food that says, "just pineapple, pear & avocado," it means there is nothing in the jar but apples and strawberries.

The Beech-Nut folks also saw that every mom fed her babies avocados because these fruits are a healthy form of fat and are easily digestible. At the time, no commercially made baby food contained avocados. Because the Beech-Nut people got out of the office, they added two avocado products to their line.

Simply shipping a MVVVP product isn't enough. Sure, you'll learn about its strengths and weaknesses from actual customers, but don't limit yourself to online comments and cumulative reports. Go and see for yourself how people are using them.

Conduct a Premortem

Doctors conduct postmortems to figure out why people died. They do this to solve a crime, prevent the death of others, and satisfy curiosity. However, once somebody dies, it's too late to help him.

Entrepreneurs and their investors also often analyze why a product, service, or company died—especially if it's someone else's company. And, as in the case of dead people, a postmortem is too late to do much good for a defunct product, service, or company. Enter the concept of premortems, coined by Gary Klein, chief scientist of Klein Associates and author of *Sources of Power: How People Make Decisions*.

His idea is to get your team together and pretend that your product has failed. That's right: failed, cratered, imploded, or "went aloha oe," as we say in Hawaii. You ask the team to come up with all the reasons why the failure occurred. Then each member has to state one reason until every reason is on a list. The next step is to figure out ways to prevent every reason from occurring.

You can't ask the team to report the issues and challenges, because regular meetings are governed by mind games and unwritten rules—for example, not embarrassing your friends, not looking like a poor team player by criticizing others, and not making enemies. You can't tell me that everyone is completely open and honest in these gatherings.

By contrast, people are not laying blame on one another and on other groups in a premortem (a properly conducted one, anyway). Everyone is compiling a list of all the *hypothetical* factors that may come into play. And "all" means "all," because it would be a shame if someone had thought of an issue but then dismissed it as not important enough to mention.

EXERCISE

Write a list of at least ten factors that could kill your launch. How many can you eliminate?

File a Provisional Patent

The final action to take during the launch of your product is to file a provisional patent application for your technology, practices, and secrets. Patent law is a complex subject for lawyers, much less entrepreneurs, so you'll need a lawyer who specializes in the area. To start, you can learn from the U.S. Patent and Trademark Office website.

The gist is that the United States is a "first to file"—as opposed to "first to invent"—country, so you need to move fast. Once you file a provisional patent, you have twelve months to decide if you're going to take it to the next level and seek a nonprovisional patent. It can take five years and $10,000 to finish the process.

If you get a nonprovisional patent, consider the practical implications of this achievement. The good news is that your parents will be proud of you. The bad news is that patents don't make your business defensible, because you won't have the time (years) or money (millions of dollars) to win and collect a judgment.

In the unlikely event that you do have the time and money, your startup is probably so successful that your success is a form of defensibility and you can hire the best lawyers to fight it out with the patent infringers. If you don't have the time and money, then it won't matter anyway.

Incubate (or Not)

When times are good, incubators and accelerators are the rage. First, some terminology: Incubators focus on providing office space and shared services. Accelerators focus on mentorship, training, and helping you make connections to customers, partners, and sources of capital.

> **"The difference between working in an incubator or accelerator versus in your garage is the difference between going away for college versus commuting from home."**

There are many variations in these programs, so here is an explanation of the various kinds of assistance they offer:

- **SEED CAPITAL**. Funding from $25,000 to $125,000 for 5 to 15 percent of your startup. This means the accelerator or incubator may invest the least amount of money of any outside investor. It's hard to say whether this is good or bad—but you should at least understand that accelerators and incubators often get great deals.

- **COMPANIONSHIP AND CROSS-FERTILIZATION.** This involves interaction with other entrepreneurs at a similar stage of development—misery loves company, and you could learn a lot from your peers. The difference between working in an incubator or accelerator versus in your garage is the difference between going away for college versus commuting from home.

- **MENTORSHIP AND EDUCATION.** This is the totality of the advice from the people running the program plus their advisers, friends, and connections. Ideally they are industry veterans and experienced entrepreneurs. Your task is to ensure that they have extensive startup and hands-on experience and are not just consultants looking for clients. (Be sure to read "Minichapter: How to Separate Contenders from Pretenders" in the previous chapter.) At many incubators, access to mentors is informal—for example, a periodic pizza night. Most accelerator programs, however, have a formal mentorship and education process that will give you more contact with such individuals.

- **BUSINESS DEVELOPMENT.** Introductions to potential customers, partners, and employees can accelerate your credibility, product development, and sales. The people who run incubators and accelerators all say they can make introductions, but you should check their claims with other startups in the program.

- **PATH TO FURTHER FUNDING.** Many incubators and accelerators hold demo days that can expose you to angels and venture capitalists. The incubator or accelerator will get you visibility but not necessarily an investment. Still, this is much more efficient than you trying to get an audience with these investors by yourself.

- **ADMINISTRATIVE TASKS.** Bookkeeping, payroll, taxes, insurance, and other nitty-gritty tasks are a pain, but a necessary pain. They drain your time, the most valuable resource you have. Some incubators and accelerators provide staff and expertise to help you with these chores that would distract you from your core duties: finishing your product and selling it.

- **OFFICE SPACE**. Shared office space, furniture, and Internet access are the main value proposition of most incubators, but these are ultimately not critical factors for your success. Therefore, don't make them a high-priority reason to join an incubator. The Ping-Pong table and espresso machine are nice, but you can always go to Sports Authority and Starbucks. The real value of coworking space is the flexibility it provides when you are not yet ready to sign a three-year lease on 2,500 square feet.

Some incubators and accelerators will ask you to grant them 1 percent or more of your company in order to compensate them for their services. This should force you to think carefully before joining one. This could be the best deal you'll ever make or a bloody rip-off, depending on how valuable those services turn out to be.

Incubators and accelerators are useful for first-time entrepreneurs who don't know where to start, but the decision to join one is not simple. You tend to hear only about the graduates of these programs that are successful—for example, Airbnb and Dropbox—and those companies will tell you that incubation was an important and valuable experience.

It's hard to make the case that joining one of these programs will decrease your chances of success. If nothing else, graduation from a well-known accelerator program such as <u>Y Combinator</u> or <u>500 Startups</u> is a proxy for quality, and everyone in the startup game is looking for a reason to believe in a company. A good analogy is college attendance: going to Harvard or Stanford can't hurt your chances to succeed, and many people use a Harvard or Stanford degree as a proxy for quality.

Graduating from an incubator or accelerator, though, is neither necessary nor sufficient to succeed. Plenty of people who didn't get into Harvard or Stanford do succeed, and plenty of Harvard and Stanford graduates don't succeed. It may increase the likelihood of success, but there are many other factors involved. Finally, correlation does not equal causation: the fact that a successful startup graduated from a program doesn't mean the program was responsible for its success.

Let's say that you don't get into any of these programs, or there aren't any in your area. There is nothing on the list of how incubators and accelerators can help that you cannot obtain in other ways—albeit, perhaps, in harder and slower (and cheaper!) ways. But alternatives do exist. There are many ways to fail, but there are many ways to succeed too.

Addenda

Minichapter: How to Be a Demo God

Acting is standing up naked and turning around very slowly.

—Rosalind Russell

Several times a year a group of executives from startups do a six-minute demo of their products to an audience of venture capitalists, analysts, and journalists. The name of this event is, logically, <u>DEMO</u>. It's a great occasion—especially if you understand the dance that's going on: entrepreneurs acting as if they don't need venture capital, and venture capitalists acting as if they don't need entrepreneurs. (This is like acting prudish in a brothel.)

This minichapter is for anyone who has to give a good demo, whether at DEMO or anywhere else. Demoing is an essential skill to launch a product, raise capital, make a sale, garner press, and recruit employees, so you must get good at it.

- **CREATE SOMETHING WORTH DEMOING.** If you want to be a demo god, create a great product to demo. Demos are excellent PR opportunities, but use them when you're ready, not when an opportunity occurs. If your product is mediocre and you don't do a demo, only you will know that it's unremarkable. If you do a demo, the whole world will know it.

- **BRING TWO OF EVERYTHING.** There is one place for duplication: equipment. Expect everything to break the night before you're on stage, so bring two, maybe even three, computers, phones, thumb drives, whatever you'll need for your demo.

> "If your demo is good, they'll hunt you down to learn more. If your demo sucks, it won't matter if you've won a Nobel Prize."

- **GET ORGANIZED IN ADVANCE.** You should never futz around during a demo—for example, looking for folders and files on your hard disk. You have weeks to prepare for these six minutes; you're clueless if you haven't set everything up in advance.

- **ELIMINATE THE FACTORS THAT YOU CAN'T CONTROL.** Should you assume that you'll have Internet access during your demo? Yes, but have a backup anyway. Sure, the hotel has Internet access, but what happens when hundreds of people use it at once? Better to simulate Internet access to your server by using a local server. You don't have to show the real system. This is, after all, a demo.

- **START WITH "SHOCK AND AWE."** I stole this from my buddy Peter Cohan, author of _Great Demo!: How to Create and Execute Stunning Software Demonstrations._ He believes, and I second it, that you have about one minute to captivate your audience, so don't try building to a crescendo. Start with "shock and awe"—the absolute coolest stuff that your product can do. The goal is to blow people's minds right up front.

- **CUT THE JOKES.** If you're wondering if your jokes are funny, they aren't. Few people are funny enough to pull off jokes in a demo. The downside of a failed joke—a loss of confidence and momentum—is much greater than the upside of a successful one.

- **DO IT ALONE.** A demo god works alone. You may think it's powerful if the two cofounders do the demo together, and you may think it will show the world how they're getting along so well. But it's hard enough for one person to do a demo. Trying to get two people to do an interactive demo is four times harder. If you want a duet, go to a karaoke bar.

- **CUT THE JARGON**. The ability to speak simply and succinctly is the best way to go. You may have the world's greatest enterprise-software product, but the consumer-device partner of your dream venture capital firm is in the audience. If she can't understand your demo, she's not going to tell her counterparts about it back in the office. What the audiences sees, not hears, should do the impressing.

- **DON'T TAKE ANY QUESTIONS UNTIL THE END**. At DEMO there's no time for questions—thankfully. But in all cases, you should always take questions at the end because you never know what people will ask you—their questions could take you down a rat hole so deep that you'll never come back up.

- **END WITH AN EXCLAMATION POINT**. Start on a high. Once you've blown their minds, then you work backward and show them the how. Not only is the what fantastic, but the how then makes it possible for mere mortals to understand that they can do it too. Then end on a high. This was part of Steve Jobs's keynote magic; he always had "<u>one more thing</u>" in his bag of tricks.

I've given this advice to hundreds of startups, and hundreds of thousands of people have read it online, but most demos still suck. This is because people think this advice applies to the great unwashed masses who don't have a curve-jumping, paradigm-shifting, patent-pending product like they do and are not gifted presenters like they are. You may believe you're one of them. You're wrong. You are the intended audience, and you're going to learn the hard way.

Minichapter: The Art of Intrapreneuring

Innovation often originates outside existing organizations, in part because successful organizations acquire a commitment to the status quo and a resistance to ideas that might change it.

—Nathan Rosenberg

Some aspiring entrepreneurs are already working for a big company. Like external entrepreneurs, they dream of creating innovative products. They, too, must prototype, position, pitch, bootstrap, recruit, fund, partner, sell, and support. The purpose of this minichapter is to explain how to do all this when you're employed by a large business.

Ironically, many entrepreneurs envy the employees of major companies— they think that these lucky souls have humongous financial resources, large sales forces, fully equipped labs, scalable factories, and established brands, plus medical and dental benefits, at their disposal. How wonderful it would be, guys and gals in garages muse, to invent a new product with the luxury of such an infrastructure already in place.

Guess again. Creating a new product within such a beast is not easier, just different. I collaborated on this minichapter with Bill Meade, director of data science at Neal Analytics. We came up with this list of recommendations for internal entrepreneurs.

"If you don't kill your cash cows, someone else will."

• **PUT THE COMPANY FIRST.** The intrapreneur's primary, if not sole, motivation should remain the betterment of the company that employs her. Intrapreneurship isn't about grabbing attention, building an empire, or setting up a way to catapult out of the company. When you have a good idea for a product, it will attract a large number of your fellow employees, from the bottom up. They will support you if you're doing it for the company but not if it's for your personal gain.

• **KILL THE CASH COWS.** Don't make enemies by telling the whole company, but your charter is often to create a product that will kill an existing product. For example, Macintosh killed Apple II. Would it have been better for Apple if a competitor had created Macintosh? Or that it never created a Macintosh and rode it to the end of the line? No way. This recommendation is another reason why it's so important to put the company first: what you're doing threatens the status quo, so it should appear to be in the best interests of the company, not your ego. If you don't kill your cash cows, someone else will.

• **STAY UNDER THE RADAR.** Two guys in a garage should try to get as much attention as they can. Awareness of their efforts makes it easier to raise money, establish partnerships, close sales, and recruit employees. However, the opposite is true for intrapreneurs. You want management to leave you alone until your project is too far along to ignore or the rest of the company realizes that it's needed. The higher you go in a company, the fewer people are going to understand what you're trying to do. This is because the higher you go, the more people want to maintain the status quo and protect their positions.

• **FIND A GODFATHER**. In many companies there are godfather figures. These are people who have paid their dues and are safe from everyday petty politics. They are relatively untouchable and have the attention and respect of top management. Internal entrepreneurs should find a godfather to support their projects by providing advice, technical and marketing insights, and, if it comes to the point where you need it, protection.

• **GET A SEPARATE BUILDING**. An intrapreneur, sitting in the main flow of a big company, will die by a thousand cuts as each department manager explains why this new project is a bad idea. "The new always looks so puny—so unpromising—next to the reality of the massive, ongoing business."* The Macintosh Division was in a building that was far enough away from the rest of Apple that it stayed out of the daily grind but was close enough to obtain corporate resources. A separate building will keep your efforts under the radar and foster esprit de corps among your merry band of pirates. The ideal distance from the corporate pukes is between one-quarter mile and two miles— that is, close enough to get to but far enough to discourage daily visits.

• **GIVE HOPE TO THE HOPEFUL**. Inside every corporate cynic who thinks that "this company is too big and dumb to innovate" is an idealist who would like to see it happen. Good people in big companies are tired of being ignored, forgotten, humiliated, and forced into submission. They may be trampled, but they are not dead. When you show them that you're driving a stake into the heart of the status quo, you will attract support and resources. Then your goal is to advance these people from wanting to see innovation happen to helping you make it happen.

---

* Peter F. Drucker, *Innovation and Entrepreneurship: Practice and Principles* (New York: Harper & Row, 1985), 162.

- **ANTICIPATE, THEN JUMP ON, THE TECTONIC SHIFTS**. Deformations in a company are a good thing for intrapreneurs. Whether caused by external factors such as changes in the marketplace or internal factors such as a new CEO, tectonic shifts may create an opportunity for your efforts.

Effective intrapreneurs anticipate these shifts and are ready to unveil new products when they occur: "Look what we've been working on." By contrast, corporate pukes say, "Now I see the shift. If you give me permission, six months, and a team of analysts, I can come up with a new product strategy."

- **BUILD ON WHAT EXISTS**. The downside of trying to innovate within a big company is clear and well documented, but there are also benefits. Don't hesitate to utilize the existing infrastructure to make innovation easier. You'll not only garner resources, but also make friends as other employees begin to feel as if they are part of your team.

If you try to roll your own solutions (as an extreme example, building your own factory), you'll make enemies. The last thing a startup inside a big company needs is internal enemies—there will be enough enemies in the marketplace.

- **COLLECT AND SHARE DATA**. The day will arrive when a bean counter or lawyer is going to notice you and question the reasons for your project's existence. If you're lucky, this will happen later rather than sooner, but it *will* happen. Prepare for that day by (1) collecting data about how much you've spent and how much you've accomplished, and (2) then sharing it openly. In big companies, data suppresses antibodies, but it might be too late to get the data once the antibodies appear.

- **LET THE VICE PRESIDENTS COME TO YOU**. Do you think that your first step should be to get your vice president to approve your project? It isn't. This is one of the last steps. A vice president will "own" your idea and support it more if he "discovers" it and then approaches you about sponsoring it. You may have to ensure that a vice president "accidentally" makes that discovery when the time is right, but this is not the same as seeking permission to get started.

- **DISMANTLE WHEN DONE**. The beauty of intrapreneurship is that it can develop new products in less time than mainstream engineering. Unfortunately, the cohesiveness that makes an entrepreneurial group so effective can lead to the group's downfall if the group remains separate and aloof.

The group's effectiveness declines further if its members come to believe that only they know what to do and if the group creates its own, new bureaucracy.* If the product is successful, consider dismantling the group and integrating it into the larger organization. Then create a new group to create the next curve.

• **REBOOT YOUR BRAIN.** Many intrapreneurs will find that the rest of this book prescribes actions that are contrary to what they've experienced, learned, and maybe even taught in big companies. The reality is that starting something within an existing company requires adopting new patterns of behavior—essentially, rebooting your brain.

FAQ

Q: When should we start talking about our product?

A: It depends on whom you're talking to. If it's to people who want you to succeed, talk as early as possible. If it's to strangers who have no connection to you, talk when you have a working prototype. If it's to celebrities or influencers, seize the day and talk whenever you can get their attention.

Q: Should we throw a launch event with food, drink, and music?

A: Dubious. Fundamentally, a launch is about making a great product, getting it in the hands of people, and hoping for the best. There's limited applicability for food, drink, and music. I would spend a few thousand dollars for a nice event for a small group of people but would never launch with a bash or blowout party.

Q: How do we launch a product if we don't have a lot of money?

A: Two words: social media. It's the best thing that ever happened to inexpensive launches.

---

* Andrew Hargadon, *How Breakthroughs Happen: The Surprising Truth About How Companies Innovate* (Boston: Harvard Business School Press, 2003), 116–17.

Q: Is it better to launch too soon or too late?

A: When you're at or near launch time, it feels as if a few weeks or a few months can make a big difference, but this is an illusion. If you are successful, someday you'll have a hard time even remembering what year you launched. If you are unsuccessful, it won't matter.

So unless you're insanely late, to the point where you've missed an entire market (such as how Motorola missed the smartphone business), you've got quite a bit of leeway. Xerox PARC launched the first graphical-user-interface computer (a.k.a. Alto) in the late 1970s. Then Apple launched a Macintosh in the mid-1980s. Microsoft shipped its Macintosh (a.k.a. Windows) even later, and it was Microsoft that ultimately owned the market.

So, given the extremes of launching a piece of crap and waiting for perfection, launch when you have enough functionality to show how you've jumped curves and you have eliminated enough bugs for your product to be stable.

There's one more factor: if you're going to run out of money, you should launch, because you should at least go down swinging. You might land a lucky punch.

Q: Do internal entrepreneurs need certain titles/credentials to be taken seriously?

A: A title is probably less important for internal entrepreneurs because in companies, employees can distinguish the performers from the bozos from firsthand experience. Titles, as a proxy for competence, are not necessary. I would also make the case that any title that is vice president or higher reduces the likelihood of being taken seriously as an internal entrepreneur.

Q: If your company decides to move forward with your idea, is there a way to make sure you can be the project manager or at least make sure that your voice isn't drowned out?

A: There is no way, and this is beside the point. The goal is not to set up a private fiefdom and new bureaucracy. The goal is to create something great.

Q: If you have great ideas for your company but are low on the totem pole, is becoming an internal entrepreneur even possible? Will your ideas ever make it out of the suggestion box? What do you do if godfather figures are out of reach?

A: First, don't put your idea in a suggestion box. A suggestion box is for requesting more gluten-free food in the cafeteria or softer toilet paper. All this talk about getting godfathers and rising to the top are distractions. You either believe and go for it, or you don't. If you want total buy-in and approval, go back to elementary school. The right attitude is to prototype now, seek forgiveness later.

Recommended Reading

Bedbury, Scott. *A New Brand World: Eight Principles for Achieving Brand Leadership in the Twenty-First Century.* New York: Viking, 2002.

Blank, Steve. *The Four Steps to the Epiphany.* Seattle: Amazon Digital Services, 2013.

Moore, Geoffrey. *Crossing the Chasm,* 3rd ed. New York: HarperCollins, 2014.

Ries, Eric. *The Lean Startup: How Today's Entrepreneurs Use Continuous Innovation to Create Radically Successful Businesses.* New York: Crown Business, 2011.

Rosen, Emanuel. *Absolute Value: What Really Influences Customers in the Age of (Nearly) Perfect Information.* New York: HarperCollins, 2014.

CHAPTER 3

The Art of Leading

Be driven not by your importance but by the work that you're trying to do.

—Sunil Thankamushy

GIST

When I was young, I thought that the hard stuff was finance, manufacturing, operations, and accounting. You had to go to school to learn these subjects. I thought the easy stuff was managing, motivating, and leading people. You didn't have to study and learn these—they were easy and would come naturally.

You know what I'm going to tell you next: I was 100 percent wrong. The easy stuff is finance, manufacturing, operations, and accounting. They are important but learnable skills. If you can't learn them, you can hire someone who has. The hard stuff is managing, motivating, and leading people.

If you think that leadership is deciding what you want and telling people to do it, I feel sorry for you. Reality is going kick your ass so far that not even Google will find you. The goal of this chapter is to help you become such a great leader that you'll appear on the first page of a Google search for "leader."

Exude Optimism

Above all, leaders cannot have a bad day. No matter how scared and depressed you are, you cannot show fear, uncertainty, or doubt. You must exude optimism every day.

> **"I cannot remember a time when Steve Jobs looked beaten."**

This isn't to say that you should not recognize issues and challenges—if you don't, you're clueless, and this is even worse than pessimism. However, I cannot remember a time when Steve Jobs looked beaten. I saw anger, frustration, and even semidelusional ranting, but never defeat.

When you have episodes of pessimism and doubt, discuss your issues with your spouse, your colleagues outside the startup, a board member who is your confidant, or, if all else fails, your mother. But don't do this with employees. They must always believe that you believe.

Establish a Culture of Execution

Do not pray for an easy life; pray for the strength to endure a difficult one.

—Bruce Lee

As the leader of the organization, you are responsible for results, and results are the product of a culture of execution. This means that everyone delivers on their promises unless there are unforeseen circumstances. Not everyone will succeed in doing so, but the corporate expectation is ultimately achieving goals, not missing them. Here's how to establish this culture:

- **SET AND COMMUNICATE GOALS.** The simple act of setting goals and communicating them increases the likelihood that your startup will achieve them. It gets everyone on the same page and provides a day-to-day guide for what employees need to do. This applies to every task: finalizing specifications, building a prototype, signing up early customers, shipping, collecting, recruiting, finishing marketing materials . . . The list is long.

- **MEASURE PROGRESS.** Goals only work if you measure progress in achieving them. As the old saying goes, "What gets measured gets done." This also means you'd better pick the right goals to begin with, or the wrong things will get done. In a startup, you should measure and report results every week. As your startup matures and uncertainties in your technology, market, and people decline, you can shift to a monthly schedule.

- **ESTABLISH A SINGLE POINT OF ACCOUNTABILITY.** If it takes more than ten seconds to figure out who is responsible for achieving a goal, something is wrong. Good people accept accountability. Great people ask for it. For the good of your entire organization, establish it. A person who knows he is being measured and held accountable is highly motivated to succeed.

- **BE PART OF THE SOLUTION.** As a leader, you're either part of the solution or part of the problem. This means that you're either establishing a culture of execution or you are establishing a culture of undisciplined, unjustified optimism. Your job is to "be the adult," set the example, and deliver what you promise too.

- **REWARD THE ACHIEVERS.** The people you reward in a startup are the ones who deliver. You can use options, money, public praise, days off, or free lunches—it doesn't matter. What does matter is that you recognize achievers, not the people who are along for the ride.

- **FOLLOW THROUGH UNTIL AN ISSUE IS SOLVED OR NO LONGER RELEVANT.** We all like to work on the newest, hottest stuff. It's human nature. Who wouldn't rather be involved with the next breakthrough product instead of fixing the current one? Don't stop paying attention to a project because it gets boring. Fixing bugs is tedium to you, but it's not to the customer who recently bought your product.

Take the "Red Pill"

This is your last chance. After this, there is no turning back. You take the blue pill—the story ends, you wake up in your bed and believe whatever you want to believe. You take the red pill—you stay in Wonderland and I show you how deep the rabbit hole goes.

—The Matrix, 1999

In *The Matrix* Neo chooses the red pill, which brings him face to face with the harsh realities of the world. If he had taken the blue pill, he could have lived in the comfortable fantasy of the Matrix.

Leaders face the same choice: reality or fantasy. If you want to succeed, take the red pill and determine how deep the rabbit hole goes. If you are serious about staying in touch with reality, these are the ten most important questions you can ask:

1. What is our top priority?

2. When will we ship?

3. When will we run out of money if we don't ship?

4. How much does it cost to acquire a customer?

5. What is our true, fully loaded cost of operations?

6. Whom do we compete with?

7. What can our competition do that we can't?

8. Who are our nonperforming employees?

9. What can we beg, borrow, or lease that we are buying?

10. How good am I as a leader?

Get a Morpheus

Every drug, even the truth, needs a delivery system. In *The Matrix* it was Morpheus, the character played by Laurence Fishburne, who delivered the truth. The question is, who is Morpheus in your organization?

"The CEO decides 'what,' while the Morpheus asks 'what could go wrong?'"

If you don't have one, you need to get one. Morpheus should have at least ten years of operating experience and a background in finance, operations, or accounting. This position requires knowledge of the real-world operation of an organization. The role isn't "naysayer" but "realist."

A background as a consultant, auditor, banker, journalist, or analyst is a bad idea because advising and analyzing are easy, but implementing is hard. The single best question to determine if a person's background is adequate is "Have you ever fired or laid off someone?" If the answer is no, keep looking.

This person is the yang to the CEO's yin. The CEO decides "what," while the Morpheus asks "what could go wrong?" Their relationship is not an opposition but a counterbalance. During different phases of your development and for different tasks, you may need a different kind of Morpheus:

- A research-and-development Morpheus to tell you that what you're creating is flawed

- An operations Morpheus to tell you that your systems can't handle the volume of business

- A finance Morpheus to tell you that you're spending too much (or too little) money

- An ethics Morpheus to tell you that you're inculcating the wrong values

Many people in a startup are in denial about something. Some denial is good—for example, denying that the "experts" are right when they say you can't succeed. The reason you need a Morpheus is to ensure that you realize that you're in denial just in case the denial is damaging the organization.

Get a Devil's Advocate

From 1587 to 1983 the Catholic Church appointed certain individuals to argue against the canonization (sainthood) of a particular candidate. The *advocatus diaboli* or devil's advocate role was created as a way to find faults in candidates to ensure saintly saints.

When the practice ended in 1983, after the election of Pope John Paul II in 1978, an explosion in canonization occurred. Specifically the church canonized five hundred people during the reign of John Paul II; it had canonized only ninety-eight people during the reign of all of John Paul II's twentieth-century predecessors.

A Morpheus and a devil's advocate are not the same thing. A Morpheus tells you the truth—good or bad. A devil's advocate tells you what's bad even if he doesn't believe it himself. The existence of this role is a positive statement because it shows that criticism is acceptable and that management is open to contrarian perspectives. Also, a devil's advocate fosters internal communication because he becomes a person that disenchanted employees can contact.

Devil's advocacy isn't necessary on every decision—just the strategic ones. (The *advocatus diaboli* reviewed only canonizations, not every doctrinal decision.)

Hire Better Than Yourself

Steve Jobs had a saying that A players hire A players, B players hire C players, and C players hire D players. Using his logic, it doesn't take long to get to Z players, and then you wind up with what's called the Bozo Explosion.

> **"Thus, great hires should not only be better than the CEO and management team; they should also differ from them."**

I've refined Steve's concept to "A players hire A+ players." If there is one thing a CEO must do, it's hire managers that are better than she is. If there is one thing managers must do, it's hire employees who are better than they are. For this to happen, the CEO (and management team) must possess three qualities:

- The humility to admit that people can perform a function better than they can.

- The ability to discern which people are A+ or A players.

- The self-confidence to recruit these "better than me" people.

Many entrepreneurs don't realize this, but startups need three kinds of A+ players depending on the stage of the organization:

- Kamikazes who are willing to work eighty hours a week to launch.

- Implementers who come in after the kamikazes and create infrastructure.

- Operators who are happy to run an ongoing system.

Thus, great hires should not only be better than the CEO and management team; they should also differ from them. Startups need people with diverse skills that complement, not overlap, each other.

If you're an engineer, imagine a startup filled with engineers who are not as good as you. This guarantees crappy products. Imagine a startup where the CEO is a better salesperson than the vice president of sales, a better marketing person that the vice president of marketing, and a better finance person than the chief financial officer. This guarantees mediocrity.

EXERCISE

Is everyone you hired better at his or her function than you?

Make People Better

It's easy to recommend that you hire A or A+ players by using an example like the Macintosh Division of Apple, but that was hardly a startup. I will not back down from stressing the desirability of hiring A and A+ players, but I realize that a startup may not always be able to woo such people.

Then what? The answer is not to pray for funding so that you can hire proven players. This will take too long, and management usually precedes funding, as opposed to catalyzing it. The answer is that you hire minimum viable people (MVPs!) who can do the job that needs doing.

The concept is the same as Eric Ries's "MVP" (minimum viable product). If you wait until you have the perfect product or person, it may be too late. So you hire minimum viable people, and much like improving your minimum viable product, you improve your minimum viable employee.

Think about this: no one came out of the womb as an A or A+ player. Everyone started somewhere, so grow your own. Consider who began their careers as interns:

- Dick Cheney: Congress (okay, this doesn't support my recommendation)

- Betsey Johnson: *Mademoiselle*

- Oprah Winfrey: WLAC-TV, Nashville

- Steven Spielberg: Universal Studios

Not everyone will ultimately become a Johnson, Winfrey, Spielberg, A, or A+ player, but one of the key tasks of the art of leading is giving people a chance and making employees better.

Focus on Strengths

Hiring better than yourself means that you hire for strengths as opposed to hiring on the basis of the lack of weaknesses. A great leader hires people for their strengths and then assigns them tasks that take advantage of those strengths. And she hires people with other strengths to provide training and assistance to address the weaknesses of other employees. This enables them to do their best work—as opposed to just getting by without exposing those weaknesses.

Your most important consideration is to distinguish between individual contribution and the ability to manage others. That is, you may decide to hire an engineer who is great at programming or a salesperson who is great at selling but neither of whom can manage. This is okay as long as you don't put such people into management positions.

The usual assumption is that over time, people should move into management and provide less individual contribution. This is a bad assumption. Many people should remain individual contributors, where their strengths lie, while some great individual contributors can, and should, make the transition to management.

Address Your Shortcomings First

Good leaders address their shortcomings before they criticize others. Perhaps your deficiencies were responsible for the shortcomings of those who work for you. There's a saying that if a manager has to fire someone, maybe the company should fire him too because the situation should not have gotten to that point.

This means you start reviews by saying, "I could have provided you with better management." People who adopt this self-criticism strategy will improve as managers because they take responsibility for lousy outcomes. Just as important, they will inspire employees to improve too, because of the good example that they set. Note: the word is "inspire," not "scare."

Poor leaders often judge their intentions against the results of others: "I intended to meet my goals, but you actually missed yours." Somehow it's easier to excuse one's own shortcomings than to understand the shortcomings of others.

You should reverse this outlook, and judge yourself by what you've accomplished and judge others by what they intended. This means you are harsher on yourself than on others. Over the long run, you cannot continue to judge people by their intentions if they consistently produce lousy results, and in that case you need to acknowledge that you made a hiring or training mistake.

Don't Ask Employees to Do What You Wouldn't Do

One of my favorite television shows was _Dirty Jobs_. Its star, Mike Rowe, went around America doing dirty jobs such as taking out the trash, mixing paint in a factory, cleaning sewers, and performing all sorts of distasteful work on farms.

"Never ask people to do something that you wouldn't do."

Rowe illustrates a key concept of leadership: never ask people to do something that you wouldn't do. This assumes that you're not a masochistic nutcase, but within reasonable limits it brings you closer to employees and reduces any feelings of "us versus them."

EXERCISE: COMPLETE THIS CHART.

Action	Do you?	Do you ask employees to?
Fly red-eye flights in coach class		
Answer all your e-mail		
Come in early and stay late		
Empty the trash can		
Make your own photocopies		

The point isn't that you should make every task fun—that's unrealistic—or even that you should take on all the grimy jobs yourself. The point is to empathize with employees and work right alongside them—that's leadership.

Celebrate Success

One win can seem to overcome the pain of a hundred losses, so celebrating the incremental successes of an organization is a powerful way to motivate employees—particularly if you emphasize team wins rather than individual ones.

According to Brenda Bence, author of _How YOU Are Like Shampoo_, celebrating success can have these positive effects:

- Motivates your employees to work even harder.

- Unifies the team around common goals.

- Uplifts employees' mind-sets from ongoing tasks to a celebration.

- Communicates the kind of goals that the organization values.

- Builds momentum by illustrating that progress is happening.

- Reminds them that they work for a winning organization.

A cautionary word about celebrations: good times tempt startups to throw blowout bashes at expensive hotels with famous entertainers. This practice is a waste of money and a bad message to employees. The operative words are "fun" and "cool," not "extravagant" and "awesome."

For example, the Industrial Extension Service of North Carolina State University celebrated its success at creating $1 billion of economic value by conducting a statewide bus tour of manufacturing companies. At each stop of the Manufacturing Makes It Real tour, NCSU people collected samples of products from the manufacturers and delivered these samples to the governor of the state. It was fun for the North Carolina State employees as well as rewarding for the employees of all the companies that the bus visited. This is an example of a good celebration.

Pick the Right Quadrant

Bob Sutton is a professor at Stanford University and author *of* <u>Good Boss,</u> <u>Bad Boss: How to Be the Best . . . and Learn from the Worst</u>. He compiled this list of the twelve beliefs of good bosses. Think of it as a Good Boss Manifesto.

1. I have a flawed and incomplete understanding of what it feels like to work for me.

"I strive to be confident enough to convince people that I am in charge, but humble enough to realize that I am often going to be wrong."

---

2. My success—and that of my people—depends largely on being the master of obvious and mundane things, not on magical, obscure, or breakthrough ideas or methods.

3. Having ambitious and well-defined goals is important, but it is useless to think about them much. My job is to focus on the small wins that enable my people to make a little progress every day.

4. One of the most important, and most difficult, parts of my job is to strike the delicate balance between being too assertive and not assertive enough.

5. My job is to serve as a human shield, to protect my people from external intrusions, distractions, and idiocy of every stripe—and to avoid imposing my own idiocy on them as well.

6. I strive to be confident enough to convince people that I am in charge, but humble enough to realize that I am often going to be wrong.

7. I aim to fight as if I am right, and listen as if I am wrong—and to teach my people to do the same thing.

8. One of the best tests of my leadership—and my organization—is "What happens after people make a mistake?"

9. Innovation is crucial to every team and organization. So my job is to encourage my people to generate and test all kinds of new ideas. But it is also my job to help them kill off all the bad ideas we generate, and most of the good ideas too.

10. Bad is stronger than good. It is more important to eliminate the negative than to accentuate the positive.

11. How I do things is as important as what I do.

12. Because I wield power over others, I am at great risk of acting like an insensitive jerk—and not realizing it.

This checklist will also help you select the right quadrant in the only two-by-two matrix you need to know as a leader:

	Incompetent	Competent
Not asshole	Third most desirable	Most desirable
Asshole	Least desirable	Second most desirable

EXERCISE

If you asked your employees to place you into one of these quadrants, which one would it be?

Change Your Mind

At the introduction of the first iPhone in June 2007, Steve Jobs announced, "Our innovative approach, using web 2.0-based standards, lets developers create amazing new applications while keeping the iPhone secure and reliable." Translation: Apple would not permit apps on the iPhone. The only way to add functionality was through Safari (the iPhone's browser) plug-in software. Apple did this to keep iPhones "secure and reliable."

Eleven months later, this was the headline of an Apple press release: "Apple Executives to Showcase Mac OS X Leopard and OS X iPhone Development Platforms at WWDC 2008 Keynote." Translation: Apple now wanted programmers to create applications for iPhones. The desired outcome was "There's an app for that."

Many people consider this kind of reversal a sign of cluelessness or weakness—changing the policy meant that Apple was wrong and didn't know what it was doing. Following this line of reasoning, leaders should not change their minds—or at least hide the fact, if they do.

Nothing is further from the truth. When leaders publicly change their minds, it shows that they're smart enough to realize they made a mistake, secure enough to admit the mistake, and willing to risk their reputation to do the right thing. All these outcomes are good, so change your mind and disclose that you did.

Think of the issue in this way: If you're running a startup and can't change your mind quickly, when will you ever? As you get bigger, it's only going to get harder to do so.

Tell Employees That They're Wanted

According to Michael Lopp, author of _Managing Humans: Biting and Humorous Tales of a Software Engineering Manager_, the three most important words during the recruitment process are "We want you." This means that it's your job to remind candidates that your startup wants them and that they are the best people for the job.

When many people are unemployed, you might think that it's a buyer's market so therefore this attitude isn't necessary. You are wrong because when it comes to great people, it's always a seller's market. _Always._

Once you've decided to hire someone, turn on the charm: communicate that you want her, invite her to come by the office, have other employees take her out for drinks, and ask her for input. The most dangerous time in the hiring process is after someone has given notice at her previous organization and hasn't yet started at yours. It's then that she'll receive a counteroffer and other forms of persuasion to remain in the old job. If the other organization doesn't make this effort, you should worry that you may have hired an inferior person.

You haven't really hired a new employee until she shows up on the first day, but even then, you shouldn't relax. Imagine that an organization hired a great employee away from you. When would you stop trying to change her mind? I wouldn't give up until she'd been on the new job for thirty days.

Say This

The last leadership tip is to encourage you to incorporate the following four phrases into your conversations with employees, customers, investors, and partners. The better the leader, the more she doesn't hesitate to use these phrases:

- "I don't know."

- "Thank you."

- "Do what you think is right."

- "It's my fault."

I'm not going to claim that some of the most heralded and wealthy leaders ever uttered these phrases, but they were probably exceptions who defied many good practices. I am not convinced that one has to be an asshole to succeed.

Addenda

Minichapter: How to Manage Your Board

> *Being in the army is like being in the Boy Scouts, except that the Boy Scouts have adult supervision.*

> —Blake Clark

This minichapter explains the art of board management. It's a skill that you need to master because it can mean your survival and at least greater leeway in managing your startup.

The first issue is deciding when you need a board. If you take outside investment, then you will have to create a board because your investors will want a say in how you manage the company. Even if they don't, you should create a board when you accept other people's money in order to establish high fiduciary standards.

"The odds that you don't need oversight because you know what you're doing and it's 'your' company are zero."

The second issue is the composition of the board. Your major investors will require a board seat, so some choices are made for you. In general you need people with two kinds of expertise: company building and deep market knowledge. Here are the typical roles that you need to fill:

- **"CUSTOMER."** This person understands the needs of your customers. He doesn't have to be a customer but should understand what your market wants to buy.

- **"GEEK."** This person provides a reality check on your development efforts. For example, is your technology defying the laws of physics? Even if you don't have a tech startup, the question remains the same: Is your task possible?

- **"DAD."** Dad (or Mom) is the calming influence on the board. He brings a wealth of experience and maturity to help mediate issues and reach closure on problems.

- **"MORPHEUS."** This is the same kind of tough guy mentioned before but who's on your board. He tells you that you're full of sushi when you're lying. This person also pushes for totally legal and ethical practices.

- **"JERRY MAGUIRE."** This is Mr. Connections. His most important asset is his Rolodex of industry contacts and his willingness to let your startup use it.

The third issue is creating a good working relationship with your board members. You should hold monthly, or at least quarterly, board meetings. You may view this as a waste of time, but you need to establish an atmosphere of discipline and responsibility. The odds that you don't need oversight because you know what you're doing and it's "your" company are zero. Here are some tips:

- **SAVE TREES.** Less paper is better than more paper. It is a mistake to bury your board in documentation, because these are busy folks. Make your accounting and financial reports about five pages long. They should include a profit-and-loss statement, cash-flow projections, your balance sheet, and a list of accomplishments and problems.

- **SAVE TIME.** The ideal length and frequency of board meetings is two to three hours once per month. You need to have your act together to make this work: reports prepared in advance, follow-up items from previous meetings locked and loaded, and a meeting—not socializing—mentality. If you want to socialize, check in with Foursquare some other time.

- **PROVIDE USEFUL METRICS.** Accounting and financial reports aren't sufficient. Nonfinancial metrics—such as the number of customers, number of installations, or number of visitors to your site—are equally important. This information should add no more than three to four pages to your reports.

- **DO THE EASY STUFF IN ADVANCE.** Board meetings are the time and place for discussing strategic issues—not for conveying the factual information contained in reports. You should spend little time in the meeting communicating the facts—and a lot of time figuring out how to improve them in the future. Thus, it's useful to send your reports in advance. However, don't assume that your directors will read them—you still need to review them in the meeting.

- **DO THE HARD STUFF IN ADVANCE TOO.** The worst time and place to announce bad news is at a board meeting—unless you want a pack of hyenas tearing your flesh from your bones. When you have bad news, meet or speak privately with each member in advance and explain the circumstances. Ask for ideas about ways to fix the problem.

- **GET FEEDBACK AND SELL YOUR IDEAS IN ADVANCE.** The corollary of never surprising a board with bad news is to prepare board members well in advance of key decisions. If you know that you are going to discuss a major issue at an upcoming meeting, then talk to each member about it before the meeting. You might get feedback that will change your perspective about the decision.

FAQ

Q: How do I know if I'm cut out to be a leader?

A: No one really knows that in advance. Usually a leadership role is thrust upon you, and you grow into it. For the time being, don't worry too much about it. Focus instead on creating a MVVVP, taking it to market, improving it, and monetizing it. That's what counts.

Q: What made Steve Jobs such an amazing leader?

A: The term "unique" means being the only one of its kind. Steve was unique. He combined the ability to create what people didn't know they would want with a mystical level of good taste. He was a perfectionist, and he took no crap from anyone. This isn't to say he was easy to work for, but I consider it an honor to have worked for him.

Q: What do I do if someone doesn't execute? Should I fire the person?

A: It's not that simple. Identify the real reason that a person failed to execute. There may be problems that were out of his control. Isolate those problems and fix what you can. A good rule of thumb is to give the person the same due process that you'd like your board of directors to give you. When due process is exhausted, make a decision and take action.

Q: How do I recruit directors?

A: The big picture is to get experienced people to believe in your dream as much as you do. This is a long process—it can take up to six months. The proper order is to get them to believe in your dream, then ask them to join your board, not the reverse.

Q: How do I get more value out of my board of directors?

A: You ask. Surprisingly many entrepreneurs are too intimidated by their boards to manage them. Give them assignments and hold them accountable. They're holding you accountable too.

   The best thing you can do is meet with them one-on-one from time to time even when problems or key issues aren't at hand. You'll get advice that you wouldn't have gotten in a group meeting, and asking for advice will help you build a special bond.

Recommended Reading

Adams, Scott. *How to Fail at Almost Everything and Still Win Big: Kind of the Story of My Life*. New York: Portfolio, 2013.

Pink, Daniel. *Drive: The Surprising Truth About What Motivates Us*. New York: Riverhead Books, 2011.

Sutton, Bob. *The No Asshole Rule: Building a Civilized Workplace and Surviving One That Isn't*. New York: Business Plus, 2007.

CHAPTER 4

The Art of Bootstrapping

It's all right to aim high if you have plenty of ammunition.

—Hawley R. Everhart

GIST

Bill Reichert, my partner at <u>Garage Technology Ventures</u>, likes to tell entrepreneurs that they're more likely to get struck by lightning while lying on the bottom of a swimming pool on a sunny day than they are to raise venture capital. He's exaggerating. The odds are worse than that.

Most entrepreneurs have to dig, scratch, and claw out a business while living on soy sauce and rice. Fortunately the costliest expenses of starting up are now cheap or even free. Bootstrapping a startup is more possible today than at any other time in history for these kinds of reasons:

- Development tools are open source or free.

- Infrastructure is cheap because of cloud-based services.

- "Middle-layer" cloud-based apps make development easier and faster.

- Employees can work virtually, or you can hire freelancers, so you need less office space.

- The most potent form of marketing is also the cheapest: social media.

It's a wonderful world! This chapter explains how to survive the critical, capital-deprived early days of a startup by lifting yourself up by the straps on your boots.

Manage for Cash Flow, Not Profitability

In the early days of the *New Yorker*, the offices were so small and sparsely furnished that Dorothy Parker preferred to spend her days at a nearby coffee shop. One day, the editor found her sitting there.

"Why aren't you upstairs, working?" demanded Harold Ross.

"Someone was using the pencil," Mrs. Parker explained.*

Entrepreneurs can bootstrap almost any business—especially if they have no choice in the matter. A bootstrappable business model has the following characteristics:

- Low up-front capital requirements

- Short (under a month) sales cycles

- Short (under a month) payment terms

- Recurring revenue

- Marketable through social media and word of mouth

"Bootstrapping involves managing for cash flow, not profitability."

These requirements point to products and target markets with these characteristics:

- People already know, or it becomes immediately obvious to them, that they need your product. You don't have to educate your potential customers about their pain.

---

* Peter Hay, *The Book of Business Anecdotes* (New York: Wings Books, 1988), 149.

- Your product is "auto-persuasive."* That is, once people recognize their pain and how you cure it, they can persuade themselves to buy what you're offering.

- A megatrend tsunami of a market is breaking down barriers for you. The Internet was an example of this. (Realize, however, that every wave eventually runs out of energy, so you must have a real business by the time that happens.)

- You can piggyback on a successful product that already has a large installed base, thus reducing your risk.

Bootstrapping involves managing for cash flow, not profitability. That isn't a long-term plan, but until you are sitting on a pile of cash, it's the way to go.

Live in the Cloud

Until approximately 2010, if you started a tech business, you needed to fill a room with servers and hire people to keep the servers running. You needed to have your application, website, and data in multiple locations so that if a disaster attack wiped out your office, backup facilities could take over.

Beginning in 2010, this all changed, and the hardware that most startups had to buy was laptops for employees. By then the main computers were in the cloud—that is, on servers at companies like <u>Rackspace</u> and <u>Amazon Web Services</u> that specialize in hosting, e-commerce, databases, and applications serving over the Internet.

This enabled startups to spend a few thousand dollars per month for all the capacity they needed instead of thousands of dollars per server. Overall, cloud-based infrastructure provides great advantages:

- **AFFORDABILITY.** When you consider the total costs of buying your own infrastructure (hardware, software, staff, redundancy), the pay-as-you-go nature of cloud-based infrastructure is a no-brainer and is its key selling point.

---

* Michael Schrage, "Letting Buyers Sell Themselves," *MIT Technology Review* (October 2003): 17.

- **ADAPTABILITY.** Capacity and performance needs can rapidly change. Cloud-based systems can adapt to these needs as they ebb and flow—ideally more of the former than the latter. In the old days (pre-2010) it would take days to increase your capacity, but cloud vendors can change a setting and increase your allocation—if it's not done automatically.

- **RELIABILITY.** There are hundreds of people at places like Rackspace and Amazon whose primary function is to ensure that everything is working well. It's true that these firms are obvious targets for cyberattacks, but cloud-based systems are ultimately more reliable than what you can piece together on your own.

Forget the "Proven" Team

Experience is the name everyone gives to their mistakes.

—Oscar Wilde

If you're bootstrapping, forget about recruiting well-known industry veterans and building a dream team. Focus instead on affordability—that is, inexperienced young people with bushels of talent, energy, and curiosity.

"Sometimes blissful ignorance is awfully empowering."

Hiring unproven people may reduce the prospects of raising venture capital, but the following table shows how easy it is to build a case for unproven people.

	Proven	**Unproven**
Salary	High, but you don't always get what you paid for	Low, and you almost always get more than what you paid for
Perks	Secretaries, four-star hotels, first-class travel, limos, and top-of-the-line equipment	Self-service, motels, coach class, Uber taxi, and equipment bought at auctions
Energy level	Still high, ideally	Controllable, ideally
Knowledge	Don't admit what they don't know, but you assume they know everything	Don't know what they don't know, so they're willing to try the impossible

Of these factors, the last one is the most important: ignorance is not only bliss; it's empowering. Consider the fantastic story of Dr. George Dantzig, Stanford professor of operations research. While a doctoral student at UC Berkeley, he arrived late for a statistics class, and there were two problems written on the board, which he assumed were homework assignments.

They were, in fact two unproven statistical theorems. Not knowing this, Dantzig took them home and solved them. According to Dantzig, when he asked his professor about a thesis topic, the professor told him to "wrap the two problems in a binder and he would accept them as [his] thesis."

Back in the eighties (1980s, not 1880s), I didn't comprehend the challenges of evangelizing a new operating system, so when Apple offered me a job, I jumped at it. Post-Macintosh, I now know how hard it is, and I would never try to do it again. This is the fundamental problem with experienced people: we know too much.

Had I known the difficulty of my task, I would not have attempted it. Had Dantzig known the difficulty of his supposed homework, he might not have attempted it. Sometimes blissful ignorance is awfully empowering.

EXERCISE

Go on the Internet and investigate the backgrounds of these entrepreneurs when they started their companies. How many had the "right" background to start their company?

Bill Gates, Microsoft

Michael Dell, Dell

Pierre Omidayar, eBay

Jerry Yang, Yahoo!

Anita Roddick, The Body Shop

Start as a Service Business

One of the advantages of a service business is that cash starts flowing within weeks. The classic example of this form of bootstrapping is a software company. The fairy tale goes like this:

- Some programmers get together to provide services to a niche market. They operate as consultants—getting down and dirty with the client. Billing is on an hourly basis and payable within thirty days.

- In the course of providing this service, they develop a software tool for the client. As they add clients, they continue to enhance the tool. Soon, they realize that there are many companies that can use the tool.

- They use the consulting fees from clients to fund further development of the tool. At this point, the consulting practice has grown and provides a steady base of cash.

- They complete development of the tool and try to sell it to nonclients. Sales take off. The company stops doing consulting because there's little leverage in consulting.

- The company goes public, or Google acquires it. The early employees buy Teslas and wineries.

Fairy tales usually don't come true. Another version of this story, slightly grimmer, goes like this:

- A couple of guys have an idea for a software startup. They are going to put Oracle, Microsoft, or Symantec out of business.

- They start creating the product. Maybe they raise venture capital. Maybe they raise angel capital. Maybe they just starve.

- For the first time in the history of mankind, development takes longer than the entrepreneurs expected. Also, customers aren't willing to buy a product from two guys in a garage. The startup is running out of money.

- To get some cash, the guys decide that they should do some consulting. They take their partially finished product and pound the pavement looking for any business they can find. They rationalize this decision as a positive step because it helps them develop a product that customers need.

- Lo and behold, customers *do* need their product. The developers complete it and start selling it. Sales take off, and they stop doing consulting because there's no leverage in consulting.

- The startup goes public, or Google acquires it. The early employees buy Teslas and wineries.

Getting customers to pay for your research and development is only a temporary strategy for a product-based company. In the long run a service business is fundamentally different from a product business. The former is all about labor and billable hours or projects. The latter is all about research and development, shipping, and spreading costs over thousands of downloads from servers.

Go Direct

Many startups try to implement a multiple-tiered distribution system in which they sell to a reseller who sells to the final user. The thinking is that an established reseller brings the benefits of a sales force, brand awareness, and existing customer relationships.

That's the concept, anyway. It usually breaks down because most re-sellers want to fill demand, not create it. They're not interested in helping you establish a market—they want to tap into a proven one. Marxist (Groucho) as this may seem, you might not need any reseller that would have you.

There are three additional issues to be weighed when considering a multiple-tiered distribution system:

- It isolates you from your customer. With a new product, you need to hear what's wrong and what's right as soon as possible and as unfiltered as possible.

- Because there's a much smaller profit margin, you need to gener-ate a larger volume of sales, and it's difficult to achieve large vol-ume as a startup.

- It takes a long time to convince distributors to carry your product and then a long time for your product to get through the system into the hands of customers.

For all these reasons, you should start by selling directly to customers. Once you've debugged your product and established sales, you can use re-sellers to accelerate, expand, or supplement your efforts. But do not think that resellers can establish your product for you or provide the quality feed-back you'd get from selling to customers on your own.

Position Against the Leader

Seth Godin, the author of <u>The Bootstrapper's Bible: How to Start and Build a Business with a Great Idea and (Almost) No Money</u>, makes a strong case for positioning against the market leader as a bootstrapping technique. Rather than trying to launch your product from the ground up, you utilize the existing brand awareness of the competition. Consider these examples of how you can do it:

- Lexus: "As good as a Mercedes or BMW, but 30 percent cheaper"

- Southwest Airlines: "As cheap as driving"

- 7UP: "The Uncola"

- Avis: "We try harder" (than Hertz)

"By spending millions of dollars and years of effort to establish its brand, your competition has done you a terrific favor."

Positioning against the leaders or standard ways of doing business can save lots of marketing, PR, promotion, and advertising dollars, so pick the gold standard in your industry and identify an important point of differentiation in your own product, such as:

- Cost

- Ease of use

- Convenience

- Industrial design

- Reliability

- Speed/performance

- Range of selection

- Customer service

- Geographic location

By spending millions of dollars and years of effort to establish its brand, your competition has done you a terrific favor. There is a catch, though, because successful positioning against a leader requires three conditions:

- The leader is, and remains, worth positioning against. Imagine, for example, if you had positioned your startup against Enron when Enron was the darling of Wall Street.

- The leader doesn't get its act together and erode your advantage—for example, if you position your computer as faster than IBM's and then IBM responds with an announcement of a radically faster model.

- Your product surpasses the competition's in truthful, perceptible, and meaningful ways. If not, no one will care about your hype. Worse, you'll lose your credibility, and credibility is hard to regain.

Still, for the near term, positioning against the market leader is a useful and cheap technique to enable you to explain what you do.

Sweat the Big Stuff

Bootstrapping goes awry when entrepreneurs focus on saving pennies to the detriment of the Big Picture. The reason for starting a company is not to build your own desks (nor is it to spend venture capital to make Herman Miller a bigger company). Here is a list of the big stuff and small stuff entrepreneurs must manage.

BIG STUFF

- Developing your MVVVP

- Selling your product

- Enhancing your product

SMALL STUFF

- Business cards and letterhead

- Office supplies

- Furniture

- Office equipment

So take care of the small stuff in rapid, good enough—not perfect—ways. Rick Sklarin, a former Accenture consultant, puts it this way: "Make one trip to Costco and be done with it." Then focus your attention and resources on the big stuff because that's what counts.

EXERCISE

The next time there's something that you can't live without, wait for a week and then see if you're still alive.

Understaff and Outsource

There's an age-old question that CEOs face: Which is worse—to leave money on the table because you can't handle all the business, or to lay people off because you overestimated revenues?

"If you want to bootstrap your organization, then understaff it."

The thought of leaving money on the table makes my ears ring, but laying off people is worse. Overstaffing causes a wicked chain reaction, so dealing with it is not simply a matter of lowering head count:

- Excess space locked in a long-term lease

- Excess furniture and computers

- Trauma in the organization as people are let go

- Trauma in the lives of the people who are let go

- Trying to hire different kinds of people (for your new reality) in the midst of letting others go

- Going through gyrations to convince the world that you're not imploding

If you want to bootstrap your organization, then understaff it. There's a short-term solution to problems you may face with a lower head count, and that's to outsource as many nonstrategic functions as you can. Outsourcing strategic functions such as research and development, marketing, and sales is riskier because they are core to your startup. Candidates for outsourcing include:

- Customer service

- Tech support

- Accounting

- Facilities management

A fantastic example of the opposite of bootstrapping is Webvan, the online grocer that went bust in the dot-com implosion of 2001. It once placed a $1 billion order with Bechtel, an engineering firm, to build facilities in twenty-six markets. When it terminated its rock star CEO, George Shaheen, the former head of Accenture, it promised to pay him $375,000 a year for the rest of his life. All I can say is, "OMG!"

Focus on Function, Not Form

To spend money wisely, focus on the function you need, not the form it takes. For example, a big-name firm (form) is not always necessary for proper legal, accounting, PR, marketing, or recruiting (function).

Area	Form	Function
Legal	Offices around the world for a Fortune 500 clientele and box seats at sporting events	Understanding your legal liabilities, protecting your assets, and facilitating deals
Accounting	Big Six status with former clients in jail and walnut walls in conference rooms	Controlling costs and ensuring fiscally sound operation
PR	Good-looking account reps who majored in Asian art history and who tell you that you're a great speaker are at the $100,000 press event they planned	Creating and proselytizing effective positioning and establishing close contacts with the press and bloggers
Marketing	A wall full of awards for television commercials and print ads with employees who do nothing but buy media	Understanding and reaching your customer and getting current customers to attract future customers
Recruiting	Established reputation for placing the CEOs of publicly traded companies that own private jets	Hiring great employees who will trade options for salary

Service providers are a big part of startup costs, so here are tips on making the right choice when assessing them:

- **SELECT A FIRM THAT SPECIALIZES IN THE TYPE OF WORK THAT YOU REQUIRE.** For example, you should hire neither Uncle Joe the divorce lawyer nor a Wall Street law firm to create your option pool.

- **PAY MORE FOR CRITICAL FUNCTIONS.** Investors, for example, may feel more comfortable dealing with companies that use the "usual" lawyers and accountants who do your type of work. But overshoot "usual" and go to "biggest."

- **CHECK THE REFERENCES OF THE INDIVIDUALS WHO ARE HANDLING YOUR BUSINESS—AND NOT JUST THE FIRM'S.** The most powerful references these providers can have are happy entrepreneurs.

- **NEGOTIATE EVERYTHING.** Everything is negotiable: rates, payment schedules, and monthly fees. Even in good times, don't be afraid to negotiate—it's part of the game. Many firms, for example, will delay billing until you're funded if you have the chutzpah to ask.

This logic of focusing on function, not form, applies to almost every element of a startup. One of the symbols of the dot-com craze, for example, was the Herman Miller Aeron chair. This was a $700 piece of office equipment that was the de rigueur indicator of cool.

It was a terrific chair, but I don't know if it was $700 terrific. It helped people work longer and harder but perhaps at the wrong tasks. By the way, 114 of these chairs were sold in the bankruptcy auction of Webvan.

Addenda

FAQ

Q: How do I know when bootstrapping has taken us as far as we can go?

A: You'll know it's time to stop bootstrapping when you're cash-flow positive and you're certain that every incremental sale generates profit.

Q: Will I forsake growth—and maybe even success—if I bootstrap too much?

A: I can't come up with a single example of an organization that bootstrapped too much. There's greater danger of screwing up because of too much money than because of too little. Negatively stated, think of venture capital as steroids: it might give you a short-term advantage, but it could kill you over time.

Remember that you're supposed to increase investor value no matter whether the money is from you or from outside investors.

Q: If I can successfully bootstrap an organization, do I even have to look for outside capital? What's wrong with doing it the old-fashioned way?

A: Respectively, no and nothing. Outside capital isn't the only way— it's simply one way. The goal is to build something great, no matter how you raise capital.

Q: If we don't have several million dollars in venture capital funding, will we not be taken seriously?

A: Only by people who don't matter. If you do raise this kind of money, use it to add to your credibility, but don't believe that it will guarantee your success. If you don't raise this kind of money, don't sweat it. Just build a great business and don't look back.

Q: Should a startup avoid getting funding from sources such as family and friends, credit cards, and home equity?

A: There are risks involved in all three strategies: ruining relationships, personal financial issues, and losing your house. However, entrepreneurship is the art of doing whatever it takes. Everyone would love to have a large and growing market, perfected technology, and infinite capital. Under those conditions, anyone can be an entrepreneur. The question is what you are willing to do and can you do when the conditions are far from perfect. If entrepreneurship was without risk, more people would try it.

Recommended Reading

Godin, Seth. *The Bootstrapper's Bible: How to Start and Build a Business with a Great Idea and (Almost) No Money.* Chicago: Upstart Publishing, 1998.

Hess, Kenneth L. *Bootstrapping: Lessons Learned Building a Successful Company from Scratch.* Carmel, CA: S-Curve Press, 2001.

CHAPTER 5

The Art of Fund-raising

At a presentation I gave recently, the audience's questions were all along the same lines: "How do I get in touch with venture capitalists?" "What percentage of the equity do I have to give them?" No one asked me how to build a business!

—Arthur Rock

GIST

Fund-raising is a necessary evil of starting an organization. It's not fun. It's not easy. And it's not quick. Bootstrapping can reduce the amount of fund-raising you have to do—and maybe even eliminate fund-raising if you're fortunate. However, few entrepreneurs can avoid the process altogether. In this chapter you'll learn about three forms of fund-raising—crowdsourcing, angel investors, and venture capital—and how to succeed in this necessary evil.

Tap the Crowd

The process of fund-raising has multiple paths. A long time ago nobility and rich people had money to start with. If they needed to raise additional capital, they had collateral and the right connections.

Fast-forward a few hundred years, and the venture capital industry made it possible for several thousand entrepreneurs per year to raise money with PowerPoint presentations, prototypes, and drawings on napkins. Angel investors democratized this process even further by funding more risky companies than venture capitalists would touch.

> **"Venture capitalists don't know shiitake about what will sell, but when people crowdfund your project, they're voting with their own after-tax dollars, not a pension fund's money that they're managing."**

Then in 2007 <u>Indiegogo</u> started and <u>Kickstarter</u> came along two years later. This marked the dawn of crowdfunding, which is about as democratic, open, and transparent as fund-raising can get. This is how crowdfunding works:

- You build a project; this involves creating a video and a description, designing rewards for participants, and providing updates as your project progresses.

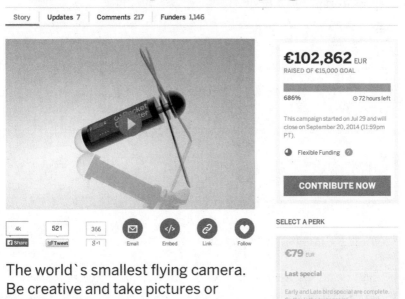

- Rather than raising funds by selling an equity share, you take pre-orders with rewards or "kickers" to encourage people to pay for something that doesn't exist. Kickers are discounts, mementos, gifts, or clever ideas such as the right to name a character in a book or to hang out with your team.

- You spread the word about your crowdfunding project through social media and e-mail. While the appeal for traditional fundraising is making money, the crowdfunding appeal is getting something cool before other people or attaining the intrinsic reward of helping others.

- People fund your project, which enables you to use other people's money to complete it. You deliver on all the orders, word of mouth spreads, and, in an ideal world, you build a great company.

Crowdfunding is most applicable for consumer deals such as devices, accessories, games, crafts, and fashion, as well as artsy projects such as films, videos, and charitable work. Crowdfunding is less applicable for biotech or enterprise software because such projects require tens of millions of dollars of funding and don't involve impulse purchases.

According to Kickstarter, in 2013 three million people from over two hundred countries pledged $480 million using its service. This resulted in 19,911 successfully funded projects—which is probably six times more than the venture capital deals that closed in the same year.

Here are some examples of successful crowdfunding—"successful" in the sense that the entrepreneurs raised money:

- Pebble watch. Total raise: $10 million.

- ElevationDock. Total raise: $1.4 million.

- Veronica Mars movie. Total raise: $5.7 million.

These examples are outliers. Crowdfunding is effective for funding to the tune of $50,000–$250,000, an amount that is often too little for a venture capital firm to invest. Not every project is going to raise millions of dollars like the examples above, but there's a lot to like about crowdfunding:

- The process is not as onerous as raising venture capital—which is often a full-time job for six months. For example, you don't have to write a business plan or go through a due-diligence process.

- There isn't equity dilution of the company. People are pre-buying or contributing—they are not investing and receiving an equity stake. A powerful advantage of not selling equity is that you don't have to report to investors, though you still have the moral obligation to deliver your project.

- Crowdfunding is a good test of viability. Venture capitalists don't know shiitake about what will sell, but when people crowdfund your project, they're voting with their own after-tax dollars, not a pension fund's money that they're managing.

Here are the key tips for succeeding in crowdfunding. There are more tips in the Kickstarter Creator Handbook, the handbook's further reading section, and Indiegogo.

- **CREATE A VIDEO.** An enchanting, enticing, and energizing less-than-two-minutes video is the most important component of your project. Make it great, because it's going to make or break your project.

- **TELL A PERSONAL STORY.** Your video, e-mails, and social media posts should tell a story. The best kind of story is a personal one. For example, how you undertook the project because you had an unmet need, such as a better way to fix flat bike tires (see the patchnride project on Indiegogo).

- **USE E-MAIL AND SOCIAL MEDIA.** Unless you're Arianna Huffington and can get on *The Ellen DeGeneres Show*, you're going to wage a guerrilla-marketing campaign to make your project a success. This means using your database of e-mail contacts and your social media accounts to get the word out.

- **ROCK THE REWARDS.** The second most important component of your project is the rewards, mementos, or kickers that you offer. The most obvious are discounts, acknowledgments, autographed copies, and physical gifts such as tote bags and T-shirts. You can push the edge by personally delivering or installing your product. Again, you're asking people to pay for something that doesn't exist, so you need to compensate them for taking this risk.

- **SHOW A BUDGET.** A powerful way to convince prospective supporters is to provide a budget to show how you'll spend their money. This will foster confidence that you know what you're doing and that you're likely to complete and ship the project.

Court Angels

The second source of funding is angel investors, the thousands of wealthy individuals who invest their money in startups. Whereas venture capitalists want to make money and perhaps pay back society, angels want to pay back society and perhaps make money.

Angels see two ways to pay back society: helping young(er) people get a start, and helping a meaningful product get to market. Here are the key concepts to raise money from angels.

- **DON'T UNDERESTIMATE THEM.** Angels may care less about financial returns than professional investors, but this doesn't mean they are suckers. Approach them with the same level of professionalism that you would a top-tier venture capitalist.

- **ENABLE THEM TO LIVE VICARIOUSLY.** A side benefit that many angels seek is a chance to relive their youth or an entrepreneurial past. Even though they can't or don't want to start another entity, they can enjoy watching you do it—call this "voyeur capital."

- **MAKE YOUR STORY COMPREHENSIBLE TO SPOUSES.** The "investment committee" of an angel is his or her spouse—not a bunch of peers, partners, or pundits. This underscores the importance of making your business understandable in plain terms. As a test, ask your spouse if he or she would invest in your venture.

- **BE NICE**. Whereas venture capitalists may invest in a jerk because money is money, many angels fall in love with entrepreneurs in a parental way: "She's a nice kid. I want to give her a start." So be approachable, enchanting, and malleable.

- **SIGN UP PEOPLE THEY KNOW OR HAVE HEARD OF**. Angel investing is often about socializing as much as profiting. Thus, if you can attract one member of the club, you can usually get more to follow. The most powerful proxy for quality for angel investors is that another angel they've heard of has invested.

Pound on Venture Capitalists

The fact is that the amount of money startups raise in their seed and series A rounds is inversely correlated with success.

—Fred Wilson

I want you to know what you're getting into: raising venture capital is a long, distracting, and frustrating process—and that's if it goes well. Let me tell you my favorite, and most illustrative, story about a venture capitalist.

"'Lady, you took your keys with you. We couldn't move your car.'"

A venture capitalist took her father to dinner at a swanky restaurant that had a valet service. On the way there her father chided her for spending too much money by buying a snazzy BMW. She pulled up in front of the restaurant, and the two of them went in and had dinner.

Several hours later they emerged and saw that her car was still standing where she had parked it. Seizing the moment, she told her father, "See? This is why I drive a BMW. Restaurants keep the nice cars out front. Now we don't have to wait for a valet to get it."

At that moment, an irritated valet approached her and said, "Lady, you took your keys with you. We couldn't move your car."

Venture capitalists can open doors to kick-start sales and partnerships. They can help you find future investors. They can prevent you from making mistakes. They can help you recruit. They can make the world take you more seriously, but . . .

- They don't necessarily know any more than you do about engineering, marketing, sales, production, finance, or operations. Still, no one can blame you for thinking this is the case, since these folks manage hundreds of millions of dollars.

- Getting their investment doesn't guarantee that you'll succeed. These firms make many bets, and they assume that most won't pay off. If venture capitalists were baseball players, none of them would be playing professionally because of their low batting average.

- Their loyalty, no matter what they say, is limited to one year from when you start failing to deliver on your promises. They are not your friends, and their primary concern is making money. They're not necessarily bad people, but you should never forget that it's just business.

Now that we've covered the three main forms of financing, let's take a look at them matrix-style. Then the rest of this chapter discusses raising money from angels and venture capitalists.

	Crowdfunding	Angel	Venture capital
Sweet spot	$25,000–$100,000	$250,000–$500,000	$1,000,000–$5,000,000
Length	90 days	180 days	270 days
Dilution per round	Not applicable: sale, not investment	20%	25–35%
Effort level	Moderate	Moderate	High
Type of product/service	Consumer-facing gadgets, gizmos, books, and other artistic and craft-oriented projects	Software and web services	Hardware, software, biotech, and web services
Due diligence	Minimal	Moderate	High
Intrusiveness	Minimal	Moderate	High
Experience	Fun	Tolerable	Miserable

Get an Intro

Thank you for sending me a copy of your book. I'll waste no time reading it.

—Moses Hadas

In publishing, movies, music, and venture capital there's a fairy-tale scenario that goes like this. You submit a draft, script, song, or business plan to an organization. Despite the mounds of other submissions on his desk, the quality of your story is so stellar that someone frantically asks you to come in for a meeting. After one meeting, you cut a deal, go on to create a blockbuster, and spend the rest of your life saving poor people.

Dream on.

As God is my witness, the following is a true story. A startup had given up on getting money from a top-tier venture capital firm because the startup sensed there was no interest. I asked a partner at the firm why it had passed, and he told me it was because his associate knew a startup in Europe that was doing the same thing that had achieved "100 percent market share in Europe and was coming to the U.S." Therefore, it was too late for another entrant.

I asked the associate for the startup's name. He didn't know it—a friend had told him about it. I contacted this friend, and he also didn't know the name. Another friend had told him about the startup and about how it had 98 percent market share—in a tiny vertical market in *Eastern* Europe.

"The point is to tilt the playing field in your direction."

Let's review: a friend told a friend who told an associate who told a partner not to bother looking at the startup. This tale illustrates why you need an introduction by a credible person to get a decision maker to take a serious look at your startup. The point is not that the submission process should be a level playing field. The point is to tilt the playing field in your direction by getting an introduction by sources that venture capitalists respect, such as:

- **CURRENT INVESTORS.** One of the most valuable services a current investor can provide is to help find additional investors. This is part of the game, so don't hesitate to ask for help. Most investors will at least listen to the recommendations of people who already have a stake in a company.

- **LAWYERS AND ACCOUNTANTS.** When you pick lawyers or accountants, look for connections as well as competence. Ask them if they will introduce you to sources of capital. Lots of firms can do the work, so find one that can both do the work and make introductions.

- **OTHER ENTREPRENEURS.** A call or e-mail from an entrepreneur to his investors saying "This is a hot startup—you should talk to them" is powerful. Go to the investor's website to figure out which companies he's invested in—you may know someone at one of them. If not, get to know someone—execs at these companies are easier to get to than their investors. For those who are starting not-for-profits, look at the organizations that the target foundations have funded.

- **PROFESSORS**. Investors are impressed by the suggestions of professors. In Silicon Valley, for example, a call or an e-mail from a Stanford engineering professor will get the attention of most venture capitalists and angel investors. I hope you did well in school!

What if you don't know these kinds of folks? It's a cruel world. Raising capital isn't an equal-opportunity activity, so get out there and get connected. There's a short course about schmoozing at the end of chapter 8, "The Art of Evangelizing," to help you.

Know Your Audience

The foundation of a great meeting with potential investors is the research that you do beforehand. First, learn what's important to your audience. You can get this information from the partner that is bringing you into the meeting by getting answers to the following questions:

- What are the three most important things you would like to learn about our organization?

- What attracted you to our idea and convinced you to give us an opportunity to meet?

- Are there any special issues, questions, or land mines I should be prepared for in the meeting?

Second, visit the venture capital firm's website, use Google searches, read reports, and talk to industry buddies to gather more information. This is the kind of information you want to learn about the firm:

- **ORGANIZATION BACKGROUND.** How did the firm start? Who were the original partners? What are its most successful investments?

- **PARTNERS.** Who works there? What organizations did they work for in their previous positions? Where did they go to school?

- **CURRENT PORTFOLIO.** What companies are currently in its portfolio? What were its big successes in the past? Are there conflicts or synergies with your startup?

In particular, LinkedIn is a great resource to prepare for the meeting. Here's how to use it:

- Find out who the firm has invested in by visiting the portfolio section of its website.

- Plug the names of those companies into LinkedIn to find people in your network who have worked for any of them.

- Reach out to these people.

Third, brainstorm with your team to find connections, hooks, and angles to make the pitch powerful and meaningful. There are many possibilities but trying to figure them out while you're pitching is difficult. The key is to conduct this research in advance, when you're under less pressure.

While angel investors may not have websites, Google and LinkedIn will provide plenty of information about them. There's also AngelList, an angel-capital marketplace. There you can search for angels and companies by name—making it a powerful resource for learning about angel investors.

Show Traction

Generally, investors are looking for a proven team, proven technology, and proven market. However, one factor cuts through all the hyperbole: actual sales. (In Silicon Valley we call this traction—in the sense that a tire grips the road and moves a vehicle forward.)

> **"Many entrepreneurs believe that saying 'I really believe in my idea' is a form of traction. They are deluded if they think this is true."**

Traction counts the most because it demonstrates that people are willing to open their wallets, take out money, and put it in your pocket. If you've been able to accomplish this, your team, technology, and market are less important. I don't know of an investor who would rather lose money on a proven team with proven technology in a proven market than make money on an unproven one.

This is also why a successful crowdfunding project is powerful. It may not only eliminate or delay the necessity of fund-raising; it can provide proof of the viability of your product and help attract investors.

Traction takes different forms in different industries. It has a straightforward definition for startups with products or services:

- Number of registrations

- Number of downloads

- Number of paying customers

- Revenues

- Website traffic

  Not-for-profits have different parameters:

- Schools: enrollment and student test scores

- Churches: attendance at services

- Museums: numbers of visitors

- Volunteer organizations: contributions and number of volunteer hours

This raises a logical question: "How can I show traction if I don't have enough money to finish my product?" There are two answers. First, no one said entrepreneurship is easy, so review chapter 4, "The Art of Bootstrapping," and do what you have to do. Second, there is a hierarchy of traction—with all due respect to Maslow's hierarchy of needs.

1. Actual sales (or the parameters discussed above for nonproduct companies)

2. Field testing and pilot sites

3. Agreement to field test, pilot, or use before shipment

4. Establishing a contact to pursue a field test

This is the pecking order of desirability. If you don't at least have a contact for a field test, you will have difficulty raising money. Many entrepreneurs believe that saying "I really believe in my idea" is a form of traction. They are deluded if they think this is true.

Catalyze Fantasy

Every—literally every—entrepreneur shows up at investor meetings with slides that "prove" the size of his market. Usually the slides contain a quote from a consulting firm stating unequivocally that the size of the llama-ranching software market will be $50 billion within the next four years.

The funny thing is that all entrepreneurs claim that they're going after a $50 billion market. However, no one in the room, even the entrepreneur, believes the number or thinks it's relevant. A better method is to catalyze fantasy. You do this by providing a product that is so needed that the audience can do the math in their own heads.

This method won't work in all cases because some markets are not obvious, but when it does, the results are spectacular. Here is an example of how the method works. Suppose your website enables people to create graphics without having to buy or rent software and without learning how to use a complicated product.

Here's how the fantasy pitch would go:

- Everyone with a website, blog, social media account, book, eBay, Etsy, or presentation needs graphics to attract attention.

- Most people, however, are not graphic designers or artists, and they are not willing to spend the time and money to become one.

- A free and easy-to-use service that produces beautiful and quick results would therefore attract many users.

- It's easy to monetize these users by selling them graphic elements, stock photos, and premium features.

This approach is more powerful than citing a study that proves the market for graphics software and services is $50 billion, because investors can conclude on their own that such a company could democratize design and become huge.

Acknowledge, or Create, an Enemy

Many entrepreneurs believe that investors want to hear that your startup has no competition. Unfortunately, sophisticated investors reach one of two conclusions if they hear such claims:

- There's no competition because there's no market. If there were a market, there would be others trying to win it.

- The founders are so clueless that they can't even use Google to figure out that other startups are doing the same thing.

Duh, a startup that aims to serve a market that doesn't exist or that exhibits cluelessness is not likely to raise money. A moderate level of competition is a good thing because it validates the possibility of a genuine market and shows that you've done your homework.

It's your job to show how you are superior to the competition, not that it doesn't exist. Use a chart like the one below to explain what you and your competition can and cannot do:

Company	We can do, it can't do	We can't do, it can do
Us		
X		
Y		
Z		

No one ever wonders why you should list what you can do but your competition can't. Many entrepreneurs wonder why you should list the things that you can't do and the competition can. The reason is to increase your credibility by showing that you're capable of four desirable skills:

- Telling the truth.

- Assessing the competition.

- Comprehending your company's weaknesses.

- Communicating knowledge clearly and succinctly.

You can also use this chart to promote the relevance of your product to the marketplace by mapping your capabilities to the particular needs of your customers—that is, the list of "what we can do" capabilities should illustrate that there's a need for your product.

> **"When people see that they can believe you about bad stuff, they are more willing to believe you about good stuff."**

Unfortunately entrepreneurs seldom take these factors into account. Instead they contrive a matrix that makes them look good—frequently with irrelevant, if not downright silly, parameters.

If you don't have direct competition, then zoom out until you find some because if you aren't competing with anything, you probably have nothing. Here are some examples of indirect competitors:

- **RELIANCE ON THE STATUS QUO.** "This is how we've always done things." "We need permission from the boss."

- **COMPETITION FOR TIME OR ATTENTION.** For example, a museum competes with other museums as well as with aquariums, online games, and shopping malls.

- **GOOGLE, APPLE, AND AMAZON.** Since at some level these companies compete with everyone.

Be bold: openly discuss your strengths and weaknesses. When people see that they can believe you about bad stuff, they are more willing to believe you about good stuff.

Don't Fall for the Trick Questions

If you're lucky, you will encounter investors who ask you trick questions—"lucky" because such questions indicate that the investors are interested and sophisticated. These questions provide an opportunity for you to show that you're sophisticated too. Here are the typical trick questions and appropriate responses.

Investor trick question	What you want to say	What you should say
"What makes you think you're qualified to run this startup?"	"What makes you think you're qualified to run this venture capital firm?"	"I've done OK so far, getting us to this point. But if it ever becomes necessary, I'll step aside."
"Do you see yourself as the long-term CEO of the startup?"	"What did your limited partners see in you?"	"I've been focused on getting our stuff to market. I will do whatever is necessary to make this successful—including stepping aside if needed. Here are the logical milestones by which we can make this transition. . . ."
"Is ownership control a big issue for you?"	"I'm going to be putting in eighty hours a week to make this successful, and you're asking me if I care how much of it I own?"	"No, it's not. I realize that to make this successful, we need great employees and great investors. They all need to have a significant stake. I will focus on making the pie bigger, not on getting or keeping a big part of the pie."
"What do you see as the liquidity path for your startup?"	"An IPO that sets a new record for valuation."	"We know that we have a lot to do before we can even dream of liquidity. We're designing this company to be a large, successful, and independent entity. Right now, our heads are down, and we're working as hard as we can to do this. An IPO would be a dream outcome—plus these five companies are possible acquirers in the future. . . ."

Bag One Cat

There may be fifty ways to leave your lover, but there are even more ways for venture capitalists to tell you no. Unfortunately, venture capitalists don't like to provide clear and unequivocal rejections; they prefer the SHITS technique: show high interest, then stall.

Here are the common responses (using the term loosely) that you'll hear:

- "You're too early for us. Show us some traction, and we'll invest."

- "You're too late for us. I wish you had come to us earlier."

- "If you get a lead investor, we'll be part of the syndicate."

- "We don't have expertise in your sector."

- "We have a conflict of interest with one of our existing companies." (Trust me, if they thought they could make money with your company, they'd resolve this conflict.)

- "I liked your deal, but my partners didn't."

- "You need to prove that your technology can scale."

Most of the time what the investor is really telling you is, "When hell freezes over." But there are some cases in which investors are genuinely interested but not yet ready to commit. You may eventually get an investment from them, but it will be as hard as herding cats to finish the process.

The key to herding the cats is to get one in the bag rather than coming close to capturing several. It's helpful if this cat is a big, beautiful, and well-known one, but any cat that isn't your relative will do, because venture capitalists—like misery—love company.

"Continuing to make contact without demonstrable, significant improvements in your story will change your status from 'persistent' to 'pest,' and nobody funds a pest."

Winning over a venture capitalist is not only about providing objective, quantifiable, and compelling information through your pitch and references. It's as much an emotional process as it is an analytic process. An uncommitted venture capitalist is still watching what you do:

- Did you follow up by answering questions that you couldn't answer during the pitch?

- Did you provide supplemental information that supports your case after the pitch?

- Have you surprised the investor by closing big customers or meeting milestones early?

- Have other high-quality investors written you a check?

Persistence along these lines can pay off, and you can provide these types of relevant updates weeks and even months after your initial pitch in your efforts to herd the cats. However, continuing to make contact without demonstrable, significant improvements in your story will change your status from "persistent" to "pest," and nobody funds a pest.

Get a Corporate Finance Lawyer

You need a lawyer, and not just any lawyer, but one who routinely does venture capital and early-stage financing deals. This means not using a friend or relative who is a divorce, criminal, family law, or real estate lawyer. Don't be stupid: you wouldn't seek brain tumor advice from a dermatologist, so why would you seek corporate finance advice from a divorce lawyer?

From due diligence to the wire transfer of money, you will need legal advice. In particular, you'll need it for the creation of a term sheet, the legal document that defines the parameters of an investment. Our friends at Wilson Sonsini Goodrich & Rosati created the fabulous WSGR Term Sheet Generator to help entrepreneurs understand this document.

The generator has forty-eight pages of questions. This should give you an idea of how complex the process is and why you need to get an experienced lawyer. I've seen many entrepreneurs risk their financing and spend tens of thousands of dollars to undo the clever decision to use a friend or relative to save money.

Pursue a Parallel Existence

The linear nature of a book may give you the impression that fund-raising—and indeed, entrepreneurship in general—is a serial process. For example, raise money from crowdsourcing, build prototype, raise money from angels, launch, raise money from venture capitalists, scale up, go public, and buy wineries and Teslas.

Fund-raising, and entrepreneurship in general, is a parallel process. For example, you may be promoting a crowdfunding project while you are meeting angel investors and venture capitalists while you're asking your friends and family for loans. And this is only one aspect of your parallel existence because you're also building a prototype, pursuing customers, forming partnerships, and recruiting and training employees.

Get used to it. This is the lifestyle you've picked.

Anticipate the Future

You're probably reading this book as you begin to raise money or after you've raised a seed round. It's useful for you to understand the total picture of what each round of capital means.

- **SEED = SIZZLE.** This is the first outside money that you raise. The order of magnitude is $100,000–$250,000. Sources include friends and family as well as angels. At this point, you're *selling* on dreams, fantasies, and delusions—in other words, this round is about sizzle.

- **SERIES A = STEAK.** In this round, venture capitalists enter the picture. Their bet on you amounts to $1–3 million dollars. You can't depend on sizzle anymore because big money is at stake (no pun intended). Now your product has to be generating revenue—in other words, this round is about steak, not sizzle. (I got the concept of applying the sizzle and steak metaphor to financing from Ben Narasin of TriplePoint Ventures.)

- **SERIES B = STEROIDS.** The steak was good. Customers are buying it and eating it. Now the company needs an injection of steroids to get to the magical $100 million a year revenue rate. You're going to use this money to scale your business. Luckily, no urine tests are required for entrepreneurs.

- **SERIES C = SYCOPHANTS.** If you make it to this round, you probably don't *need* money anymore. This additional series is just in case the capitalist system collapses or Google/Apple/Amazon decides to enter your business. At this point, investors are *buying*—you're not *selling*—so they are sucking up to you in order to jump on a winner.

Spend Like You Can't Raise Money Again

My final recommendation pertains to what you should do after you manage to raise money—no matter what amount. Many entrepreneurs, after subsisting on fumes for months, go wild after a capital infusion and waste money on nice furniture, cool office space, free food, and MBAs from big companies.

"The best mentality is to assume that you'll never be able to raise money again."

If you find yourself having the following kinds of thoughts, you are stepping onto a slippery slope:

- *The investors gave us the money to invest, so let's invest it.*

- *If we feed our employees, they won't go out for lunch, and we'll get more work out of them.*

- *We need to build infrastructure now to support the amazing future growth we're sure to achieve.*

- *We can always raise more money.*

The best mentality is to assume that you'll never be able to raise money again. How could this happen? You could miss shipping dates. You could fail to meet sales forecasts. Your investors could lose confidence in your team. Your investors could run out of money. An economic depression or a pandemic could occur. You never know. . . .

Anyone can survive when everything is going right. Great entrepreneurs can survive when everything is going wrong. If you knew that you couldn't raise more money, how would you spend what you have?

LOL

Just for grins, to conclude this chapter, let me tell you about some of the more unusual pitches that I've had the honor of hearing:

- Make Israel into an amusement park for the rest of the Middle East.

- Build a geodesic dome over Los Angeles. (I forget whether the dome's purpose was to contain the pollution in Los Angeles or prevent more pollution from entering Los Angeles.)

- Build a dirigible to function as a hospital in the sky.

- Sell plots of land on the moon.

- Float a giant inflatable turtle above San Francisco that's a hotel.

- Enlarge breasts using hypnotherapy.

- Manufacture an invisible car—pitched with the warning that it would be given to the Iraqis if it wasn't funded by a U.S. firm.

- Sell a battery-powered device that you clip to your nose to keep you warm.

- Print out sandwiches.

- Create a new currency for the world; the entrepreneur was seeking a trillion-dollar investment.

  As crazy as these ideas sounded, 3-D printing and Bitcoin happened!

Addenda

Minichapter: Top Ten Lies of Venture Capitalists

Venture capitalists are simple people: they've either decided to invest and are convincing themselves that their gut is right (a.k.a. due diligence), or there's not a chance in hell that they'll do so. While they may be simple, they're not necessarily forthcoming, so if you think it's hard to get a definitive yes out of a venture capitalist, you should try to get a conclusive no.

Alas, entrepreneurs are also simple people: if they don't hear a conclusive no, they assume the answer is yes. This is why there's so much miscommunication between venture capitalists and entrepreneurs. To foster greater understanding between the two groups, here is an exposé of the top ten lies of venture capitalists.

1. "We can make a quick decision." Sure, the firm *could* make a quick decision—after all, it's not their money they're risking, but the firm never *does* make a quick decision because the partners are not the bold, swashbuckling, innovation catalysts they purport to be. They are risk averse like most people in the financial sector and like to follow the crowd.

2. "I liked your company, but my partners didn't." In other words, "No." What the sponsor is trying to get the entrepreneur to believe is that he's the good guy, the smart guy, the guy who gets it; the others didn't, so don't blame him. This is a cop-out; it's not that the other partners didn't like the deal as much as the sponsor wasn't a true believer. A true believer would get it done.

> "If your aunt had balls, she'd be your uncle."

3. "If you get a lead, we will follow." In other words, "No." As the Japanese say, "If your aunt had balls, she'd be your uncle." She doesn't have balls, so it doesn't matter. The venture capitalist is saying, "We don't really believe, but if you can get Sequoia to lead, we'll jump on the pile." In other words, once the entrepreneur doesn't need the money, the venture capitalist would be happy to give him some more. What you want to hear is, "If you can't get a lead, we will." That's a believer.

4. "Show us some traction, and we'll invest." In other words, "No." This lie translates to "I don't believe your story, but if you can prove it by achieving significant revenue, then you might convince me. However, I don't want to tell you no because you might be the next Google, and then I'd look like a total orifice."

5. "We love to co-invest with other venture capitalists." Like the sun rising and Canadians playing hockey, you can depend on the greed of venture capitalists. Greed in this business translates to "If this is a good deal, I want it all." What entrepreneurs want to hear is, "We want the whole round. We don't want any other investors." Then it's the entrepreneur's job to convince them why other investors can make the pie bigger as opposed to reconfiguring the slices.

6. "We're investing in your team." This is an incomplete statement. While it's true that they are investing in the team, entrepreneurs are hearing, "We won't fire you—why would we fire you if we invested because of you?" That's not what the venture capitalist is saying. What she is saying is, "We're investing in your team as long as things are going well, but if they go bad, we will fire your ass because no one is indispensable."

7. "I have lots of bandwidth for your company." Maybe the venture capitalist is talking about the fiber-optics line into his office, but he's not talking about his personal calendar because he's already on ten boards. Counting board meetings, an entrepreneur should assume that a venture capitalist spends between five to ten hours a month on a company. That's it. Deal with it. And make board meetings short!

8. "This is a vanilla term sheet." There is no such thing as a vanilla term sheet. If term sheets are ice cream, the most common flavor is Rocky Road. You need an experienced corporate finance attorney— as opposed to Uncle Joe the divorce lawyer—to navigate the complexities and traps of terms sheets.

9. "We can open up doors for you at our client companies." This is a double whammy of a lie. First, a venture capitalist can't always open up doors at client companies. The client company might hate him, and the worst thing in the world would be a referral from him. Second, even if the venture capitalist *can* open the door, entrepreneurs can't seriously expect the company in question to commit to their MVVVP.

10. "We like early-stage investing." Venture capitalists fantasize about putting $1 million into a $2 million pre-money startup and ending up owning 33 percent of the next Google. That's early-stage investing. Do you know why we all know about Google's amazing return on investment? For the same reason that we all know about Michael Jordan: Googles and Michael Jordans hardly ever happen. If they were common, no one would write about them. If you scratch beneath the surface, venture capitalists want to invest in proven teams (for example, the founders of Cisco) with proven technology (for example, the basis of a Nobel Prize) in a proven market (for example, e-commerce).

FAQ

This FAQ is the longest in this book. Its length reflects how difficult the process of raising money is for most people. I answered the most common questions about this topic within the main body of the chapter, and I've included only the most specialized ones here.

Q: How much money should I try to raise?

A: There are two answers. First, you could raise only as much as you need to get to the next major milestone—for example, from first prototype to first shippable product. The rationale is that accomplishing this milestone will enable you to raise money at a much higher valuation.

Second, if investors are throwing money at you at a high valuation, then you could take as much as they're offering. The goal would be to never have to raise money again, so you'd have one less thing to worry about.

However, no matter what valuation, the more money you take, the more you have to return. For example, when you hear that a company raised $50 million, there are two consequences: First, the company has amassed a large arsenal of funding. Second, the company has to return $500 million to make the investors happy. The latter creates a lot of pressure.

The likelihood that investors will be throwing money at you in the early stages is low, so for most startups, the answer is to take enough to reach the next milestone.

Q: How do I set a valuation for my startup?

A: I used to tell people that every full-time engineer is worth $500,000 and each MBA is worth $250,000. (And I have an MBA). People thought I was joking—I wasn't.

Some advice. First, *you* don't set the valuation unless you're one of the rare startups that is turning away investors. For the rest of us, investors try to set the valuation, and you try to raise it. This is called negotiation.

Second, information about the valuation of private companies is imperfect. It's not as if you can pick up the *Wall Street Journal* and find out what their stock is trading at. The best you can do is use approximations based on companies that are comparable.

The calculation works like this. Suppose a similar firm raises $3 million. Usually, a startup sells 20 to 25 percent of its equity during such a financing. Backing out the math, if $3 million is 20 to 25 percent, then 100 percent is $12 million to $15 million. This provides an initial starting point, and you negotiate from there.

You can find out about these financings by reading websites such as *Mashable, TechCrunch,* and the *Verge.* Wilson Sonsini Goodrich & Rosati also publishes <u>a useful report based on their clients' financings</u>.

Third, you don't need an 800 in the math component of the SAT to think that owning a larger percentage of the startup is better. However, this isn't the whole story—what counts is how much your stock is worth, not how much of the company you own. For example, it's much better to own .001 percent of Google than 51 percent of a $10 million company.

Therefore, don't make yourself crazy trying to maximize the valuation of your startup to minimize the dilutive effects of raising money. You're either going to make more money than you ever dreamed of or you'll end up with nothing. How much your company is worth is more important than what percentage you own.

Q: **Do entrepreneurs have to accept the valuation proposed by the venture capitalist who wants to invest into their business?**

A: Whatever the first offer, ask for a 25 percent higher valuation because you're expected as part of the negotiation to push back—

in fact, if you don't push back, you may scare the venture capitalist into thinking you're not a good negotiator. It would be nice to also be armed with some arguments to show why you believe your valuation should be higher—saying that this book told you to push back isn't sufficient.

At the end of the day, though, if the valuation is reasonable, take the money and get going. Valuation and owning a few more percentage points seldom make a difference.

Q: I've got a venture capitalist that wants to invest $5 million in my company! What should I expect in terms of how he will want to interact with the company?

A: As long as things are going well, a venture capitalist will leave you alone. Understand a venture capitalist's life: he's on as many as ten boards that meet at least quarterly and sometimes monthly; he has to raise money to invest and keep about twenty-five investors informed and happy; he's looking at several deals a day; and he's dealing with five other partners. He doesn't have the time to micromanage you—and if he thought he'd have to, he wouldn't have invested in you in the first place.

The more important question is, "What support can I expect from a *good* venture capitalist?" Here is the answer: five hours a month of mindshare during which he opens doors for you with prospective customers and partners and interviews candidates for high-level positions at your company.

Q: How can I identify the venture capital firms that have new funds with a maturity sufficiently far out so they align with my liquidity time frame?

A: You're thinking too much. The timing of a fund is rarely a big factor. You can either convince the firm that you can make money for it or not. If you do, they'll find funds for you. Also, the firm is going to pick you, and not vice versa, and there is no way to predict a liquidity time frame.

Q: What is the order of approaching the tiers of venture capitalists: tier one, then two, then three, or the other way around?

A: You're thinking *way* too much. Pitch almost any firm you can get into. After trying to raise money for nine months, you'll realize that all money is green. Plus, it's not obvious who is a tier-one, -two, or -three firm.

Q: What is the internal rate of return expected from tier-one, -two, or -three venture capitalists? How firmly do they stand by that projection?

A: You're thinking way, *way* too much. First, it is unlikely that a venture investor will admit that his firm is not a tier-one firm. Even if he did, he isn't saying to his partners and investors, "Since we're a tier-two firm, let's just try to get ten percent."

All venture investors are looking for a high return on your specific investment, not a return that matches their target average. (Remember: they know there is a high likelihood that your company will flame out.) But your question misses another point. Although venture firms are ranked against one another by their IRR performance, venture investors do not evaluate individual deals by calculating prospective IRRs.

Practically speaking, investors look at cash-on-cash returns— that is, if they put in $1 million today, what can they expect to get back in four or five years? (Five million dollars would be a 5× return.) Expectations for cash-on-cash returns vary by the type of investor and the sector of investment, not by the prestige of the firm. For an early-stage, high-tech investment, you had better be able to convince the investor that there is a realistic plan for returning 5× to 10× his money in three to five years.

Q: Should I admit that our sales to date are lackluster (or even nonexistent)?

A: Yes, but I would spin it: Your sales aren't lackluster—you're "early in the sales cycle with an innovative product." Also, this is why the longer you can bootstrap, the better.

Q: Should I admit to the venture capitalist that I am new to all this?

A: You won't have to because it will be obvious. Thus, you might as well tell the truth. However, to ameliorate this situation, surround yourself with directors and advisers who are experienced. Also, say, "I'll do what's right for the organization and step aside if this is the right thing to do," and mean it.

Q: How much do venture capitalists talk among themselves? Will my faux pas in front of one be the talk of the watering hole and poison the well for me with the others?

A: It's unlikely that venture capitalists will talk about you because there isn't enough time in the day to discuss all the lousy meetings they've taken and the clueless entrepreneurs they've met. You'd have to do something astoundingly stupid to be a topic of conversation.

Q: Is it necessary to have hired a law firm and accounting firm before fund-raising?

A: It's not necessary, but it's better if you have a law firm for three reasons: First, assuming you pick a law firm that's recognized for its corporate finance / venture capital work, it shows that you know what you're doing. Second, a good lawyer can help you find investors. Third, you need an experienced corporate finance lawyer to work through the paperwork of a financing. An accounting firm is less important because there's not much to account for yet.

Q: Is it better to ask for the cash to support the whole project up to a liquidity event or just what is needed for the first one or two years?

A: Neither. You can't possibly know if there will be a liquidity event, when it will occur, and how much money you'll need to get there. However, what you want to get, and what investors want to give, is enough capital to get to the next big milestone, plus six months of cushion for when you're late.

Q: Does my business need to be fully functioning and profitable in order to attract investment capital?

A: The venture capital business is cyclic—some would say bulimic. During times of feast, venture capitalists will fund anyone who can boot PowerPoint. During times of purging, most venture capitalists turn cautious and want "fully functioning and profitable" companies.

Your job is to find venture capitalists who make early bets on unproven startups. When venture capitalists tell you that they only invest in proven companies, they're lying. What they are saying is, "We don't get it, so we're blowing you off by telling you this. If we really got it and believed, we'd take the chance with you."

Q: Does the existence of a clear leader in my target market preclude me from getting funding?

A: I can unequivocally say, "It depends." If it's early in the life cycle of the market, and it's clear that the market will be huge, you can get funding. Commodore was the clear leader in personal computers, and plenty of companies got funded after it. On the other hand, it would be difficult in a mature, capital-intensive industry such as automobiles.

It also depends on the investor. Some will be scared off by a market leader. Others will see the existence of a market leader as proof that there is a market and be willing to take the leader on.

There's one more thing to think about. Your question is about funding. However, fundability and viability are not the same thing. Your idea to take on the market leader may not be fundable, but it could still be viable, so don't let negative responses from investors stop you.

Q: Is it better to have fewer, bigger investors, or numerous, smaller ones?

A: You should be so lucky to have the choice. Fewer investors means that there are fewer relationships to manage. Also, bringing in more investors may mean you're also getting less sophisticated ones.

However, there are several compelling reasons to get additional investors: (1) More investors means that there are more people helping you by opening doors, recruiting, and generating buzz. (2) When you need additional capital, it's nice to have several sources already in the deal. (3) It's dangerous to have one investor calling the shots when (not if) you have disagreements.

Q: When accepting angel money, is it reasonable and customary to have a buyout clause, to allow me to retain my stock if I am able to pay back the angel's loan with interest?

A: You can try for this, but it's tacky. Angels aren't banks trying to make a spread between the cost of capital and the interest you'll pay. Angels are putting money into your company at the riskiest time, so they should reap the upside. If you do pull off a buyout clause, you'll rack up bad karma points—and a startup needs all the good karma it can get.

Q: Should current investors attend company pitches to prospective investors?

A: If it's okay with the prospective investor, this is usually viewed positively: "The current investors care enough to come with the company to our meeting." If the current investor is a famous person, by all means bring him or her.

Q: Which would appeal more to investors: a product concept that has a proven billion-dollar market in which there are already some big players, or a product idea that will create a new, potentially billion-dollar market that has no competitors in the short run?

A: This depends on the investor. There are a handful of investors who like "brave new world" investment, but the vast majority are similar to buffalo: running with their heads down toward a cliff because the rest of the herd is too. At some level, raising money is a numbers game: you've got to make a lot of pitches to find one investor to write a check, so you can't be picky.

Q: Which should we put more focus on: Pitching how the product addresses pain and a competitive analysis, or pitching how the investors can get X percent return?

A: The former, never the latter. No one can predict when and how liquidity will occur. Attempting to do so will make you look silly.

Q: When should an entrepreneur give up on getting capital from an investor?

A: I've never seen an entrepreneur reverse a negative decision by arguing. When an investor says no (in so many words, as discussed in the list of venture capitalist lies), accept the decision gracefully.

Do go back, however, when you can produce proof. Proof means finishing your product, opening prestigious accounts, raising money from other sources, and building a great team. Persistence, with proof, can succeed.

Q: What is a reasonable salary that a CEO should set himself up with that will not scare an investor away?

A: This is hard to answer in absolute numbers. Circa 2014, for technology startups, the answer is probably $125,000 per year. An answer that can better stand the test of time is this: the CEO should not be paid more than four times the lowest-paid full-time employee.

Q: Angels want entrepreneurs to have some skin in the game. I don't have any money to invest in the business. How do I overcome this? What do venture capitalists look for these days as far as skin in the game?

A: An entrepreneur's skin in the game, for a venture capitalist or an angel, is nice to have—but not a necessity. Certainly you shouldn't believe that because you were stupid enough to put money into a lousy idea, other investors will follow suit.

If you think that the only reason a potential investor declined was because you didn't have skin in the game, you were going to get a negative answer anyway. What's more important is how long you've been working on the product and what progress you've made.

Conversely, if the investor agrees to provide capital primarily because you have skin in the game, then the investor is a fool, and you wouldn't want him. Also, in almost all cases, you will have a lot of skin in the game in the form of months of sweat equity.

Q: If an angel investor asks what his return will be, what is the best answer?

A: The best answer is to tell him that he must not be a sophisticated investor, because such an investor would know better than to ask a question that has no answer. I'll bet, however, that you don't have the guts to do this. Instead, you can ask him to go over your financial projection with you and then ask him, "What do you think is realistic?"

Q: What do I wear to meetings with venture capitalists?

A: It depends on what part of the country you're in. On the East Coast, you should wear a jacket and tie. On the West Coast, you can be much more casual—Dockers and a polo shirt will do. No matter where you are, if you're the geek genius, you can get away with a clean T-shirt and jeans.

Q: Would investors ever be interested in making their return through profit sharing or a buyout from the founders of the company in five to ten years?

A: Only if the investor is your mother. If the investors are professional investors, you can forget about raising money without a shot at an IPO or acquisition. If they're angels, investing in your startup might represent a flight of fancy or sympathy—then liquidity doesn't matter as much. But profit sharing or buying out investors is attractive to few investors.

Q: How can one protect an idea, given that few investors will sign an NDA (nondisclosure agreement)?

"Implementation is hard—and where the money is."

A: You're right. Few investors will sign one, and even if they did, hearing your idea had better not render it defenseless. I've never seen a case where an entrepreneur told an investor about an idea and the investor ripped it off.

Investors are looking for people who can implement ideas, not only come up with them. Ideas are easy. Implementation is hard—and where the money is. Quite frankly, few investors are capable of implementing an idea—that's why they're investors . . . but I digress.

Here are the fine points of using an NDA:

If you're asking for an NDA to merely present your idea, keep your day job because you're clueless. No one who would sign one just to hear your idea is an investor that you'd want.

Freely circulate your executive summary and PowerPoint pitch. These documents should entice investors to go to the next step. They should not reveal your magic sauce.

Ask for an NDA if an investor is interested in your deal and wants to learn more at the source-code or pure-science level. It is reasonable for an investor to ask for this kind of information in the due-diligence stage. It is reasonable for you to ask for an NDA at this stage too.

Once patents are filed, you should feel pretty safe in discussing your magic sauce under an NDA—not that you'll have the time or resources to sue for patent infringement. The best protection of an idea is great implementation of the idea.

Q: When do I stop trying to find/negotiate a better deal and take what's offered?

A: It's a good idea to stop looking and negotiating if you can't meet payroll. If the deal that you're offered is within 20 percent of what you wanted, take it. Focus on building your business, not finding the best deal. In the long run, the quality of your business determines how much money you'll make, not the deal you cut years before with an investor.

Q: Should I worry more about dilution, the real needs of my business, or the amount the investor wants to put in?

A: Here's the priority: the real needs of your business, the amount the investor wants to put in, and, last and least, dilution.

Recommended Reading

Stross, Randall E. *eBoys: The True Story of the Six Tall Men Who Backed eBay, Webvan, and Other Billion-Dollar Start-Ups.* New York: Crown Business, 2000.

CHAPTER 6

The Art of Pitching

Mend your speech a little, lest it may mar your fortunes.

—William Shakespeare, *King Lear*

GIST

Forget "I think, therefore I am." For entrepreneurs, the operative phrase is "I pitch, therefore I am." Pitching isn't only for raising money—it's for reaching agreement, and agreement can yield many good outcomes including sales, partnerships, and new hires.

Question: How can you tell if an entrepreneur is pitching?

Answer: His lips are moving.

In this chapter, you'll learn how to pitch your startup and product in shorter, simpler, and more effective ways.

Be Prepared

If there's no projector available when you show up for a meeting, it's your fault. If your laptop and the projector don't work together, it's your fault. If the projector bulb blows out in the middle of your pitch, it's your fault. If you start slowly, seem disorganized, and lose your audience, it's your fault.

Are you seeing a pattern?

It's almost impossible to recover from a bad start, so get there early and set the stage. Bring your own projector. Bring two laptops loaded up with your presentation. Bring two VGA adapters. Bring a copy of your presentation on a USB drive. Bring printouts of your presentation in case nothing works.

Set the Stage

When the meeting starts, you should set the stage for the rest of the pitch. The thing to ask is, "How much of your time do I have?" This question shows that you respect the value of the audience's time by not running over your limit. It also makes the audience commit to a minimum allotment of time.

> **"If you set the stage so that everyone has the same expectations, you're way ahead of the game."**

Then you ask, "What are the three most important pieces of information that I can provide?" You may find out that they already know or believe in something that you were going to try to communicate, so you can skip that. And you may find out that you can't skip something that you thought was understood.

Finally, you ask, "May I quickly go through my presentation and handle questions at the end?" You're trying to make the audience commit to not interrupting you so that your pitch can flow better.

You should have gotten this information before the meeting from your sponsor, but getting these answers should take about five minutes, and if you set the stage so that everyone has the same expectations, you're way ahead of the game.

Explain Yourself in the Sixth Minute

I've never sat through a pitch and wished that the speaker had spent the first fifteen minutes explaining her life story and then another fifteen minutes giving me the background of every team member in the room.

Unfortunately, many entrepreneurs believe that a pitch is a narrative whose opening chapter must always be autobiographical. These personal tales are supposed to convince the audience that this is a great team. Meanwhile, everyone is wondering, *What does this startup do?* To use an aviation analogy, the presentation feels like a 747 rumbling along for two miles. Instead, you should emulate an F18 catapulting off a three-hundred-foot aircraft carrier deck.

By no later than the sixth minute of your presentation, you should be explaining what your startup does. (Remember that the first five minutes are to get answers to the three questions mentioned above.) Once the audience has learned what you do, they can listen to the rest of your pitch with calm and focused minds.

Don't go crazy with statements along the lines of "patent-pending, curve-jumping, enterprise-class, scalable, revolutionary, first-mover advantage, paradigm-shifting, customer-focused solutions." Use three- to five-word statements like these instead:

- "We sell software."

- "We sell hardware."

- "We teach underprivileged kids."

- "We prevent child abuse."

EXERCISE

Set a timer to one minute. Explain what your startup does to some friends until time runs out. Ask them to write down what your startup does. Collect the answers and compare them to what you think you said.

Observe the 10/20/30 Rule

I have Ménière's disease, the medical term for the combination of tinnitus, hearing loss, and vertigo. There is no cure, but there are many theories about its cause and treatment. I am convinced that my Ménière's is the result of listening to thousands of crappy pitches.

"I am convinced that my Ménière's is the result of listening to thousands of crappy pitches."

Pareto's Principle is that 80 percent of the effects come from 20 percent of the causes. Metcalfe's Law is that the value of a network is proportional to the square of the number of users. The 10/20/30 Rule of Presentations is that you should use ten slides in twenty minutes with a minimum of thirty-point text. It's the most important rule you can learn about pitching, and it will help prevent a Ménière's epidemic.

Ten Slides

The purpose of a pitch is to stimulate interest, not to cover every aspect of your startup and bludgeon your audience into submission. Your objective is to generate enough interest to get a second meeting.

Thus, the recommended number of slides for a pitch is ten. This impossibly low number forces you to concentrate on the absolute essentials. You can add a few more, but you should never exceed fifteen slides—the more slides you need, the less compelling your idea. The ten slides are:

• **TITLE.** Organization name; your name and title; address, e-mail, and cell phone number. When this slide is showing, you ask the three questions that set the stage and then explain what your startup does. Cut to the chase!

"'If a picture is worth a thousand words, a prototype is worth ten thousand slides.'"

• **PROBLEM AND OPPORTUNITY.** Describe the pain that you're alleviating. The goal is to get everyone buying into the utility of your product. Avoid looking like a solution searching for a problem. Minimize or eliminate citations of consulting studies about the future size of your market.

If you're not alleviating pain but enabling people to do things that they could never do before, this is the time to paint a picture of the brave new world that you're offering.

- **VALUE PROPOSITION**. Explain how you alleviate pain and the meaning that you make. Ensure that the audience understands what you sell and your value proposition.

This is not the place for an in-depth technical explanation. Provide the gist of your startup—for example, "We are a discount travel website. We have written software that searches all other travel sites and collates their price quotes into one report."

- **UNDERLYING MAGIC**. Describe the technology, secret sauce, or magic behind your product. The less text and the more diagrams, schematics, and flowcharts the better. With this one slide, you must convince people that you have a technically viable idea.

If you have an MVVVP, working prototype, or demo, this is the time to transition to it. If you're lucky, you'll never get to the rest of your slides. As Glen Shires of Google said, "If a picture is worth a thousand words, a prototype is worth ten thousand slides."

- **BUSINESS MODEL**. Explain how you make money: who pays you, your channels of distribution, and your gross margins. Generally, a unique, untested business model is a scary proposition. If you have a revolutionary business model, explain it in terms of familiar ones. This is your opportunity to drop the names of the organizations that are already using your product.

- **GO-TO-MARKET PLAN**. Explain how you are going to reach your customer and summarize your marketing leverage points. Convince the audience that you have an effective go-to-market strategy that won't break the bank. (Resist the temptation to use "go viral," because that's wishful thinking, not a strategy.)

- **COMPETITIVE ANALYSIS**. Provide a complete view of the competitive landscape. Too much is better than too little. Never dismiss your competition. Everyone—customers, investors, and partners—wants to hear why you're good, not why the competition is bad.

- **MANAGEMENT TEAM**. Describe the key players of your management team, board of directors, and board of advisers, as well as your major investors. It's okay if you have less than a perfect team—if you were the cofounder of Cisco or YouTube, you would not need to raise money.

You only have to show that your education and work experience are relevant to the market you're going after. All startups have holes—what's important is whether you understand that there *are* holes and are willing to fix them.

• **FINANCIAL PROJECTIONS AND KEY METRICS.** Provide a three-to-five-year forecast containing not only dollars but also key metrics, such as number of customers and conversion rate. Do a bottom-up forecast (see chapter 4, "The Art of Bootstrapping"). Take into account long sales cycles and seasonality. Making people understand the underlying assumptions of your forecast is as important as the numbers you've fabricated.

• **CURRENT STATUS, ACCOMPLISHMENTS TO DATE, TIMELINE, AND USE OF FUNDS.** Explain the current status of your product, what the near future looks like, and how you'll use the money you're trying to raise. Share the details of your positive momentum and traction. Then use this slide to close with a bias toward action.

A word about liquidity: no entrepreneur knows when, how, or if she will achieve liquidity, and yet many insist on including a slide that says, "There are two liquidity options: an IPO or an acquisition." Duh. If an investor asks about your exit strategy, it usually indicates he's clueless. If you answer with these two options, you have a lot in common.

The only time you should include a slide about liquidity is when you can list at least three acquirers whom the investor has never heard of—this shows that you know the industry. By contrast, saying that Google, or the Google of your industry, will buy you will make all but the dumbest investors laugh at you.

In addition to your ten slides, you can have more that go into greater detail about your technology, marketing, current customers, and other key strategies. It's good to have these done in advance in case you're asked for a more in-depth explanation. However, don't use them unless you're asked about their subject matter.

Twenty Minutes

Most appointments are made for an hour; however, you should be able to give your pitch in twenty minutes. There are three reasons for this:

- If you're using a Windows laptop, you may need forty minutes to make it work with the projector. If you've recently upgraded Windows, you may need the full hour.

- You may not get a full hour if the previous meeting is running long, and I've never seen a previous meeting end on time. Unfortunately, your meeting may have to end on time to get back on schedule.

- You want ample time for discussion. Whether it's twenty minutes of presentation and then forty minutes of discussion or a sequence of slide/discussion, slide/discussion, slide/discussion isn't critical.

You're thinking, *Guy's referring to the hoi polloi, great unwashed masses, and bozos. They should use ten slides and twenty minutes, but not us. We have curve-jumping, paradigm-shifting, first-moving, patent-pending technology.*

I am referring to *you.* I don't care if you sell dog food, permanent life, nano particles, optical components, or the cure for cancer: ten slides and twenty minutes is all you get.

Thirty-Point Font

This recommendation applies to any pitch you're giving with a projector. Think about it: most investors are older and have deteriorating vision. A good rule of thumb for font size is to divide the oldest investor's age by two and use that font size. Another good rule of thumb is that the larger the font, the better the speaker—Steve Jobs used a 150-point font. You use an eight-point font.

The large size of the font and the paucity of text is because slides are to lead, not read. They should paraphrase and anchor what's coming out of your mouth. Because people can read faster than you talk, if you put too much detail on the slide, the audience will read ahead of you and not listen to what you're saying.

EXERCISE

Pretend that someone offered to pay you a hundred dollars for each word that you deleted from your pitch. What would your pitch look like?

If you have to use a small font to accommodate your material, you're putting too much detail on the slide. Each slide should portray one primary point. All the text and bullets should support this point.

Master the Fine Points

In some cases . . . the knife can turn savagely upon the person wielding it. . . . You use the knife carefully because you know it doesn't care who it cuts.

—Stephen King

If you obey the 10/20/30 Rule, your pitches will be better than those of 90 percent of entrepreneurs. To come even closer to perfection, master these fine points:

- **NEVER. READ. YOUR. SLIDES.** Never read your slides. The text on slides is your anchor point. The words out of your mouth are explanatory and embellishment.

"Do you think that a faded fly-in from the bottom left is going to make a presentation better?"

- **USE A DARK BACKGROUND.** A dark background communicates seriousness and substance. A white or light background looks cheap and amateurish. Also, staring at a white screen for twenty to sixty minutes (depending on what kind of computer you use) gets tiring. Have you ever seen movie credits that use black text on a white background?

- **ADD YOUR LOGO TO THE MASTER PAGE.** Every presentation is a chance to build brand awareness for your startup, so put your logo on the master slide page. By doing this, your logo will appear on every slide.

- **USE COMMON, SANS-SERIF FONTS.** A presentation is not the place to show that you've accumulated the world's largest collection of fonts. Use common fonts because someday you may present your pitch on someone else's computer. Use sans-serif fonts because they are much easier to read than the delicate serif font you love. You can never go wrong with Arial.

- **ANIMATE YOUR BODY, NOT YOUR SLIDES.** PowerPoint has more than sixty ways to animate text and graphics. This is fifty-nine too many. Many entrepreneurs use animations and transitions between slides to jazz up their presentations. Do you think that a faded fly-in from the bottom left is going to make a presentation better? Use your body, not PowerPoint effects and animations, to communicate expressiveness, emotion, and enthusiasm.

- **BUILD BULLETS.** Most entrepreneurs don't use bullets. They display and read big blocks of long text. That's a mistake. Use bullets instead: snippets of text that capture the main point. Even when many entrepreneurs use bullets, they put them all up at once, which enables people to read ahead. That's also a mistake. Build your bullets: click, bullet one, explain; click, bullet two, explain; click, bullet three, explain. This is all the animation you need anywhere in a presentation.

- **USE ONLY ONE LEVEL OF BULLETS.** The use of bullets with bullets means that you're trying to communicate too much information on a slide. Each slide should communicate one point, with bullets to support that point. If you observe the "30" part of the 10/20/30 Rule, it will be hard to have bullets with bullets anyway.

- **USE DIAGRAMS AND GRAPHS.** Better a bullet than a block of text, but better a diagram or graph than a bullet. Use diagrams to explain how your business works. Use graphs to explain trends and numerical results. And build your diagrams and pictures by bringing in these elements with clicks, just like bullets.

- **MAKE PRINTABLE SLIDES.** There is a cautionary aspect to adding diagrams and graphics. Sometimes these graphic objects build upon each other, and in the process, cover previous ones. This is okay during a presentation but not when the file is printed, so ensure that your slides work when printed too.

Let One Person Do the Talking

Many entrepreneurs believe that investors invest in teams, so they should demonstrate teamwork in their pitches. Using this line of reasoning, four or five employees attend the pitch, and each has a speaking role.

The logic that everyone should have a speaking role is terrific for a school play. Parents and grandparents see their precious jewels in action, and there are plenty of opportunities for video. Life is good, fair, and equitable. A pitch, however, is not a school play.

In a pitch the CEO should do 80 percent of the talking. The rest of the team (and there should be no more than two others) can present the one or two slides pertaining to their specific area of expertise. They can also provide detailed answers if any questions arise. However, if the CEO can't handle most of the pitch by himself, he should practice until he can, or he should be replaced.

Often team members try to rescue the CEO when the audience pushes back on something he said. For example, suppose someone wants to debate a multiple-tier distribution system for selling products. A team member, with all good intentions, asserts, "I think you're right. I've thought for a long time that we should sell directly to the customer."

Bad move. This doesn't show flexible thinking, an open environment, or a broad-based set of expertise. It shows a lack of cohesion. The right answer is for no one else to say anything and for the CEO to say, "You raise a good point. Can we follow up with you on that?"

Get to One Thousand Feet and Stay There

I promise that this is the only war analogy in this book. Consider three methods to deliver lethal force:

- **B-1B LANCER.** This is a long-range bomber for intercontinental missions that is capable of penetrating sophisticated defense systems. It can fly up to thirty thousand feet above the ground. It costs $200 million.

"If pitches were weapons, the majority, unfortunately, would be B-1 Lancers or Navy Seals."

- **NAVY SEALS.** These people specialize in on-the-ground special operations in enemy territory. They provide unconventional warfare capabilities and real-time eyes on targets by striking from, and returning to, the sea.

- **A-10 WARTHOG.** This plane is for close air support of troops. It is simple and rugged. Its sweet spot is flying at a thousand feet, and it costs $13 million.

If pitches were weapons, the majority, unfortunately, would be B-1 Lancers or Navy Seals. The B-1 pitch is up in the clouds. It features a lot of hand waving, cool PowerPoint animations, and use of terms such as "strategic," "partnership," "alliance," "first-mover advantage," and "patented technology." An MBA with a finance or consulting background delivers it.

Geeks, propeller heads, and engineers deliver the Navy Seal pitch. They explain the technical nuances and use a lot of acronyms that only they understand. It's clear that they know every bit of their technology—and would love to explain it all.

The B-1 pitch is too high because listeners want to learn what the business does and why it will succeed, not learn about megatrends and megalomaniac ambitions. The Navy Seal pitch is too low because it focuses on bits, bytes, and nits.

The right analogy for pitching is the A-10 Warthog (a thousand feet). Your pitch shouldn't be in the clouds or on the ground with a knife in your teeth. Simply provide enough detail to prove you can deliver and enough aerial view to prove you have a plan.

Answer the Little Man

When Bill Joos, a former colleague at Garage Technology Ventures, started his career, IBM trained him to imagine there was a little man sitting on his shoulder. During presentations, every time Bill said something, the little man would whisper, "So what?"

You should imagine this little man on your shoulder and listen to him, because the significance of what you're saying is not always self-evident, much less awe inspiring. Every time you make a statement, imagine the little man asks his question.

After you answer, follow with the two most powerful words in a pitch: "For instance . . ."* Then discuss a real-world use or scenario of a feature of your product. Here are some examples:

---

* Richard C. Borden, *Public Speaking as Listeners Like It!* (New York: Harper & Brothers, 1935), 53.

You said	Little man asked	You replied	You elaborated
"We use digital signal processing in our hearing aids."	"So what?"	"Our product increases the clarity of sounds."	"For instance, if you're at a cocktail party with many conversations going on around you, you'll be able to hear what people are saying to you."
"We provide 128-bit encryption in a portable device."	"So what?"	"It's harder than hell to break into our system."	"For instance, if you're in a hotel room and want to have a secure telephone conversation with your headquarters."
"Ms. (big name celebrity) is on our advisory board."	"So what?"	"What we're doing is interesting enough to attract top talent."	"For instance, she has already opened doors for us in her industry."
"We use Montessori methods in our new school."	"So what?"	"Our school focuses on children as individuals and enables them to learn to manage their own study independently."	"For instance, we enable children who are gifted in specific areas to proceed in advance of the rest of the students."

Pitch Constantly

Familiarity breeds content. When you are totally familiar and comfortable with your pitch, you'll be able to give it most effectively. There are no short-cuts to achieving familiarity—you have to pitch a lot of times.

"If you're lousy in practice, you're lousy in the pitch."

Twenty-five repetitions are what it takes for most people to reach this point. All these pitches don't have to be to your intended audiences—your cofounders, employees, relatives, friends, and even your dog are fine auditors.

Forget rising to the occasion without practice. Steve Jobs practices his product introductions for hours, and you're not Steve Jobs. If you're lousy in practice, you're lousy in the pitch, so get going—because if there's anything worse than getting Ménière's, it's causing it.

EXERCISE

Videotape yourself giving your pitch. If you can watch it without being embarrassed, you're ready to go.

Provide the Right Numbers

Socialism never took root in America because the poor see themselves not as an exploited proletariat but as temporarily embarrassed millionaires.

—John Steinbeck

Investors don't spread pitches across the table and pick the ones to fund based on financial projections and rates of return. Most pitches submitted to venture capitalists are more similar than they are different anyway. Specifically, they all project fourth- or fifth-year sales of $50 million. Anyone who can boot Excel can achieve these theoretical results.

Generally venture capitalists want three to five years of projections to help them do three things: first, understand the scale of your business; second, examine the assumptions of your business model; and third, determine how much capital you'll require. Here is how three leading investors describe what they look for in financial projections.

- **MOHANJIT JOLLY—DRAPER FISHER JURVETSON.** "I look for a five-year forecast with some detailed assumptions for the first couple of years where some level of visibility exists. The later years are more to understand revenue growth as a proxy for whether the entrepreneur is thinking big as well as an understanding of the key drivers such as capital intensity, head count growth, etc. In totality the financials are more of a 'gut check' than anything else: Can the business be big enough in a reasonable amount of time to provide the kind of returns that we are looking for? And are the underlying assumptions sane?"

- **DOUG LEONE—SEQUOIA CAPITAL**. "Believe it or not, financials for startups have become irrelevant," was Doug's answer, so I asked, "So in a business plan or pitch to Sequoia, people don't even have to cover it at all? You don't care at all?" To which he responded, "Not at all in startups. We care about how big is the market, how long to build it, how many engineers, the usage and engagement and so on."

- **IAN SOBIESKI—BAND OF ANGELS**. "I know my early/seed stage investments will not meet their five-year pro forma, but I still want the entrepreneur to have one in sufficient detail to show how she is thinking about the business. It's not science, but it is a sort of Impressionist painting by the numbers of what the entrepreneur is trying to build. I want to then see how this plan is broken down into provable hypotheses and experiments that allow the entrepreneur to test pieces of the model as the company grows. These pieces are natural inflection points in the business plan where pivots can be made, and they are also natural places for different rounds of fund-raising: the series A, B, and C."

The point is that investors are not looking for detailed forecasts containing every conceivable line item. They're looking for the big picture and trying to understand the kinds of assumptions that you're making about your business.

One way to improve your forecasts is to build them from the bottom up instead of from the top down. First, let's review the wrong way: taking a huge number at the top and multiplying it by an easy-to-achieve market share. Let's apply this method to selling dog food:

- According to the Humane Society there are 85 million owned dogs in America.

- Each dog eats two cans of dog food per day.

- The total market, therefore, is 170 million cans per day.

- Let's assume, conservatively, that you can achieve 1 percent market share or 1.7 million cans per day.

- Let's also assume that each can costs one dollar.

- This means your company will have $1.7 million in revenue per day—again being conservative. This is a mere $620 million in annual revenue.

Now let's examine the right way, which is to start from the bottom at zero dollars and estimate how many customers you can reach and close:

- Using every SEO trick, partnership, and social media technique, you can get 50,000 visitors to your site per month.

- One percent or 500 will buy all sixty cans needed for the month, so monthly revenue is 500 people x 60 cans x $1/can = $30,000.

- You may get more visitors and improve your percentage of closed sales, but this is a realistic baseline: $30,000 per month or $360,000 per year.

Three hundred and sixty thousand dollars is a long way from $620 million. Maybe $360,000 is too pessimistic, but your actual results will be a lot closer to $360,000 than $620 million.

Disclose Everything

If there's crud in your company that you haven't or can't clean up immediately, disclose it to investors early in the fund-raising process. The later you reveal it, the harder it is to disclose, and the more it will harm your credibility.

For example, Garage Technology Ventures once invested in a company that disclosed that a potential investor had a consulting agreement with the company. This arrangement came to light a few days before financing was closing. This investor was buying stock, as well as receiving stock and cash for consulting services. No other investor had a similar deal.

When the other investors found out about this arrangement, the deal almost collapsed. Had the company made a full disclosure earlier and explained why it made sense for everyone (which, in fact, it did), things would have gone much more smoothly. Unfortunately a high-value investor bailed out because of this last-minute issue.

What if there's a cloud in your background, such as you started, or worked for, a company that failed? There's no use in trying to hide this fact because investors will uncover it. It's also poor form to blame anyone or anything else for its failure, whether the market, other employees, customers, or, in particular, the investors, no matter what the truth actually is.

My recommendation is that you do a *mea culpa*. That is, you accept as much blame for the failure as is justified and confess your sins. Sophisticated investors find such honesty admirable, and many investors have made boatloads of money with entrepreneurs who failed in previous efforts. What's important is that you learned from your failures and are eager to try again.

Shut Up, Take Notes, Summarize, Regurgitate, and Follow Up

There are very few people who don't become more interesting when they stop talking.

—Mary Lowry

I once accompanied a startup's CEO and COO on a pitch to a venture capitalist. A few days after the pitch, I met with the venture capitalist. When we began to discuss the Management (with a capital M), he said, "I noticed that the CEO did a lot of talking, but the COO was sitting there taking notes. The CEO didn't write down a thing. I think the COO is a quality guy."

"The visible act of taking notes says, 'I think you're smart. You're saying something worth writing down. I'm willing and anxious to learn. I'm conscientious.'"

I don't remember whether what the venture capitalist was saying in the meeting was noteworthy, but that's not the point. Shutting up, taking notes, and listening for ways to improve are good things to do in a pitch because even the smallest actions can create a big impression.

The visible act of taking notes says, "I think you're smart. You're saying something worth writing down. I'm willing and anxious to learn. I'm conscientious." Taking notes provides these benefits, plus the value of the information that you're recording. It can't get much better than this.

Also, at the end of the meeting, summarize what you heard and play it back in order to make sure you got the correct information. Then follow through, within a day, on all the promises that you made during the pitch—for example, providing additional information.

Rewrite from Scratch

After World War II many U.S. military Jeeps were given or sold to people in the Philippines. These vehicles, called Jeepneys, were altered by the Filipinos to increase their seating capacity and were decorated with wild colors until they were beautiful but unrecognizable from their original form. Some Jeepneys even made the transition to become Mercedes.

After a while, many pitches begin to resemble these cars. They started as basic, utilitarian documents, but entrepreneurs kept editing and patching them in response to feedback from potential investors. Each meeting leading to more edits, fixes, and patches, until it's difficult to recognize the fundamentals of the pitch at all.

My recommendation is that after five or so pitches you throw away your pitch and start with a clean slate. Let this version 2.0 reflect the gestalt of what you've learned instead of being a patchwork quilt.

Pitch, Then Plan—and Why There Is No Chapter about Business Plans in This Book

I have not seen a plan in five years. Only presos.

—Doug Leone, Sequoia Capital

<u>According to the British Library</u>, there were magical vessels in Celtic myths that "satisfied the tastes and needs of all who ate and drank from them." These myths led to the legend of the Holy Grail. Until recently the modern-day equivalent of the Holy Grail for entrepreneurs was a business plan.

In the old days entrepreneurs wrote a business plan and then pulled PowerPoint slides out of it. They viewed the business plan as the be-all and end-all, and the pitch as a subset of this magnificence. The business plan was supposed to satisfy the tastes and needs of all who read it and induce magical effects—specifically, the irresistible urge to fund.

This is outmoded thinking, and Holy Grail business plans remain unattainable and mythological. In practice, the days of writing business plans are gone. Few sophisticated investors will read one as the first step—everyone wants to hear your pitch, not read your plan.

For early-stage companies, all you need is a PowerPoint or Keynote pitch. There's a small chance that potential investors will ask you for a business plan, but even then they've already made up their minds without it.

Much later, when raising a mezzanine round just before going public, you may have to produce a business plan, but at that point you'll be using investment bankers and lawyers to write drivel to cover your ass.

Addenda

Minichapter: A Pitch Makeover

I advise a company called Enthrill. It provides book publishers with a way to sell e-books through brick-and-mortar retailers. The CEO of the company, Kevin Franco, asked me to review his ninety-second pitch for the TechShowcase2014 in Calgary, Alberta. I am providing what he originally sent me and how I edited (to put it mildly) it as an illustration of how to make an effective pitch.

BEFORE (my comments/$.02 to Kevin are in *italicized* text):

> Hello, my name is Kevin Franco. I am the cofounder and CEO of Enthrill Distribution Inc.

We are seeking $750,000 in equity capital to help commercialize our e-book distribution technology. **MY $.02:** *Don't give a number. What if someone wants to invest $2 million?*

One of the biggest problems in the publishing industry today is the barrier presented by the "walled gardens." **MY $.02:** *"Walled Gardens" is not clear to people unless they are really familiar with publishing. I'm really familiar, and I'm not sure what you mean. . . .*

Amazon, Apple, Kobo, Nook, and Sony cannot deliver into each other's devices. This limits publishers to just consumer trade sales, only a portion of total publishing sales. **MY $.02:** *How many people will understand what "consumer trade sales" means?*

Enthrill has solved this problem. Our technology delivers e-books to all device types. We have two applications that help publishers sell e-books:

A. B2B sales (or bulk e-book sales to corporations) **MY $.02:** *I completely understand publishing. I completely understand what B2B means. I'm trying to figure out what B2B in publishing means.*

B. Retail sales (or e-book sales in retail chains)

In the B2B segment, we see a white-space sales opportunity of over $4 billion globally for publishers to capitalize on using our SaaS (software as a service). **MY $.02:** *What is "white-space sales"? Now you have me thinking, "Huh, what is SaaS about enabling a publisher to sell books? Oh, you mean Enthrill is SaaS, not what publishers will do. But SaaS is like Salesforce.com. How is Enthrill like Salesforce? What the hell is this guy talking about?"*

In the retail segment, we see a huge opportunity for publishers to leverage the traffic of brick-and-mortar retailers and the exploding gift card market by selling digital content through e-book gift cards.

In a few weeks, Enthrill will be officially launching our technology in the market. Walmart will be unveiling an Enthrill-powered online e-bookstore and an Enthrill gift card in-store e-book program in all their Canadian stores. Enthrill will be selling e-book gift cards in over a thousand retail locations in Canada for this holiday season. **MY $.02:** *Three-quarters done and finally it's getting interesting. This is ass-backward.*

We have signed contracts with HarperCollins, Macmillan, Harlequin, Scholastic, and many more publishers, as well as Walmart, Target, Safeway, Air Miles, Toys "R" Us, Home Hardware, InComm, Air Miles, Blackhawk Network, and CMMI.

I would love to meet with you one-on-one so that we may discuss this opportunity further.

This is the version that I wrote to replace what he sent me.

My name is Kevin Franco. I am the cofounder and CEO of Enthrill Distribution. We are probably the only company at this event with a signed, sealed, and about-to-launch service with Walmart.

In a few weeks, Walmart shoppers will be able to buy an e-book from publishers such as HarperCollins, Macmillan, Harlequin, and Scholastic. You're familiar with gift cards. [Hold up a card at this point.] Our product is similar but instead of a cash credit, it's for a specific book.

People buy the card for an e-book, go home, get online, enter the code number on the card, and download their e-book. Or give them as gifts. Without our technology publishers cannot offer e-books through brick-and-mortar stores. They are completely dependent on online sales by Amazon, Apple, Kobo, Nook, and Sony—and you know how they feel about that.

Our product is a win-win-win. Publishers love us because Amazon and other retailers no longer control their e-book distribution. Walmart and retailers love us because they can tap the e-book market, not just the printed-book market. Also, our cards take a lot less space, so retailers can offer more titles and it's easier to handle the return of cards as opposed to shipping pallets of books.

And people love us because they find out about new e-books while they're out shopping.

> Oh, one more thing . . . We have signed contracts with Target, Safeway, Toys "R" Us, and Home Hardware too. By Christmas, Enthrill cards will be available in over a thousand locations in Canada.

The lessons to derive from my rewrite are:

- **START STRONG.** If you're about to do business with a giant like Walmart, you should scream this at the top of your lungs. Start with whatever is your best news.

- **CUT THE INDUSTRY JARGON.** Tell people what you do, how you do it, and who your customer is in the simplest language possible.

- **DROP ALL THE BIG NAMES YOU CAN.** If you have other big-name relationships, blast them out too. The audience is looking for proof that you'll succeed. Big-name customers go a long way toward making this happen.

- **CATALYZE FANTASY.** Notice that there are no industry revenue numbers and market-sizing bullshiitake. A solution like this would appeal to lots of publishers, so you don't need to be a mathematician to know that lots of e-books are sold.

- **FINISH STRONG.** As Steve Jobs used to say, "One more thing . . ." Save something great for the end.

Minichapter: How to Win a Business-Plan Contest

Organizations around the world run business-plan contests to promote innovation and entrepreneurship. The good news is that these contests force entrepreneurs to get their acts together because of a deadline, and they are learning experiences that force entrepreneurs to simulate a startup team.

The bad news is that business plans are no longer necessary, so business-plan contests are using the wrong format. Organizations should run business-*pitch* contests instead. I've been a judge for many business-plan contests, and

I only read the first executive summaries and listen to the pitches to cast my votes.

Another issue is that these contests are geared toward making startups attractive to investors. IMHO, this emphasis is a disservice to entrepreneurs. What's more important than making a startup attractive to investors in a beauty-contest format is to make them viable in real life.

For example, by not targeting a proven market with a proven management team and proven technology (the three qualities most investors say they're looking for), an entry might not appeal to investors. But unproven teams in unproven markets with unproven technologies often produce epic startups.

In the real world, viability is more important than fundability for three reasons: First, you need less startup capital because everything is free or cheap—infrastructure, marketing methods, and tools. Second, crowdfunding can provide up to several hundred thousand dollars in cash. It doesn't matter if you don't have the most fundable startup if you don't need funding. Third, the hard part of starting a company is achieving viability, not fund-raising. What does it matter if you have the most fundable startup if it isn't viable?

But I digress.

I can't build a case that it's bad to win a business-*plan* or business-*pitch* contest, because visibility is always a good thing. These competitions are the last bastions of business plans, so you may have to *write* one to enter, but final judging is based on pitching, so to win one of these, you should focus on your pitch:

- **PRACTICE**. Practice until you're sick of your presentation. Few people can wing it. The probability that you're one of them is zero.

"You're going to win or lose in the first minute or so."

- **GET TO IT**. Explain what your product does in the first thirty seconds. Explain the problem or pain that it addresses in the second thirty seconds. You're going to win or lose in the first minute or so. Remember: F18 not 747.

- **TELL A STORY.** Provide a logical reason for your interest in your product, service, and sector. Stories such as "My girlfriend wanted to sell her collectible toys online" have launched a thousand checks.

- **CATALYZE FANTASY.** Forget trying to prove that there's a huge market for your product by citing statistics and consulting studies. Every other team is going to do this. Paint a story that's so compelling and so cool that the judges fantasize about your potential and do the math in their heads.

- **USE A BIG FONT.** The judges are probably old and can't read small text on slides. There's probably a large audience, so the people in the back need to read your slides too.

- **USE BIG GRAPHICS.** Your competition is going to use small text and no graphics. Think different. Use as many graphics and photos and as few words as possible. Screenshots are also powerful because they make your idea seem more real.

- **DO YOUR RESEARCH.** You'll know who the judges are in advance. Find out all that you can about them and then tailor your presentation to them. The obvious benefit is a more relevant presentation, but there's an added outcome: the judges will see that you were clever and diligent enough to have done this.

- **LIGHTEN UP ON THE REALITY DISTORTION OF THE QUALITY OF YOUR TEAM.** By definition if you're in one of these contests, you and your team probably don't have heart-stopping résumés. Trying to minimize weakness doesn't produce strength. Just show that your backgrounds are relevant to your business.

- **PRACTICE SOME MORE.**

Minichapter: Top Ten Lies of Entrepreneurs

In a typical day an investor meets with two or three startups and sees another four or five executive summaries. Each company claims to represent a unique and earth-shattering opportunity with a proven team, proven technology, and proven market. No company claims to be a bunch of losers who don't know what they're doing.

For the sake of investors who are tired of hearing the same old lies and for the sake of entrepreneurs who hurt their cases by telling them, here are the top ten lies of entrepreneurs. Study them so you can at least tell new lies.

1. "Our projection is conservative." Your projection is conservative, but you claim you'll be doing $100 million by year three. In fact, the company is going to be the fastest-growing company in the history of mankind.

The truth is, you have no clue what your sales will be, and I fantasize about the day an entrepreneur tells me, "Our projection is a number we're picking out of the air. We're trying to make them high enough to interest you, but low enough so that we don't look like idiots. We really will have no clue until we ship the product and see how it's accepted." At least that entrepreneur is honest.

2. "Experts say our market will be fifty billion dollars in five years." Don't cite numbers like this and expect to impress investors. No one ever comes in and says, "We're in a crappy little market." Everyone says the same thing. It's much better to catalyze fantasy.

3. "Amazon is signing our contract next week." Traction is good. It makes you fundable. But until a contract is signed, it's not signed. If the investor asks about the contract the following week, and it still isn't signed, you've got a credibility problem. In five years I've never seen a contract signed on time. Talk about Amazon and your big deals after they're done.

4. "Key employees will join us as soon as we get funded." Let me get this straight: You're two guys in a garage, you're trying to raise a few hundred thousand dollars, your product is twelve months from completion, and

you're telling me that these well-known people are going to resign their $250,000-per-year, plus bonus, plus stock-option jobs to join your company?

When investors contact these key employees who are supposedly set to join a company, the response is often, "I vaguely remember meeting the CEO at a cocktail party." If you're going to tell this lie, make sure that these potential employees are locked and loaded and ready to join.

5. "Several investors are already in due diligence." That is, "If you don't hurry, someone else will invest in us, and you won't have the chance." This works well in times of irrational exuberance, but during other times it is a laughable tactic. The reality, and what the listener is thinking, is, *You've pitched a few other investors, and they haven't gotten around to rejecting you yet.*

The odds are that the investors know one another better than you know them. They can call up their buddies and find out how interested another firm is in your deal. To pull this lie off, you'd better be either a great bluffer or smokin' hot, or you won't have a chance against the investor network.

6. "Microsoft is too old, big, dumb, and slow to be a threat." Microsoft, Oracle, Apple, Facebook . . . Pick a successful company. Many entrepreneurs think that by making such a statement, they are (a) convincing the investor of their moxie, (b) proving that they can defeat an entrenched competitor, and (c) establishing a competitive advantage.

In reality all they are showing is how naïve they are about what it takes to build a successful business. There's a reason why people such as Larry Ellison can keep the San Jose airport open late for his private jet while you and I are munching peanuts on Southwest Airlines. And it's not because his company is old, big, dumb, and slow.

It's scary enough to investors that you are competing with an established company. Don't seal your coffin by showing how clueless you are by denigrating such competition. Instead, explain how you can avoid the competition by serving different segments or fly under the competition's radar. If nothing else, acknowledge that you're undertaking a high-risk and difficult venture, to at least indicate that you're aware of the magnitude of the challenge.

7. "Patents make our business defensible." Patents do not make a business defensible. They might provide a temporary competitive advantage—particularly in material science, medical devices, and biotech companies—but that's about it.

By all means, file for patents if you can, but don't depend on them for much more than impressing your parents unless you have the time (years) and money (millions) to go to court.

When talking to investors, the optimal number of times to mention that your technology is patentable is one. Zero is bad because it implies you don't have anything proprietary. More than one mention means that you're inexperienced.

8. "All we have to do is get one percent of the market." This is what venture capitalists call the Chinese Soda Lie. That is, "If just one percent of the people in China drink our soda, we will be more successful than any company in the history of mankind."

There are problems with this line of reasoning: First, it's not that easy to get even 1 percent of the people in China to drink your soda. Second, few entrepreneurs are truly going after a market as large as all the people in China. Third, the company that came in before you said something similar about another market, and so will the company after you. Fourth, a company that is shooting for only 1 percent market share isn't that interesting.

9. "We have first-mover advantage." There are at least two problems with this lie: First, it may not be true. How can you know that no one else is doing what you're doing? As a rule of thumb, if you're doing something good, five other startups are doing the same thing. If you're doing something great, ten are.

Second, first-mover advantage isn't all that it's cracked up to be. Being a fast second might be better—let someone else pioneer the concept and learn from their mistakes—then leapfrog them.

10. "We have a world-class, proven team." The acceptable definition of "world-class" and "proven" in this context is that the founders created enormous wealth for investors in a previous company, or they held positions in highly respected, large companies. Riding the tornado of a successful

company in a minor role, working for McKinsey as a consultant, or putting in a couple of years at an investment bank doesn't count as a proven entrepreneurial background.

EXERCISE

Give the list of lies to a friend and ask him to listen to your pitch. How many of these lies do you tell? You fail the exercise if you tell more than two.

FAQ

Q: How do I make my pitch memorable?

A: The problem is not that pitches are not memorable. In a vacuum many are exciting because of their promises of first-mover advantage, patented technology, a $50 billion market, and proven teams of highly motivated geniuses.

The problem is that pitches all begin to sound alike because they all make the same claims. You can make yours memorable by adhering to the basics: a short (ten-slide, twenty-minute) presentation with a compelling story of how you aim to solve real pain or tap an attractive opportunity.

There's one more thing you can do: a demo that makes heads explode because it is so cool. Then you don't have to worry about your PowerPoint slides at all. In fact, you may never get back to your slides after the demo because there will be so much discourse.

Always imagine that your audience is at the end of a long day of boring meetings; everyone is barely awake, much less attentive; and people just want to go home. More often than not, this is what you'll walk into, so be prepared for it.

Q: Should I print my pitch in color and bind copies to give to investors?

A: Colorful, bound crap is still crap. I would worry about more important things, such as the content and delivery, rather than printing and binding.

Q: Should I send my presentation in advance to the attendees?

A: No. A good presentation typically features only snippets of text (in a big font!), so recipients will most likely find it difficult to comprehend without your riveting oral presentation.

Q: Should I hand out my presentation at the beginning of the meeting?

A: No. If you do this at the beginning, people will skip ahead because they can read faster than you can talk. This does, however, make it more difficult for the audience to take notes, so an alternative strategy is to hand out the presentation at the start of the meeting but ask people not to skip ahead.

Recommended Reading

Nesheim, John. *High Tech Start Up: The Complete Handbook for Creating Successful New High Tech Companies.* New York: Free Press, 2000.

Reynolds, Garr. *Presentation Zen: Simple Ideas on Presentation Design and Delivery.* New York: New Riders, 2008.

PROLIFERATION

CHAPTER 7

The Art of Building a Team

It is essential to employ, trust, and reward those whose perspective, ability, and judgment are radically different from yours. It is also rare, for it requires uncommon humility, tolerance, and wisdom.

—Dee W. Hock

GIST

Few tasks are more exciting than recruiting great people for a hot startup, and there are few factors that are more critical to success than great people. It's not enough that candidates are qualified to work for your startup; they must also believe in your product, because working for a startup is closer to a religion than a way to make a living. This chapter explains how to build an awesome team.

Ignore the Irrelevant

There is a shortage of great employees in the world. Therefore, it's stupid (and in many places illegal) to make recruiting decisions based on irrelevant considerations. The art of building a team requires looking beyond race, creed, color, sexual orientation, and religion. I'd even add formal education and work experience to this list. Instead, focus on these three factors:

1. Can the candidate do what you need?

2. Does the candidate believe in what you're doing?

3. Is the candidate likeable and trustworthy?

> **"Early employees of Apple, Google, Facebook, Twitter, and Microsoft won't necessarily make great employees for a startup."**

Many people put too much emphasis on the formal experience and background of candidates. Sometimes it pays to ignore the lack of a perfect and relevant background, while at other times it pays to ignore the presence of the perfect and relevant background:

- **EXPERIENCE IN A SUCCESSFUL STARTUP.** People who worked at a company when it achieved success didn't necessarily contribute to its success. Early employees of Apple, Google, Facebook, Twitter, and Microsoft won't necessarily make great employees for a startup. For one thing, at this point, they may be too rich to want to work hard again.

- **EXPERIENCE IN A BIG ORGANIZATION.** Employment in big organizations is not a reliable predictor of success in a startup environment. The skills needed in each context are different. A vice president of Google (with its established brand, infinite resources, and 80 percent market share) may not be the right person for a "two guys in a garage" operation.

- **EXPERIENCE IN A FAILED ORGANIZATION.** This is the flip side of experience in a successful startup or large organization. Many factors could have caused the failure—perhaps the candidate was one of them. Or not. Failure, however, is often a better teacher than success—especially when it's a failure on some other company's dime.

- **EDUCATIONAL BACKGROUND.** You want smart people, not necessarily degreed people. The two are not the same. Steve Jobs never finished Reed College. Steve Case, the founder of AOL, went to Punahou (an inside joke for people from Hawaii). Half the engineers of the Macintosh Division didn't complete college. I dropped out of law school, and Stanford Business School rejected me.

- **EXPERIENCE IN THE SAME FUNCTION.** Functional experience is also a double-edged sword. Apple once hired an executive from the tampon business because we thought we needed packaged goods–marketing expertise to sell Macintoshes like sanitary napkins. However, his experience did not transfer to the computer business—duh. There are positions like accounting that require a specific skill set, but for many positions in a startup, drafting the "best athlete" is effective.

- **EXPERIENCE IN THE SAME INDUSTRY.** Industry experience is another double-edged sword. On the one hand, understanding the industry and possessing preexisting relationships are helpful. On the other hand, a candidate who is stuck in his way of thinking about an industry ("A computer manufacturer cannot support its own chain of retail stores") can be a problem. Again, consider the best athlete approach.

There is one final characteristic to ignore: weakness. You wouldn't say that one of Steve Jobs's strengths was compassion. Nor was Bill Gates's strength aesthetic design. Should you therefore not hire the next Steve Jobs or Bill Gates? There are two theories:

- Find the candidate who lacks major weaknesses (even though he lacks major strengths).

- Find the candidate who has major strengths (even though he has major weaknesses).

The first line of reasoning is flawed because everyone has major weaknesses—it's just a matter of finding out what they are. Performing well in one area is tough enough; trying to find people who can do everything is Mission: Impossible.

The second line of reasoning is the way to go. A team of people with major and diverse strengths is what you want in the early days when head count is low and there's little room for redundancy. High achievers tend to have major weaknesses. People without major weaknesses tend to be mediocre.

EXERCISE

Think back to your first few jobs. True or false?

___ I was perfectly qualified.

___ I am holding candidates up to standards higher than the person who hired me used.

Dramatize Your Expectations

Make it clear to anyone you hire that working in a startup is different from what they are used to (if they came from large companies) and different from the movies and sitcoms (if they watch a lot of TV).

For the former, you need to ask, "Can you fly coach, function without a secretary, and stay in cheap motels?" You might scare off a few desirable prospects, but it's worth risking this to avoid ending up with people who cannot function in a startup environment.

Big organization skill	Startup skill
Sucking up to the boss	Being the boss
Generating paper profits	Generating cash flow
Beating charges of monopoly	Establishing a beachhead
Evolving products	Creating products
Market research	Shipping
Squeezing the distribution channel	Establishing a distribution channel

For the latter, startups are not about Ping-Pong, free food, fun parties, and a quick path to wealth. A realistic description is that startups take four to five years of long hours at low pay with incredible highs and depressing lows with the constant fear of running out of money. And this is if things go well.

Collect Adequate Data

You'll encounter two recruiting scenarios when you are compelled to use your intuition. First, a candidate's education and background aren't quite right, and others on your team will argue you shouldn't hire him. Your rational side says, "Don't hire him. He doesn't have the right experience," but your intuition says, "Grab him."

Second, a candidate's education and background look perfect, and the rest of your team urges you to grab her. Your rational side says, "Grab him," but your intuition says, "Pass."

> "You should use reference checking as a means to decide whether the candidate is good, and not as a confirmation of a choice that you've already made."

According to conventional wisdom, you should trust your intuition in these kinds of situations. Unfortunately, intuition is often wrong—perhaps you liked a candidate because he was physically attractive, went to the same college as you did, or shared your passion for hockey, so you softened up on the interview questions and reference checking.

Or, maybe you have an inflated perception of the quality of your intuition because you remember when your intuition was right and forget when it was wrong. Here's a procedure to help you make good decisions:

- **STRUCTURE THE INTERVIEWS.** You and your team should decide on the attitude, knowledge, personality, and experience that are necessary for the position before you conduct interviews. Don't let employees conduct unstructured interviews because they think they are good judges of people.

- **ASK ABOUT SPECIFIC JOB SITUATIONS.** Fit and chemistry are important but so is competence. Start with determining if the person can do the job before you decide you like her. For example, for a vice president of marketing position, these are good questions:

  - How did you manage a product introduction?

  - How did you determine the feature set of a new product?

  - How did you convince engineering to implement these features?

  - How did you select your PR firm?

  - How did you select your advertising firm?

  - How did you handle a crisis such as a faulty product?

- **STICK TO THE SCRIPT.** Minimize spontaneous questions. You want to get a sample of candidates who answered the same questions in order to accurately compare them.

- **CONDUCT INITIAL INTERVIEWS BY PHONE.** One way to create a level playing field for candidates is to conduct initial interviews by phone. This reduces the effect of factors such as physical attributes, dress, and race.

- **DON'T GET TOO TOUCHY-FEELY.** A half-decent candidate can bluff through questions such as "Why do you want to work for this startup?" More pointed questions are better: "What are the accomplishments you're most proud of?" "What were your biggest failures?" "What was your most gratifying learning experience?" Again, worry about competence first.

- **MATCH THE PERSON AND THE POSITION.** Beware of the false positive: hiring a likeable person who is incompetent. And beware of the false negative: rejecting a less likeable person who is competent. For example, the best engineers aren't necessarily charismatic, and people who are charismatic aren't necessarily the best engineers.

- **TAKE NOTES.** Take notes during the interview to remember what each candidate said. Don't depend on your memory, because the passing of time and your subjective reactions will make it hard to accurately and fairly assess candidates.

- **CHECK REFERENCES EARLY.** Many organizations check the references of candidates they've already decided to hire. This is a setup for a self-fulfilling prophecy because at that point you want to hear comments that affirm your decision. Big mistake. You should use reference checking as a means to decide whether the candidate is good, and not as a confirmation of a choice that you've already made. (More tips on reference checking are at the end of this chapter.)

- **USE LINKEDIN.** Candidates will provide references who will say good things about them (although you may be surprised), but you can use LinkedIn to find people who worked for companies at the same time. This can provide more of a 360-degree view of the candidate.

The beauty of this process is that its rigid and standardized nature will help you garner better information, and this can improve your intuition. Now you can follow your intuition. Going with my intuition has served me well (granted, my memory is selective), and I would be a hypocrite to tell you to rely on just the facts, because Apple hired me—an ex–jewelry schlepper with a psychology degree—to evangelize the most important product in the company's history.

(Early testers of this book asked for more information about my hiring process. If you want to know the full story, Apple hired me because my roommate from college, Mike Boich, made the decision. On paper, there was no reason for Apple to hire me as the second software evangelist. When Steve first interviewed me, he told Mike, "I like him, but he has no relevant experience, so unless you want to bet your job on it, I'd say no.")

Use All Your Tools

In good times or bad, it's hard to hire the A+ players, so prepare to use all the tools at your disposal. Most people think their recruiting arsenal is limited to salary, equity, and fringe benefits, but there is more that you can offer:

- **YOUR VISION.** For many people, money isn't the most important motivational factor. They will work for less to do more by making meaning and changing the world.

- **YOUR TEAM.** Don't limit the candidate's interviews to her prospective immediate supervisor and coworkers. If you've got directors, advisers, and investors, add them to the seduction process.

- **RÉSUMÉ-BUILDING POTENTIAL.** Let's face it: few people work for one organization for their entire career. There's nothing wrong with getting a few good years out of people and having them building their résumés at your organization. And you never know: they may stick around longer than you anticipated.

Evangelize All the Decision Makers

Going to work for a startup is seldom a solo decision. While more-enlightened employers consider the spouse of the candidate as well, a candidate's decision process usually involves a complex web of relationships.

Key decision makers can include parents, friends, and colleagues of the candidate. It's easy to imagine a young person asking his parents if he should go to work for a startup and being told, "Don't. It's too risky. Get a job in a nice, safe company that will be around a long time—like Lehman Brothers, Arthur Andersen, or Enron."

Therefore, ask candidates who all their important decision influencers are and then address their potential concerns. However, be aware that some candidates may interpret this as a trick question—*If I admit that my parents are part of the process, they'll think I'm a wimp and won't hire me*—so do your best to assure them that this is a way to increase the likelihood of successfully recruiting candidates that you like.

Wait to Compensate

Many startups make the mistake of sending an offer letter too early in the hiring process. They use it as a straw man, getting compensation details on paper in order to show how interested they are and to reach closure. This is a mistake.

An offer letter should come at the end of the recruiting process. It is not a negotiating tool to get the candidate to say yes, but rather a way to confirm a verbal agreement where she has already said yes. Think of an offer letter as you would a marriage proposal: make it when you know the answer will be yes, not to show that you're serious.

Interpret the Lies

When she worked at Garage, Amy Vernetti, who's now a partner at True Capital, came up with this list of the top ten lies of job candidates. Study them. They will help you avoid making hiring mistakes. This is a definitive list of lies, so if your candidate tells you different ones, at least he is creative.

Lie	Truth
"I've got three other offers, so you'd better move quickly."	I've had three other interviews, and no one has flat out rejected me yet.
"I was responsible for my company's strategic alliance with Google."	I picked up the FedEx envelope from Google.
"I'm leaving my current organization after only a few months because the organization isn't what the CEO told me it was."	I don't know how to do due diligence.
"I've never been with a company for more than a year because I get bored easily."	It takes people about a year to figure out that I'm a bozo.
"I didn't really report to anyone at my old company."	No one wanted me in her department.
"Most of my references are personal friends because they know me best."	No one I worked for is willing to give me a reference.
"You've never heard of my last three employers because they were in stealth mode."	All the companies I worked for imploded.
"I'm no longer with the organization, but I maintain an excellent relationship with people there."	I was forced to sign a nondisparagement agreement to get my severance package.
"I am a vice president, but no one reports to me."	I've been put out to pasture.
"I'm expecting to at least double my prior compensation package."	I was overpaid and understand that I may have to take a cut for a good opportunity.

Apply the Shopping-Mall Test

There's one more test to apply to candidates, the Shopping Mall Test. Its genesis is that I was at the Stanford Shopping Center when I caught sight of a Macintosh software developer, but he had not yet seen me. I made an abrupt turn in order to avoid having to talk to him because he was a pain in the ass. This experience led me to conceive the Shopping Mall Test.

"Life is too short to work with people you don't like—especially in a startup."

This is how it works. Suppose you are at a shopping mall. You see a candidate before he notices you. At that point, you can do one of three things:

1. Scoot over and say hello.

2. Figure that if you bump into him, fine. If not, that's okay too.

3. Get in your car and go to another shopping center.

No matter what your intuition and a double check of your intuition tells you, I'm telling you to only hire people that you'd hustle over to and engage in a conversation. If you find yourself picking option 2 or 3, don't make the hire. Life is too short to work with people you don't like—especially in a startup.

(By the way, if you pick option 2 or 3 for someone already employed at your startup, either fix the situation or get rid of the person.)

Define an Initial Review Period

Despite your best efforts, your recruiting process (or your intuition) is sometimes wrong and a new hire does not perform to your expectations. For me, one of the hardest tasks is to admit this mistake and correct it.

However, if there's one thing that's harder than firing someone you don't want it's laying off people you do want. If you don't make a course correction or terminate people who aren't working out, you increase the probability of having to lay off people who are working out if your startup fails.

To make this process easier on both the organization and the employee (because it's also the right thing for the employee to stop working for the wrong organization), you should establish an initial review period with incremental milestones. The more concrete the performance objectives, the better. For example, objectives for a salesperson might include:

- Completion of product training

- Completion of sales training

- Participation in five sales calls

This period needs to be longer than that of the hiring afterglow but shorter than the time it takes for the predominant feeling to become, *Why did we hire this person?*

In short, ninety days.

Establish an understanding that after ninety days, there will be a joint review in which both sides discuss what's going right, what's going wrong, and how to improve performance. Some issues will be your fault!

Don't Assume You're Done

In 2000 Garage recruited a well-known investment banker from a big-name company. It took weeks of wooing and two rounds of offers and counteroffers as his current employer sweetened his current compensation.

Finally we landed him. He and his family came to our company BBQ. Life was good. Several weeks later he started at our firm. He showed up for work for a few days but then called in sick. Late one night I got an e-mail from him saying that he was resigning.

He left Garage to work for a former client of the investment bank. A few months after that he returned to his original employer. I learned that you should never assume you're done. Recruiting doesn't stop when a candidate accepts your offer, or when he resigns from his current employer, or on his last day at his current employer—not even after he starts at your organization. Recruiting never stops.

Every day is a new contract between startups and their employees.

Addenda

Minichapter: The Art of Reference Checking

You can't build a reputation on what you're going to do.

—Henry Ford

Reference checking is a crucial part of recruiting a great team. However, most startups do it in a cursory and casual way—after the company has made a hiring decision. Courtesy of Amy Vernetti, here's a short course on reference checking to improve your results.

The goal of referencing is not to disqualify a candidate but to look for consistency in how the candidate represented himself and what his references have to say. You are also looking for clues about whether the candidate can be effective at your startup.

In order to get a complete picture of a candidate, you should speak with at least two subordinates, two peers, two superiors, and two customers. Investors or board members of his current company are also interesting references. These are suggested questions:

- How do you know this person? How long have you known him?

- What are your general impressions of him?

- How would you rank him against others in similar positions?

- What contributions has he made to the organization?

- How do others in the organization view him?

- What are his specific skills? What is he best/worst at?

- What are his communication and management styles?

- In what areas does he need improvement?

- Is he capable of functioning effectively in a small organization?

- How would you comment on his work ethic?

- Would you hire / work for / work with him again?

- Should I speak with anyone else about him?

In addition to following Amy's suggestions, you should get unsolicited references from other people the candidate did not provide too. LinkedIn is great for this. Find someone who knows someone at the company and check out the candidate via her.

FAQ

Q: Should I be honest about our startup's weaknesses as well as our strengths?

A: Let me get this straight: You're wondering if you should lie to candidates, knowing that if they take the job, they'll eventually discover that your startup sucks?

Always tell it like it is. Lower their expectations. You'll encounter three types of responses to your candor:

- Some candidates need only an honest assessment of any problems. Chances are, they just want to know what they're getting into, and you won't scare them off.

- Other candidates want the challenge. For them, problems are opportunities. You should tell this type, "People like you are going to make us successful. Can you step up and be a hero?"

- You will scare off the third kind of candidate. This person wasn't well suited to a startup, so you've done yourself a favor.

Q: Does it look bad to the outside world if we only have a few employees? Is it better to have six part-time employees rather than three full-time employees, for the sake of numbers?

A: Having six part-time employees for the sake of looking bigger is insane. If you're doing this for other reasons—offering flexible hours to get better people, for example—it's okay, but not for a silly reason like this.

Q: Is the right time to recruit CXO-level people before or after receiving funding?

A: Many people think that the process of starting a startup is serial: Remember: entrepreneurship is a parallel process. You do A, B, and C at the same time. The answer to your question is that you're recruiting before, during, and after the funding process.

However, don't fall into this trap of reacting to an investor who tells you that he would put money in your company if you had a "world-class" CXO. You could take this as a yes, recruit the person, and go back to the investor. Then the investor could add another test: "Good job. Now show us that customers are paying for your product." The lesson is this: don't recruit to make an investor happy. Recruit to build a great startup.

Q: Should I spend money on retainer-based searches or rely on my own capability to attract the best talent?

A: Before funding, your job is to tap your own network to find the right person without paying fees. After funding, do whatever you have to—including retainer-based searches. But before funding, don't pay a headhunter to find any employees, because you don't have the funds to do so.

Q: If asked, should I provide a salary range early in the recruitment process?

A: No. If you're asked, respond by saying, "We will pay what it takes to get a great candidate." Then ask, "What is your current salary level so we know where to start?" This will teach them to ask tough questions.

The beginning of the interview process is too early to start mentioning numbers. Candidates will remember what you said—especially the top end of the range. And whatever number you do throw out could affect the candidates' answers in the interviews.

Q: If my goal is to recruit people better than myself, how do I retain control of the venture and avoid getting ousted from my own business?

A: This question says more about you than you intended. Your goal shouldn't be to "retain control" and "avoid getting ousted." Your goal should be to build a great startup. There may come a time when you should step aside. Deal with it. Would you rather have a failed startup that you controlled until the bitter end?

Q: I'm working with my best friend. Do I need a legal agreement?

A: Yes, absolutely and even more so because it's your best friend. Times change, people change, and organizations change. Difficult and inappropriate as it may seem, you must do this. Such a legal agreement may turn out to be the best thing for your friendship and your startup.

You should do this at the beginning of the startup, before there is much to fight over. The longer you wait, the harder it's going to get to put a legal agreement in place. Difficulty will peak around the time you need it the most.

Q: What is a reasonable enticement and compensation for a member of my board of directors?

A: The range is usually 0.25 to 0.5 percent, but for an absolute superstar, I'd go as high as 1 percent of the company. If it takes more than this to get the candidate, move on. The person is more interested in making money than in making meaning.

Q: **What do you do when you have to fire the partner who conceived the business, brought you in to help run it, trusts you, and is now in over his head?**

A: You take him aside and have a private conversation explaining the situation. You offer the person some choices about how to take a smaller role, but you are clear that such a move is necessary.

A smaller role can mean taking a different position or serving only on the board of directors or board of advisers. Try to preserve the person's dignity. In most cases, there will be a blowup. Expect that. It might take years to heal your relationship, but that's how it goes.

Recommended Reading

Lewis, Michael. *Moneyball: The Art of Winning an Unfair Game.* Waterville, ME: Thorndike Press, 2003.

Myers, David G. *Intuition: Its Powers and Perils.* New Haven, CT: Yale University Press, 2002.

CHAPTER 8

The Art of Evangelizing

Instead of imposing new obligations, (Christians) should appear as people who wish to share their joy, who point to a horizon of beauty and who invite others to a delicious banquet.

—Pope Francis

GIST

Evangelism comes from the Greek word that means, approximately, "to proclaim the good news." I was Apple's second software evangelist, and I proclaimed the good news that Macintosh could make people more creative and productive.

"When people believe in your product, they will help you succeed through credible, continuous, and cost-effective proselytization."

Evangelism is not mucked up with desires to kill competitors and make fortunes. Customers don't care if you want to destroy the competition. They want to know what benefits they derive from using your product. Also, evangelism is about what you do for your customers—not about what you want to become.

At Apple, and subsequently as an entrepreneur, I learned that when people believe in your product, they will help you succeed through credible, continuous, and cost-effective proselytization. This chapter explains both how to use evangelism and how to recruit evangelists.

Touch Gold

I've tried to evangelize people with great stuff, and I've tried to evangelize people with crap. Evangelism is much easier with great stuff. I call this "Guy's Golden Touch." It doesn't mean that whatever I touch turns to gold. I wish. It means, "Whatever is gold, Guy touches."

I explained the concept of DICEE products earlier, but let's review it here. If you want to use evangelism, you need to create or find a product that rolls the DICEE:

- **DEEP.** A deep product has lots of features because you've anticipated what people need as they come up the power curve.

- **INTELLIGENT.** An intelligent product reflects your insights on how to ease people's pain or increase their pleasure.

- **COMPLETE**. A complete product embodies everything a customer needs, such as support, documentation, and enhancements.

- **EMPOWERING**. An empowering product makes people better. Great stuff doesn't fight you—it becomes one with you.

- **ELEGANT.** An elegant product is not just functional; it's also well designed so that people can use it easily and quickly.

Get High and to the Right

Another way to understand and position an evangelistic product is get it high and to the right:

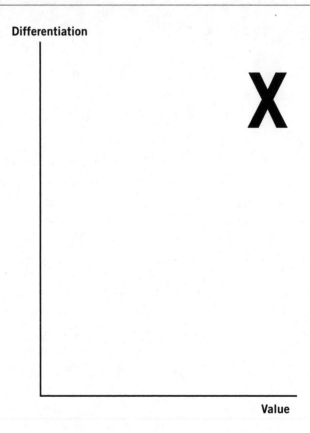

The vertical axis measures the degree of differentiation, and the horizontal axis measures value, so you want a unique and valuable product. In total, there are four types of products:

- **VALUABLE BUT NOT UNDIFFERENTIATED**. These products fulfill a need, but they work the same way as existing products. You can sell a lot of them, but your margin is always under pressure because people can buy similar products from other companies.

- **DIFFERENTIATED BUT NOT VALUABLE**. These products are stupid. They serve a market that doesn't exist, or they provide functionality that no one wants.

- **UNDIFFERENTIATED AND NOT VALUABLE**. These are the worst products of all. There is no demand for what they do, and multiple companies are making a similar product.

- **DIFFERENTIATED AND VALUABLE**. This is the Holy Grail of evangelism. When you provide a valuable product that no one else can, evangelism is easy. This is the corner of the chart where meaning, margin, and money are made.

If you're an engineer, you should be thinking about how to make a product that is valuable that no other company can make. If you're an evangelist, you should be thinking about how you can convince the world that the product is valuable and different from everything else on the market. Here are examples of such products:

- **BREITLING EMERGENCY**. This watch can broadcast an emergency signal that airplanes receive. It's one of the few watches that can save your life, so if you're a hardcore adventurer, it's differentiated and valuable.

- **SMART CAR**. There are lots of cars that are easy to park parallel to the curb when there's abundant space. The Smart Car, however, can park perpendicular to the curb. There aren't many cars that are this small.

- **TESLA MODEL S**. Another car example: There aren't many that can go zero to sixty miles per hour in under four seconds on battery power with a 275-mile range and that can hold five people. If you want a car that doesn't burn gasoline and can take your family fast and far, Tesla Model S is your only choice.

Put the Best Interests of Others at Heart

The difference between evangelists and most people is that evangelists have the best interests of others at heart. They believe in their product so much that they want others to use it too.

The Tesla Model S provides an example of this concept. Circa 2014 the state government of Iowa prevented Tesla from selling cars to residents because Tesla doesn't have licensed auto dealers in the state. Tesla owners from Minnesota drove to Urbandale, Iowa, and invited Iowa residents to see and test-drive their cars. These owners were not Tesla employees, and unless they were stockholders, you can't make the case that they would derive financial benefit from this action.

Even if they were shareholders, I doubt that the primary motivation was increasing the price of Tesla's stock. No, these were Tesla evangelists, and they did this because they wanted people to buy a car they loved. That's the power of evangelism.

Achieve Humanness

Consider several great brands: Virgin, Levi Strauss, Nike, Harley-Davidson, and Etsy. They've all achieved humanness—for example, the enchantment of Virgin, the youthfulness of Levi Strauss, the gutsiness of Nike, the rebelliousness of Harley-Davidson, and the artisanal goodness of Etsy.

To be sure, there are high-awareness brands that don't exhibit such qualities—Microsoft, Oracle, and United Airlines, to name a few. Call me a romantic, but it's much easier to evangelize a product that's rooted in human values. If you agree, here's how to achieve this:

- **TARGET THE YOUNG.** No matter who buys your product, targeting young people forces you to build a human brand. I have no data to back this up, but it seems that lots of old people are buying products that were targeted to the young. For example, there are many baldheads driving Toyota Scions and MINI Coopers.

- **MAKE FUN OF YOURSELF.** Most companies are incapable of making fun of themselves. It's an attitude that they view as suicidal: "People won't take us seriously if we don't take ourselves seriously." Or, they are so caught up in their self-image that appearing to lack total control scares them. As the saying goes, "To err is human," so don't be afraid to err and make fun of your startup.

- **HAVE FUN TOO.** The market capitalization of a particular company, circa 2014, is approximately $400 billion. In order to celebrate anniversaries and holidays as well as the lives of interesting people, the company alters its logo for the day. How fun and human is that?

Another, even better example, Richard Branson once lost a bet to Tony Fernandes, the owner of AirAsia. Because he lost, Branson had to shave his legs, apply lipstick, dress up as a flight attendant, and work on an AirAsia flight. Have you seen the CEO of United in a skirt? Do you even know who the CEO of United is?

- **FEATURE YOUR CUSTOMERS**. Organizations that feature their customers in marketing materials exude humanness. Is there a better example than GoPro? The customer videos that it features on its <u>website</u> and <u>YouTube channel</u> make it seem as if anyone can shoot a great video with a GoPro camera.

- **HELP THE UNDERSERVED AND UNDERPRIVILEGED**. Corporate philanthropy efforts are a double win: not only are you fulfilling a moral obligation to society, but you are also increasing brand awareness. Actually, it's a triple win because corporate philanthropy programs are also an important tool for the recruitment and retention of employees.

EXERCISE

Go to the websites of your favorite companies and try to find information about how to apply for grants and volunteer for the company.

Make It Personal

To his dog, every man is Napoleon; hence the constant popularity of dogs.

—Aldous Huxley

I once met an entrepreneur who wanted to start an online service for people to create trusts for their pets. Her pitch hinged on the fact that nine million pets are euthanized every year in the United States.

My first reaction was that nine million pets may get euthanized, but only a few because their owners died. Therefore, the market wasn't as big as she thought. My second reaction, as a dog owner, was that she was right:

What would happen to Bane and Jersey if we all died? We hadn't included any of our pets in our wills and trusts.

> **"Positioning is more powerful when it's personal, because it's easier for potential customers to imagine how a product fills a need."**

Here's the lesson: position your product in a personal way. "What happens to Bane and Jersey?" is more powerful than "What happens to the pets of two and a half million people who die each year in the United States?" If you connect people to a personal concern about their pets, they can extrapolate their own emotions to those of millions of other people who are concerned about their pets. Positioning is more powerful when it's personal, because it's easier for potential customers to imagine how a product fills a need.

Impersonal	Personal
Our operating system is an industry standard that enables MIS departments to maintain control and reduce costs.	Apple: "Our operating system makes you more creative and productive."
We're committed to reducing the size of the global ozone hole.	We prevent you from getting melanoma.
We have dozens of airplanes flying in a hub-and-spoke pattern around the United States.	Southwest Airlines: "You are now free to move about the country."
We increase the mean test scores for children in your school district.	We ensure that your son can read.

Learn to Schmooze

It's not what you know or who you know, but who knows you.

—Susan RoAne

It's much easier to evangelize people you already know—or, more accurately, people who already know you. The process of building such social connections is called schmoozing.

If you're hesitant about schmoozing—either because you're shy or because you consider it offensive or manipulative—you need to change your mind. In his book <u>The Frog and Prince: Secrets of Positive Networking to Change Your Life</u>, Darcy Rezac defines networking (which is "schmoozing" for goyim) as "discovering what you can do for someone else."

"No one is more fascinating than a good listener."

World-class schmoozers adopt Rezac's outward, what-can-I-do-for-you attitude. It is the key to building extensive, long-lasting connections. Upon this foundation, here's how to get more people to know you:

- **GET OUT.** Schmoozing is a contact sport. You can't do it from the office, so force yourself to attend trade shows, conventions, seminars, conferences, and cocktail receptions. For all the wonderfulness of Skype and Google Hangouts, pressing flesh is still the best platform for schmoozing.

- **ASK GOOD QUESTIONS; THEN SHUT UP.** Good schmoozers don't dominate conversations. They initiate with interesting questions and then listen. No one is more fascinating than a good listener.

- **MAKE IT EASY TO GET IN TOUCH.** This is ironic, but many people who want to be or are great schmoozers often make it hard to contact them. For example, they don't print their cell number on their business cards, or they don't include contact information in the signature area of their e-mails.

- **FOLLOW UP.** Follow up within twenty-four hours of meeting someone. Send an e-mail. Give her a call. Send her a copy of your new book. Few people ever follow up, so the ones who do can distinguish themselves as worth knowing.

- **UNVEIL YOUR PASSIONS.** If you can talk only about your job, you're a boring person. Good schmoozers are passionate about multiple and diverse interests. A benefit of these passions is that they provide additional ways to connect to people. I'm not saying you should take up a hobby because it will be good for business. For example, I'd rather be poor than play golf. However, I've made many business connections through hockey—and I've made many hockey connections through business.

- **GIVE FAVORS.** There's a karmic scoreboard in the sky (more about this in chapter 13, "The Art of Being a Mensch"). This scoreboard tracks what you do for people. If you want to be a world-class schmoozer, ensure that you're hugely positive on that scoreboard.

Learn How to Use E-mail

I have made this [letter] longer because I have not had the time to make it shorter.

—Blaise Pascal

E-mail is a key tool of a good evangelist. It is fast, almost free, and ubiquitous. Unfortunately, most people use it poorly. Here's how to improve your e-mail effectiveness to make it a powerful evangelism tool:

- **OPTIMIZE YOUR SUBJECT LINE**. If people don't recognize your name on an e-mail message, the next thing they look at is the subject line. Think of it as an executive summary of your message. If it doesn't entice people to read your e-mail, then you've failed before you even started. Subject lines that work on me are: "Enjoyed your book," "Enjoyed your speech," and "Referred to you by [someone I know or have heard of]."

- **TIME IT FOR TUESDAY**. Stephen Brand, a professor of entrepreneurship at Olin College of Engineering, promotes an interesting concept that Tuesday mornings are the best time to send e-mails. This is because by Tuesday people have worked through their backlog from the weekend but have not yet received the deluge of the rest of the week.

- **RESEND UNANSWERED E-MAILS**. Another Stephen Brand idea is to resend unanswered e-mail to the recipient with a brief note saying, "Did you have a chance to read this?" He believes that when a person receives the same e-mail twice, it jars (or guilts) the recipient into action.

- **ANSWER WITHIN FORTY-EIGHT HOURS**. As I said before, responsiveness is a big factor in cementing a contact. You need to answer while the topic of the e-mail is fresh. Messages that are below the first screen of a person's inbox are often forgotten.

- **DON'T USE ALL CAPS.** All-caps text is more difficult to read, and it is considered SHOUTING. If nothing else, it's a sure sign that you're clueless about e-mail, and cluelessness is not conducive to successful schmoozing.

- **QUOTE BACK.** Select the question or section of the e-mail that you're responding to and quote it back in order to refresh the sender's mind. People get dozens of messages per day, so a simple "Yes, I agree" is useless.

- **KEEP IT SHORT AND SIMPLE.** Cut the crap and get to it. The ideal length for e-mail is five sentences. If you can't say what you have to say in five sentences, you don't have much to say.

- **USE PLAIN TEXT, NOT HTML.** I assume that HTML e-mails are spam and give them no more than a glance. If you have something significant to say, you don't need bold, outline, shadow, red text, and graphics to say it.

- **DON'T ATTACH FILES OVER FIVE MEGABYTES UNLESS YOU HAVE PERMISSION.** Imagine that your recipient is sitting in a hotel room using a slow connection and you've sent a ten-megabyte PowerPoint file. Do you think you'll get a positive reaction? Also, many people assume attachments from strangers are viruses.

- **BLIND CARBON COPY (BCC) LARGE GROUPS.** When you send an e-mail to more than two people, it should be a BCC to prevent inadvertent responses to everyone and to prevent revealing e-mail addresses to the other recipients.

- **REDUCE CARBON COPIES (CC).** When I get a CC, I assume that other people are taking care of the issue. Either a person needs to get the e-mail or not. A CC is in a dubious middle ground. The most common purposes of a CC are to cover one's butt ("But you were CC'd!") or to implicitly threaten ("I CC'd your boss, so you better do what I ask").

- **INCLUDE A GOOD SIGNATURE.** A signature is the information that your e-mail software includes at the end of every outgoing message. A good signature provides your name, organization, postal address, phone number, e-mail address, and website. This is useful for copying and pasting into a calendar or database. God forbid someone should want to make more contact with you, and they have to hunt down the information.

- **WAIT WHEN YOU HATE.** Although you should answer e-mail in under forty-eight hours, there is one case where you should wait longer: when you're angry, offended, or argumentative. E-mails written when you're in these moods tend only to exacerbate problems.

Ask for Help

Let's move on from using evangelism to recruiting evangelists. The starting point is to ask your customers for assistance. Tell them you want to achieve critical mass and you need their help to spread the word. This is a sign of intelligence, not weakness.

If your product is outstandingly contagious, you may not even have to ask for help—customers may have already started evangelizing it. That's what happened with Macintosh. But if you do ask, you can get help much faster and in larger amounts. However, many companies hesitate to ask:

- "If we ask for help, people will think we're weak. A strong company never asks its customers for help."

- "People will expect something in return: discounts, special treatment, etc. Then what will we do?"

- "Our customers, much as we love them, can't help us. We know what to do, and we can do it ourselves."

- "It will cost too much to maintain special programs. These programs are not as cost-effective."

These reasons are bogus, and stupidity and arrogance are an ironic combination. When customers want to help you, you should rejoice, not refuse them. So stifle your paranoia and pride and accept the help. Evangelists will be your best salespeople.

Create a Program

In the late 1990s a group of businesspeople and community leaders started an organization called the Calgary Flames Ambassadors. They were Flames fans who were alarmed by the prospect that their National Hockey League team might move to another city. According to the chairman of the group, Lyle Edwards, "The Ambassadors ran around Calgary and twisted arms so that people bought more tickets."

> **"Don't be picky about how evangelists help you. Let them help in any way they can."**

Circa 2014, the Flames no longer need much help selling tickets, but the program continues. Members provide volunteer time, support community programs, and sponsor meet and greets at the arena entrances as well as help with ticket sales. All members must buy season tickets—in other words, they are paying fans, and they perform these services for free. That's evangelism!

The goal of recruiting evangelists is to build a community around your product. Companies that have such communities include those in the following list. Take a look at what they do, and adapt their programs to your needs.

- Adobe groups

- Apple user groups

- Articulate

- Flipboard Club

- <u>Google Android developers</u>

- <u>Google Top Contributors</u>

- <u>Harley Owners Group</u>

- <u>HubSpot user groups</u>

- <u>Ubuntu LoCo teams</u>

These communities provide customer service, technical support, and social relationships that make owning a product a better experience. You can proactively bring a community into existence by implement these practices:

- **"LET 100 FLOWERS BLOSSOM."** This principle applies to evangelism as well as it does to rainmaking. Don't be picky about how evangelists help you. Let them help in any way they can. They will show you ways to market your product that you never would have developed yourself.

- **ASSIGN TASKS AND EXPECT THEM TO GET DONE.** Have you ever volunteered to help an organization and then it never took you up on your offer? If there's anything worse than being asked to do too much, it's not being asked to help at all. If evangelists have signed up for your cause, it's your obligation to make good use of them.

- **GIVE THEM THE TOOLS TO EVANGELIZE.** Make it easy for believers to help you by providing stacks of information and promotional material. For example, <u>SCOTTeVEST</u>, the "tech-enabled" clothes company, includes several VESTimonial cards in each garment. These cards show a customer and his or her testimonial as well as information about how to buy SCOTTeVEST products.

Tropiformer Jacket
Steve "Woz" Wozniak,
Co-Founder of Apple

SCOTTeVEST

- **RESPOND TO THEIR REQUESTS**. You should revise your product to reflect the wishes of your evangelists for two reasons: First, they know what it takes to make your product better. Second, it demonstrates that you are listening to them, which fosters even greater loyalty and enthusiasm.

- **GIVE THEM STUFF**. You would be amazed at the power of a free T-shirt, coffee mug, pen, or notepad. (At one point, Apple had a $2-million-per-year T-shirt expense.) Evangelists love these goodies.

It makes them feel as if they're part of the team and special. This is money well spent, but never give away anything that costs more than twenty-five dollars, which is where the line between a gift and a bribe gets blurry.

- **HIRE SOMEONE WHOSE SOLE PURPOSE IS TO FOSTER A COMMUNITY.** An internal champion who looks after the needs of the community will both evangelize evangelists and lead the fight for the necessary resources. As you achieve success, build a department around this person to institutionalize community support.

- **CREATE A BUDGET FOR SUPPORTING THEM.** You won't need much, and the intent is not for you to buy evangelists, but you'll still need a budget for travel, entertainment, meetings, and the stuff mentioned above.

- **INTEGRATE EVANGELISTS INTO YOUR SALES, MARKETING, AND ON-LINE EFFORTS.** The existence of evangelists is a proxy for quality and coolness—"The product is so successful that people have formed user groups for it." Thus, you should publicize this both to help you close sales and to provide an additional resource to your customers.

- **HOST THE COMMUNITY'S EFFORTS.** This means letting members use your building to hold meetings, as well as providing digital assistance, such as a section of your website, hosting webinars, and hosting chats.

- **HOLD A CONFERENCE.** No one loves electronic communication more than I do, but face-to-face meetings are important for evangelism. At these conferences, evangelists can meet one another as well as interact with your employees.

- **CONTINUE FELLOWSHIP.** The model for effective evangelism is the relationship between a good parent and child. Your kids will always be your kids—they never leave the nest. Evangelists are the same—they need frequent and perpetual lovin'.

Addenda

Minichapter: How to Get a Standing Ovation

> *No hables al menos que puedas mejorar el silencio. (Don't speak unless you can improve on the silence.)*
>
> —Jorge Luis Borges

When I started working at Apple in 1986, I was afraid of public speaking. For one thing, working for the division run by Steve Jobs was intimidating: "How could I possibly measure up to Steve?" But if you want to succeed as an evangelist and CEO, you must learn how to make speeches.

"It's much easier to give a great speech if you have something to communicate. End of discussion."

It took me twenty years to get comfortable with public speaking, and this chapter explains what I've learned. I am not content that you merely survive speeches. I want you to get standing ovations.

• **HAVE SOMETHING INTERESTING TO SAY.** This is 80 percent of the battle. It's much easier to give a great speech if you have something to communicate. End of discussion. If you don't have anything to say, decline the speech. If you don't want to decline, then do some research and get something interesting to say.

• **REMOVE THE SALES PITCH.** The purpose of most keynotes is to entertain and inform the audience. It is seldom intended to provide an opportunity to pitch your product. The worst speech you can give is one that people interpret as a sales pitch.

• **CUSTOMIZE.** The technique that has helped me the most in public speaking is customizing the first three to five minutes of every speech. This demonstrates that you've done your homework and have made an effort to craft a speech that is a valuable and special experience. I do this in two ways:

- First, I try to find a personal link to the audience. For example, when I spoke for Acura, I showed pictures of the two Acuras and two Hondas that I own. When I spoke for S. C. Johnson, I showed them pictures of its household cleaners in my cabinets.

- Second, when I travel to a foreign country, I typically get to the location the day before and sightsee. Then I show my pictures of the sites that I visited and express my appreciation for local culture—here's an example of a picture I used when I spoke in Istanbul.

- **FOCUS ON ENTERTAINING.** Many speech coaches will disagree with this, but they don't speak fifty times a year like I do. My theory is that the goal of a speech is to entertain. If people are entertained, you can also slip in a few nuggets of information. But if your speech is dull, no amount of information will make it great.

- **OVERDRESS.** My father, who was a politician in Hawaii, was a good speaker. When I started speaking, he gave me a piece of advice: never dress beneath the level of the audience. For example, if they're wearing suits, you wear a suit. To underdress is to communicate this message: "I'm smarter/ richer/more powerful than you. I can insult you and not take you seriously, and there's nothing you can do about it." This is hardly the way to get an audience to like you.

- **DON'T DENIGRATE THE COMPETITION.** Don't criticize your competition in a speech, because it indicates that you are taking undue advantage of the privilege of the audience's attention. You are not doing the audience a favor. The audience is doing you a favor, so do not lower yourself by using it as an opportunity to slander your competition.

- **TELL STORIES.** The best way to relax when giving a speech is to tell stories. Stories about your youth. Stories about your kids. Stories about your customers. Stories about things that you read about. When you tell a story, you lose yourself in the storytelling. You're not "making a speech" anymore. You're making conversation. Good speakers are good storytellers; great speakers tell stories that support their message.

- **PRECIRCULATE WITH THE AUDIENCE.** True or false: the audience wants your speech to go well. The answer is "true." Audiences don't want to see you fail—why would people want to waste their time listening to you fail? The way to heighten your audience's concern for your success is to circulate with the audience before the speech. Talk to people. Let them make contact with you. Especially the ones in the first few rows; then, when you're on stage, you'll see these friendly faces. Your confidence will soar. You will re- lax. And you will be great.

- **SPEAK AT THE START OF AN EVENT.** If you have the choice, speak at the beginning of an event. The audience is fresher then, so they're more apt to listen to you, laugh at your jokes, and follow along with your stories. On the third day of a three-day conference, the audience is tired, smaller, and thinking about going home. It's hard enough to give a great speech—why increase the challenge by having to lift the audience out of the doldrums?

- **ASK FOR A SMALL ROOM.** If you have a choice, use the smallest room possible. If you're in a large room, ask that it be set classroom style—that is, with tables and chairs—instead of theatre style. A packed room is a more emotional room. It is better to have two hundred people in a two-hundred-person room than five hundred people in a thousand-person room.

• **PRACTICE AND SPEAK ALL THE TIME.** This is obvious but nonetheless relevant. You need to give a speech at least twenty times in order to get good at it. You can give it nineteen times to your dog if you like, but it takes practice and repetition. As Jascha Heifetz said, "If I don't practice one day, I know it. If I don't practice two days, my critics know it. If I don't practice three days, everyone knows it."

I hope it takes you less than twenty years to get to this point. Part of the reason it took me so long is that no one explained the art of giving a speech to me, and I was too dumb to do the research. Now my goal is to get a standing ovation every time I speak.

Minichapter: How to Rock a Panel

Man clamors for the freedom to express himself and for knowing that he counts. But once offered these conditions, he becomes frightened.

—Robert C. Murphy

At any conference, there are ten times more panelists than there are keynote speakers, so the odds are higher that you're on a panel instead of giving a keynote speech. Therefore, rocking a panel is an important skill for evangelists too.

A panel looks easy. There are four or five other people on it, and it lasts only sixty minutes. How hard could it be? Herein lies the problem: because everyone thinks a panel is short and easy, no one prepares for it. In reality, a panel is harder than an individual speech because you cannot control a panel like your own keynote speech, and you get much less air time.

"Make love to the microphone."

This is what to do if you want to be the person everyone comes up to talk to after a panel:

- **KNOW THE SUBJECT.** If you're invited to a panel about a subject that you don't know, decline the invitation. I don't care how wonderful the opportunity seems to be. If you can help it, never provide a way for people to learn that you're clueless.

- **CONTROL YOUR INTRODUCTION.** The first mistake that most panelists make is assuming that the moderator has an up-to-date and accurate bio. The moderator either knows nothing about you or has done a cursory Google search and found a bio that is incorrect. Therefore, before the panel starts, hand the moderator a three-sentence bio and ask her to read it verbatim.

- **SPEAK UP.** The optimal distance between your lips and the microphone is one inch. This is because you're sitting down, you're hunched over, and you're not projecting. So get close to the mike and speak up. Make love to the microphone.

- **ENTERTAIN, DON'T JUST INFORM.** As in keynotes, your primary goal is to entertain, not inform. The funnier you are, the more people will think you're smart because it takes intelligence to be funny. I'd go so far as to pick a friendly fight with the moderator or another panelist. Have fun.

- **TELL THE TRUTH, ESPECIALLY WHEN THE TRUTH IS OBVIOUS.** If you're lucky, the moderator will try to provoke you with tough questions. This is a good thing because it provides an opportunity to be (a) funny and (b) a straight shooter. "The truth will get you glee." If everybody knows the truth, don't try to lie. It would be far better to say, "I take the Fifth Amendment." At least that will get a laugh.

- **ANSWER THE QUESTION THAT'S POSED, BUT DON'T LIMIT YOURSELF TO IT.** When asked a question, answer it as quickly as possible, but then feel free to take the conversation in the direction you want it to go. For example, let's say that the moderator asks, "Do you think smartphones will get viruses soon?" It's okay to answer, "Yes, I think this is an issue, but the real issue is the lack of good cell phone coverage," if that's what you want to talk about.

- **BE PLAIN, SIMPLE, AND SHORT.** Let's assume you are on a panel of experts. Let's further assume the moderator is an expert. The moderator asks a question. You direct your answer to her and to the other panelists—all experts, so you launch into an alphabet soup, acronym-du-jour response. Big mistake. The audience is the audience, not the moderator or the panelists. Reduce the most complex and technical issues to something plain, simple, and short, and you'll stand out.

- **FAKE INTEREST.** This may be one of the hardest aspects of a panel. Let's say the other panelists are in the middle of a long, boring, jargon-filled response. The temptation is to check e-mail or resist looking bored. Don't do it. Fake rapt interest because the moment you look bored, a photographer is going to snap a picture or the cameraman is going to put your face on the fifty-foot screen.

- **NEVER LOOK AT THE MODERATOR.** The moderator is a proxy for the audience. When you answer, look at the audience because the audience doesn't want to see the side of your head. (FYI, a good moderator will not make eye contact with you—forcing you to look away from him and toward the audience.)

- **NEVER SAY, "I AGREE WITH THE PREVIOUS PANELIST."** A moderator will often ask everyone on a panel to answer the same question. If you're not the first to reply, there's a temptation to say, "I agree with what my colleague just said." That's a dumbass response. Come up with something different, or say, "I think that question has been answered. For the audience's sake, let's move on."

FAQ

Q: Are the religious connotations of "evangelist" an issue?

A: In some parts of the world, the word has too many connotations to use comfortably. In the tech sector, though, it's fine. Christianity, after all, does have 30 percent market share, which is more than most companies.

Q: What if people like our product but don't want to help us spread the word?

A: You can't bludgeon people into becoming evangelists. They either get it or they don't. And they either want to help or they don't. If people like a product but not enough to want to evangelize, they probably don't like it as much as you think.

Q: Are evangelists born or made?

A: Evangelists are made—made by creating, finding, or being found by a great product. Almost anyone, short of a psychopath, can be an evangelist for a product that moves her soul.

Recommended Reading

Kawasaki, Guy. *Selling the Dream: How to Promote Your Product, Company, or Ideas and Make a Difference—Using Everyday Evangelism.* New York: HarperCollins, 1991.

CHAPTER 9

The Art of Socializing

Finally finished invention. Disappointed to find that no one can read.

— @JGutenberg, October 3, 1439. Historical Tweets

GIST

Social media is the trifecta of marketing: fast, free, and ubiquitous. When I was evangelizing Macintosh, by contrast, phones, faxes, and airplanes were the powerful marketing tools. Leverage was gathering a few hundred people in a hotel ballroom.

Social media is the best thing that ever happened to entrepreneurs. Today startups can reach millions of people anywhere in the world in seconds at no cost, but using social media is not necessarily easy. This chapter explains how to use this awesome resource.

Make a Plan

I'm not a believer in social media planning if you define "planning" as spending six months cogitating or hiring an agency to map out and achieve strategic goals. My version of strategic planning is:

- Figure out your business model.

- Figure out what kind of people you need to attract to make this business model work.

- Figure out what kind of stuff those people want to read.

- Share that kind of stuff.

Few people will give you such breezy advice, but don't confuse gravitas with knowledge. Consultants and agencies will tell you to create a strategic plan or retain them for three months. This is total bullshiitake. You don't have time to cogitate, nor should you waste money on consultants and agencies. You should dive into social media, see what works, and change things as you go.

What's more important than planning is grinding—that is, working long and hard and experimenting. In other words, social media is like everything else you're doing!

Grok the Platforms

As of 2015, the primary social media platforms to consider are Google+, Facebook, Instagram, LinkedIn, Pinterest, and Twitter. Here is a synopsis of each:

- **FACEBOOK**. This is the McDonald's of social networking, with "over one billion served." It's the platform that most companies use to reach customers. Unfortunately, some black magic called Edge-Rank determines which followers see your posts based on mysterious Facebook algorithms. Supposedly only 10 percent of followers see what you've shared—I think it's lower than this. However, you can pay to promote your posts to more people.

- **GOOGLE+**. Many "experts" love to hate Google+. They believe it's too small because in raw numbers it's one half the size of Facebook. However, because Google+ doesn't have an analogue to Facebook's EdgeRank, everyone who "circles" your company can see its posts; this makes up for its smaller size. Also, this is Google after all, and it would be silly to ignore anything Google does.

- **INSTAGRAM**. Instagram is for visual storytelling. Companies share pictures of their products or their fans' photos. You can't link to your website in an Instagram post, but many brands excel by connecting with their fans and building solid communities using this service.

- **LINKEDIN**. This is the unsung hero of social media. It added social media features late in the game, but the seriousness of its content and comments makes it a useful marketing tool. Stop thinking of LinkedIn as just a place to look for jobs, because it's a social media platform too.

- **PINTEREST**. Pinterest is a visual platform where people discover and save the things they love. Brands connect with customers by creating campaigns and Pinterest boards that showcase their products. It is by far the prettiest social media platform.

- **TWITTER**. Think of Twitter as a river: it can get you places fast, but it can also drown you. Twitter is a great platform for promoting and supporting your product in 140-character messages. Twitter is also a potent resource for monitoring your competition and the degree to which your company or product is in the social media conversation.

- **YOUTUBE**. Google's YouTube website is a powerful tool if you can produce interesting and educational videos. This isn't too hard these days, because YouTube videos from enthusiastic amateurs are often more effective than ones from slick professionals. You can create your own YouTube channel, and your customers can subscribe to it.

Which of these platforms should your startup support? All of them. I'd be giving you bad advice if I told you to focus on one or two. But I'd also be giving you bad advice again if I told you that this would take a team of four to six people. One or two people working hard can do it.

Perfect Your Profiles

Social media platforms provide a profile page to describe your company.

These are vital because people use them to make a snap judgment about the quality of your business. Here's how to optimize these one-page résumés for your business:

- **OPTIMIZE FOR FIVE SECONDS.** People do not *study* profiles. They spend a few seconds looking at them and then make a snap decision. If this were online dating, think <u>Tinder</u> (swipe right for yes, swipe left for no), not <u>eHarmony</u> (complete a Relationship Questionnaire).

- **TELL YOUR STORY WITH PICTURES.** A profile contains two graphic elements to tell your story. The first is an avatar, a small round or square picture. For personal accounts, it's your face. For corporate accounts, it's your logo.

Cadbury

www.cadbury.co.uk

3,566,710 followers | **122,027,489** views

A second, larger photo is called a "cover" (Facebook, Google+, and LinkedIn) or a "header" (Twitter). This should be a picture that communicates your startup's identity. These companies have excellent avatars and covers/headers:

- Cadbury

- Audi

- Nike

Platforms change the optimal dimensions for cover/header photos all the time, so be sure to monitor the standards. You can consult a blog post called "Quick Tips for Great Social Media Graphics" whenever you want to check the optimal sizes.

Also, Canva, the company where I'm chief evangelist, has created hundreds of cover and header designs for Google+, Facebook, Twitter, and Pinterest. You can check them out at Canva.com.

• **CRAFT A MANTRA.** Most platforms enable you to add a tagline to your profile. Make this your mantra: two to four words that explain why your startup exists. (Refer to chapter 1, "The Art of Starting Up," for more information about mantras.) Here are three theoretical mantras for companies that would work well as taglines:

- Nike: "Authentic athletic performance"

- FedEx: "Peace of mind"

- Google: "Democratizing information"

• **PROVIDE ALL THE INFO.** Your avatar, tagline, and cover/album/header photo determine people's initial impressions of your company. Then, if you've attracted their interest, people will read the rest of the info in your company's profile, so provide as much information as you can. Again, think of the profile as a résumé.

• **GET A VANITY URL.** You can get a vanity URL for your Google+,

Facebook, and LinkedIn account. It means that people will see this kind of link: https://plus.google.com/+canva/posts.

If you don't get a vanity URL, people will see this kind of link, which is much harder to remember, copy, and share: https://plus.google.com/+112374836634096795698/posts.

Google+, Facebook, and LinkedIn all explain how to do this. As is the case with domain names, many vanity URLs are no longer available, but almost anything is better than twenty-one random numbers. Also, coming up with a vanity URL is a good test of your cleverness.

- **GO ANONYMOUS.** When you're happy with your company's profile, view it in an "incognito window." This is a browser window that enables you to see the profile the way other people do.

To get an incognito window in Chrome, launch "New Incognito Window" from the File menu. There's a way to do this for every browser. Search Google for "anonymous" plus your browser name to find out how.

Pass the Reshare Test

The Reshare Test is the most important concept of social media marketing. It's nice when people "like" and "+1" your posts. It's swell when people add comments. These actions are akin to tipping a waiter or waitress.

However, resharing your posts is the ultimate compliment because it means that people are risking their reputations on what you've shared. This is akin to telling your friends to eat at a restaurant. Resharing is caring! So the most important test of anything you do in social media is:

WILL PEOPLE RESHARE YOUR POSTS?

Every post should pass this test. To do so, they need to add value to people's lives. There are four kinds of content that do this:

- **INFORMATION**. "What happened?" For example, Secretary of Defense Chuck Hagel said he's open to reviewing the role of transgender people in the military.

- **ANALYSIS.** "What does it mean?" For example, *Mother Jones* explains why Uruguayan soccer star Luis Suárez's biting incident is a big hygienic deal.

- **ASSISTANCE.** "How can I do that?" For example, CNET explained how texting to 911 works.

- **ENTERTAINMENT.** "What the hell?!!!" For example, every year two churches in Vrontados, Greece, stage a mock rocket war to celebrate Easter.

Try to emulate what I call the NPR model. NPR provides great content 365 days a year. Every few months NPR runs a pledge drive to raise money. The reason NPR can run pledge drives is that it provides great value.

By passing the Reshare Test, you earn the privilege to run your own pledge drive, which in your context is a promotion for your product.

Feed the Content Monster

The biggest daily challenge of social media is finding content to share. This is called "feeding the Content Monster." There are two ways to do this: content creation and content curation.

Content creation involves writing long posts, taking pictures, or making videos. It's difficult to create more than two pieces of content per week on a sustained basis, and two pieces are not enough for social media because of the intense competition for attention. Unfortunately, helping you master content creation is outside the scope of this book.

> **"Most companies define too narrowly what they believe will be relevant and interesting to their followers."**

Content curation involves finding other people's good stuff, summarizing it, and sharing it. Curation is a win-win-win: you need content to share, blogs and websites want more traffic, and people want filters to reduce the flow of information. These techniques can help you curate content to feed the Content Monster:

- **PIGGYBACK ON CURATION AND AGGREGATION SERVICES**. I cofounded a website called Alltop to help me curate content. It is an aggregation of RSS feeds ranging from A (adoption) to Z (zoology), organized into more than a thousand topics. For example, there's <u>food</u>, <u>photography</u>, <u>Macintosh</u>, <u>travel</u>, and <u>adoption</u>.

- **SHARE WHAT'S ALREADY HOT**. You could say this is cheating, and you'd be right, but there's nothing wrong with content that's already hot. No matter how many people have already seen something, *everyone* has not seen it yet. I've shared YouTube videos that are several years old with great success. Check out the "<u>Explore</u>" <u>area of Google+</u> for good stories.

- **USE LISTS, CIRCLES, COMMUNITIES, AND GROUPS**. People and brands that share a common interest comprise "lists" (Twitter and Facebook), "circles" (Google+), "communities" (Google+), and "groups" (Facebook and LinkedIn). These groupings are a great way to find good content.

- **SHARE USER-GENERATED CONTENT**. You should share photos that people create of your product. This practice is good for everyone: you get social proof when people take a photo of your product, and the photographers receive warm-and-fuzzy acknowledgment and attention.

Most companies define too narrowly what they believe will be relevant and interesting to their followers, which hinders their ability to feed the Content Monster. Here are examples of how posts can remain on-brand and be more interesting at the same time—generating more re-sharing:

Type of business	Desired followers	Examples
Restaurant	Foodies	Atomic particles help solve wine fraud and the scientific way to cut a cake.
Motorola	Android fans	The hundred best Android apps of 2014 and six great Android tips.
Airline	Travel lovers	The last drive-in theaters in America and mindful travel photography. Or you could make people happy even if you don't serve Japan.
Design agency	Marketers	Why it's okay to have an ad below a web page's fold and key findings about retail-customer loyalty.
Monster products	Music and sports enthusiasts	"Weird Al" Yankovic's parody of "Happy" and fun/scary jumps.

Use an Editorial Calendar

I'm not a believer in calendaring because I subscribe to the "spray and pray" approach to social media (that is, throw out a lot of stuff and hope something works). However, if you desire a more organized approach, several tools can help you manage an editorial calendar:

- **EXCEL**. You can use this old standby product to store draft posts according to the date of publication.

- **GOOGLE DOCS**. The strength of Google Docs for social media calendaring is that you can collaborate with team members in real time, and everyone can access the calendar from many devices. This eliminates the need for back-and-forth e-mail and reduces the likelihood of changes getting lost.

- **HUBSPOT EDITORIAL CALENDAR**. The HubSpot editorial calendar can act as a guide to brainstorm ideas for your blog, monitor the content, and track the progress of your writers. This is an Excel template designed for a team to calendar social media activities. You can add keywords, themes, and calls to action for each post.

- **BUFFER**, **SPROUT SOCIAL**, **AND HOOTSUITE**. All three provide calendaring functionality that's oriented toward sharing posts. Buffer is a scheduling-only platform, so you can't respond to comments with it. Sprout Social and Hootsuite allow you to schedule and monitor your social media as well as comment and respond. (Disclosure: I advise Buffer.)

- **STRESSLIMIT DESIGN WORDPRESS PLUG-IN**. This is an editorial calendar that you can add to a WordPress blog. The Stresslimit Design plug-in enables you to plan your blog content and review what's scheduled for the future.

Share Like a Pro

A scrupulous writer, in every sentence that he writes, will ask himself at least four questions, thus: 1. What am I trying to say? 2. What words will express it? 3. What image or idiom will make it clearer? 4. Is this image fresh enough to have an effect?

—George Orwell

After you've created or curated material, it's time to share it through your company's social media accounts. Here are the basics of sharing that are generally accepted as best practices. (In the next section I provide ideas that are not generally accepted.)

- **BE BRIEF.** Brevity beats verbosity in social media. You're competing with millions of posts every day. People make snap judgments and move right along if you don't capture their interest at a glance. My experience is that the sweet spot for posts of *curated* content is two or three sentences on Google+ and Facebook and 100 characters on Twitter. The sweet spot for content that you create, such as blog posts, is 500 to 1,000 words.

• **BE VISUAL.** Every post—literally *every* post—should contain eye candy in the form of a picture, graphic, or video. According to a <u>study from Skyword</u>, "On average, total views increased by 94 percent if a published article contained a relevant photograph or infographic when compared to articles without an image in the same category."

• **BE EARLY.** The best time for me to share posts is mornings Pacific time because that's when most of my audience is awake and on the computer. Try some experiments to see if mornings are good for your posts too. In the next section, you'll learn about automating posts, so scheduling is easy to do.

• **BE THANKFUL.** Every post with curated content should link to its source. Here's what these links accomplish:

- Enables readers to learn more from the source

- Sends traffic to the source as an act of gratitude

- Increases your visibility and popularity with bloggers and websites

When you find content because of someone else's post, use this protocol: compose and share a post with a link to the source and then add a "hat tip" or "h/t" to the person who brought it to your attention.

• **BE BULLETED.** If your post on Google+, Facebook, and LinkedIn is longer than four paragraphs, use a bulleted or numbered list. This makes it easier for people to read because the information is organized into smaller chunks and reduces the TLDR effect (too long; didn't read).

Maybe I'm the only person in the world who does this, but when there's paragraph after paragraph of text, I tune out. If I want to read a novel, I'll buy a Kindle e-book. On the other hand, when there's a bulleted or numbered list, I am much more likely to read the post.

• **BE SLY.** Posts that are titled "How to . . . ," "Top Ten . . . ," and "The Ultimate . . ." are difficult to ignore. Something about these words says (at least to me), "This is going to be practical and useful." The folks at <u>Twelveskip</u> compiled <u>a list of more than a hundred great titles</u>, so be sly and use it.

My favorites from this list are:

- "How to Rock . . ."

- "Quick Guide: . . ."

- "A Complete Guide to . . ."

- "Questions You Should Ask Before . . ."

- "Rules for . . ."

- "Essential Steps to . . ."

- "Most Popular Ways to . . ."

- "Tips for Busy . . ."

- "Tactics to . . ."

- "What No One Tells You About . . ."

• **BE FOUND.** Hashtags are a beautiful thing. They connect posts from people all over the world and add structure to an unstructured ecosystem. When you add a hashtag to a post, you are telling people that the post is relevant to a shared topic.

For example, the #socialmediatips hashtag on Google+ connects posts that are about social media. Twitter, Instagram, Facebook, Tumblr, and Google+ all support hashtags, so this is a common and well-accepted practice.

Consider adding two or three hashtags to your posts. However, if you use more than that, you look like an #idiot who's trying to #gamethesystem. Also, don't use hashtags on Pinterest because people hate them there—perhaps because hashtags interfere with the minimal-text sensibilities of Pinterest posts.

• **BE PROMOTIONAL.** I hardly ever do this as a matter of pride and principle, but paying to promote posts on Pinterest, Facebook, and Twitter can work. This ensures that more people see your posts. Facebook, in particular, is becoming a pay-to-play platform.

The decision comes down to a calculation of whether the revenue justifies the expense of paying for these views. For example, you could promote a post with a call to action to buy your product. Then the additional sales (and perhaps brand awareness) are either worth it or not.

If you refuse to promote your posts (I'd respect you if this was your decision), you can "pin" your posts to the top of your page on Facebook and Twitter. This means that the post remains as the first visible story at the top of your timeline. This isn't as effective as paying for promotion, but it's free.

• **BE ANALYTICAL.** You can improve the relevance of your content by analyzing the characteristics of people who follow you. For example, Facebook's analytics are a rich resource to find out who your fans are, and this is a great place to start for planning future content for Facebook.

- LikeAlyzer is useful to check your Facebook pages and to tweak the content, types of posts, and when you're sharing.

- For Twitter, you can use a service such as SocialBro to get reports on who follows you, to find new people to follow, and to determine how your content is doing. You can also get similar reports in Sprout Social and Hootsuite.

Automate Your Posts

Using tools to automate and schedule posts isn't cheating. It's what smart companies do to optimize sharing. Anyone who insists that you must manually share posts is silly. Most followers can't tell how a post was shared, and if you have duties other than social media, you can't manually share posts throughout the day.

This is a list of services to automate your posts. In thirty minutes, you could plan a day's worth of posts by using any of them:

- **BUFFER.** This schedules posts for Google+ pages, Facebook pages and profiles, LinkedIn, and Twitter. It enables you to add posts at a specific time or to put them in a queue. Team management and analytics are available in the "Buffer for Business" plan. Buffer suggests stories to share, and it's the prettiest of the services.

- **DO SHARE**. If you don't have a Google+ page, this is the only product that enables you to schedule posts on a personal profile. It is a Chrome extension and requires that Chrome be running in order to work. Do Share is great but limited by that requirement; for example, if you're traveling and your computer isn't running, Do Share won't share your posts. Your company's account is probably a page, not a profile, so Do Share may not apply to your needs.

- **FRIENDS+ME**. This product enables you to share your Google+ posts to other platforms. It currently supports Facebook (groups, profiles, and pages), Twitter, LinkedIn (profiles, groups, and company pages), and Tumblr. The ability to tweet with the image from your Google+ post is useful. Using hashtags, you can control how and where each post is shared or if you want it to post only to Google+.

- **HOOTSUITE**. You can schedule content, monitor comments, and respond to comments with Hootsuite. You can share to Facebook profiles and pages, Google+ pages, LinkedIn profiles, and Twitter. Using the ViralTag app, you can schedule pins on Pinterest. Useful features include bulk-scheduling posts from a spreadsheet, dragging and dropping from the calendar for scheduling, and collaborating with multiple users.

- **POST PLANNER**. Although Post Planner only works with Facebook, it also provides stories to share and suggests when to share too. With easy access from an app inside Facebook, you can find viral photos and trending content for story ideas. You can also add feeds for blogs that you like and share from Post Planner. It's a great service for managers of Facebook pages.

- **SPROUT SOCIAL**. This is a powerful product that works with Facebook pages and profiles, Twitter, Google+ pages, and LinkedIn profiles. There is team-management functionality and integration with Zendesk. The ability to repeat the same tweet with an image and create a team calendar is powerful. It costs a minimum of fifty-nine dollars a month.

- **TAILWIND**. You can schedule and monitor posts for only Pinterest with Tailwind. The display of rich data of popular pins, trending boards, and other people's popular content is a powerful feature. Tailwind has access to Pinterest's API, so there's bound to be more features in the near future.

- **TWEETDECK**. This is a stand-alone application to monitor activity and schedule tweets. It has a columnar orientation that displays search results. For example, you can create a column for "@mentions" (an @mention is when people tweet the "@" symbol and your name) and another column for @mentions of your competition. The next time you go to a tech conference, look at how people are monitoring Twitter, and you'll see that most are using TweetDeck.

Repeat Your Posts

Now we come to the not generally accepted stuff. I share a total of fifty posts per day via my accounts on Google+, Facebook, Twitter, LinkedIn, and Ello. Many of these posts are exact repeats of previous ones.

"This is an IQ test: Would you rather have 1,300 clicks or 7,600?"

Very few people or companies approach this level of activity, but my experience is that as long as your posts are good, you can share as much as you want. I checked my assertion that more is more by sharing four identical tweets over two days. Each tweet contained a different link to the same source story. These were the results:

Date and Time	Clicks	Responses	Retweets	Favorites
7/6, 7:41 p.m.	1,300	22	18	41
7/7, 2:11 a.m.	1,300	20	17	43
7/7, 12:50 p.m.	2,300	24	23	26
7/8 8:00 a.m.	2,700	16	10	15
Total	7,600	82	68	125

This is an IQ test: Would you rather have 1,300 clicks or 7,600? Would you rather risk complaints about repeated tweets and threats of unfollowing your accounts or achieve 5.8 times more clicks? I choose the latter every day of the year.

Some people will complain about the higher volume, but don't sweat this. They will either get used to the increase or unfollow. What matters is the net effect: you are either building a brand by adding followers and racking up reshares, or you're not. If you're not pissing someone off on social media, you're not using it aggressively enough.

Respond to Comments

Don't take anything personally. Nothing others do is because of you. What others say and do is a projection of their own reality, their own dream. When you are immune to the opinions and actions of others, you won't be the victim of needless suffering.

—Don Miguel Ruiz

You will encounter insightful, funny, and flattering comments in response to your posts, and you will encounter stupid, mean, and insulting comments.

The mix will be skewed toward the former if you post good stuff, but everyone gets negative comments.

Responding to comments requires diligence and effort. In particular, negative comments take effort, patience, and understanding. Here is how to change responding to comments from a pain into a way to foster engagement, build your reputation, and even have fun:

• **USE THE RIGHT TOOLS.** The first step is to find comments that you need to address. There are two scenarios: First, monitoring comments in your Google+, Facebook, LinkedIn, Pinterest, and Instagram posts. This is easy because these platforms organize or "thread" the discussion, so you can share a post and go back to see if there are comments.

The second scenario is monitoring comments on Twitter. Because it doesn't feature the same level of threading, you'll need to set up a search for your startup's name to monitor comments about you and responses to you. You can save this search so that you don't need to reenter it.

Twitter also provides <u>advanced search capabilities</u> to make finding comments more efficient. For example, I use a saved Twitter search that <u>finds mentions of @GuyKawasaki or @Canva but not the retweets of our tweets</u>. (You don't need to respond to retweets, and ideally there'll be so many that you couldn't respond to them all even if you wanted to.)

> "You can never go wrong by taking the high road, because winning the war for class and credibility is more important than winning the battle with one commenter."

People will also make comments about your startup that are unrelated to your posts. You need to monitor these too. In a perfect world, whenever people would mention your startup they would do so by typing "@" (Twitter and Facebook) or "+" (Google+) before its name. If they did, the platforms would notify you via e-mail or when you're on your page. However, most people are unaware of this capability.

Many services can, however, monitor mentions and text in comments, including <u>Commun.it</u>, <u>Google Alerts</u>, <u>Hootsuite</u>, <u>Social Mention</u>, <u>SocialBro</u>,

<u>Sprout Social</u>, and <u>Viralheat</u>. And, as mentioned before, <u>TweetDeck</u> is a great application for monitoring @mentions and search terms.

• **CONSIDER THE TOTAL AUDIENCE.** The audience for your response is anyone who will read it—not only the commenter. This is different from e-mail, in which the recipient and anyone he or she might forward your e-mail to are all that matters.

In social media, many people are lurking and will judge you by the tone of your responses. These lurkers may be more important than the original commenter himself or herself because they may have more followers than the trolls—online bullies who are looking for fights in order to compensate for inadequate organs or pathetic lives—who are trying to drag you into a fight. How you respond will be analogous to a politician answering a question in a town hall meeting: everything is on the record.

• **STAY POSITIVE.** Since others are watching, you should stay positive and pleasant no matter how banal, blasphemous, or baiting the comment. You can never go wrong by taking the high road, because winning the war for class and credibility is more important than winning the battle with one commenter. Truth be told, I sometimes forget to follow this recommendation, so do as I write, not as I do.

• **ASSUME PEOPLE ARE GOOD UNTIL PROVEN BAD.** As is the case with e-mail, it's easy to misinterpret social media comments. What you interpret as criticism or an attack may in fact be innocuous or just sarcastic. Or perhaps you are oversensitive. It pays to give people the benefit of the doubt.

• **AGREE TO DISAGREE.** If you can't stay positive, then you can at least agree to disagree. Life is too short to fight all the time, and most battles are not worth the trouble. Also, agreeing to disagree pisses off trolls.

• **ASK THE PENETRATING QUESTION.** When someone expresses a strong negative opinion, ask if he or she has firsthand experience with the issue. For example, if you shared a story about Android and an iOS fanboy attacks you, ask him if he's ever used or owned an Android phone. The odds are good that he hasn't, and he's only repeating what he's heard. On social media, the combination of certainty and ignorance is common, so get used to it! Indeed, it's often the case that the more certain a person is, the more ignorant he is too.

• **GO THREE ROUNDS.** The best (and worst) interactions often occur between commenters. It's enchanting to watch strangers develop relationships and take posts in deeper and serendipitous directions. That's the good news. The bad news is that commenters sometimes get into bitter fights and make mean-spirited comments that they would never utter in person.

My suggestion is to embrace the rules of amateur boxing and fight for only three rounds. The opening bell is when you share a post. Ding-ding. Round 1: commenter comments. Round 2: you respond. Round 3: commenter responds to the response. End of fight.

• **DELETE, BLOCK, AND REPORT.** If all else fails, ignore, delete, block, or report trolls and spammers. You don't have a moral obligation to interact with them, and there's little upside to lowering yourself to their level. If you need help identifying someone who's a troll versus someone who's passionate, read "<u>Top 12 Signs You're Dealing with Trolls</u>."

I have a one-strike rule, so I delete inappropriate comments (profanity, racism, and off-topic rabbit holes) and flag trolls and spammers without hesitation. Life is too short to deal with orifices.

Get More Followers

Do not yearn to be popular; be exquisite. Do not desire to be famous; be loved. Do not take pride in being expected; be palpable, unmistakable.

—<u>C. JoyBell C.</u>

There are only two kinds of people and organizations on social media: those who want more followers and those who are lying. In 2014 a Google search for "how to get more followers" yields 284 million results, which tells you something. There are only two things you need to do to get more followers:

1. First, share good stuff. This is how to get more followers. End of discussion.

2. Second, jump on new platforms. It's much easier to amass followers when a platform is young because there are fewer people to follow and much less noise.

I have 6.4 million followers on Google+ as of July 2014—I jumped on Google+ within weeks of its introduction. If I were to start afresh on Google+ or any other existing platform, I could not catch up to people who started earlier.

Every new platform creates a new set of stars. I cannot catch up with <u>Joy Cho on Pinterest</u> now that she has more than thirteen million followers. But she would also have difficulty catching up with me on Google+, where <u>she has a few hundred followers</u>.

The lesson is that a new platform is a land grab. If you want lots of followers on it, you have to join before it's clear that the platform will succeed.

Avoid Looking Clueless

The whole problem with the world is that fools and fanatics are always so certain of themselves, but wiser people so full of doubts.

—Bertrand Russell

Social media has its own set of expectations and faux pas, and people expect a company to observe the niceties. This section will help you fake not being clueless until you're no longer clueless:

• **DON'T BUY FOLLOWERS, LIKES, OR +1S.** Only losers and charlatans buy followers, likes, and +1s. (Can I tell you how I really feel?) I don't deny that people think a large number of followers is social proof of goodness, but buying followers is silly. Here's how large companies slide down the slippery slope:

• The CEO attends a conference and decides that her company has to use social media more.

> "You may never be caught buying your way in, but doing so is pissing on your karma, and karma is a bitch."

- She tells the CMO that she wants to see some results, where results are an increase in the number of followers, likes, and +1s.

- The CMO realizes there's no one who understands social media in the company (which is not true, but I digress), so the easy, safe, and logical choice is to hire someone from one of the company's agencies, since these agencies are full of experts.

- The first thing the newly hired social media exec does is retain his former agency to achieve the objectives of the CMO.

- The agency asks for and receives a large budget that includes enough money to buy followers, likes, and +1s to achieve the stated objectives.

- The agency spends the budget and, big surprise, achieves the numbers. Victory is declared, and everyone is happy.

Purchased followers, likes, and +1s provide few lasting benefits, since they don't interact with your content and have no interest in your content. You may never be caught buying your way in, but doing so is pissing on your karma, and karma is a bitch.

There is one exception to my distaste for buying your way in, and that's paying to promote Facebook posts or pages. This is the way Facebook works—it's the same as buying advertising in other media.

• **DON'T ASK PEOPLE TO FOLLOW YOUR COMPANY.** If you want more followers, earn them with the quality of your posts. If Groucho Marx were alive today, he'd amend his famous quote and say that people who ask you to follow them aren't worth following. Maintain your dignity, don't grovel for followers, and share good stuff in large quantities.

• **DON'T ASK PEOPLE TO RESHARE YOUR POSTS.** If your posts are good, this will happen naturally. With all the techniques we've explained, people will read your posts, and if those posts are good, they'll reshare them. It's that simple. The only time that it's acceptable to ask for reshares is when the post is philanthropic in nature.

• **DON'T BE A PIMP.** Social media is a great way to promote your product, service, or website—that's why we're making all this effort. You'll look clueless, however, if more than 5 percent of your posts are promotional. If you're familiar with American media channels, you want to be NPR, not QVC. Imagine if NPR ran pledge drives every day of the year.

• **DON'T ABDICATE TO AN AGENCY.** If you hire a digital agency that puts ten people into a "war room" to "measure sentiment" along your "brand ethos" and then needs forty-five days to compose a tweet, I have failed you.

Do not abdicate your social media to "experts" who have a hundred followers, tweet once a month, and charge you more than the GNP of a small nation for their services. A good rule of thumb is to never take the advice of someone who has fewer followers than you.

If you follow the recommendations of this chapter, you won't need an agency. If you follow the recommendations of this chapter and you are an agency, perhaps you can now justify your rates.

• **DON'T DELEGATE YOUR SOCIAL MEDIA TO AN INTERN.** The fact that you found a young person who uses Facebook who will work for less than a fast-food employee doesn't mean that he or she should manage your social media. This is like saying that having a penis makes a person a urologist or owning a car makes a person a mechanic.

Don't get me wrong: I love interns. They bring fresh perspectives and sensibilities to social media. I just want to ensure that you take social media seriously and put good people on it, because for many people, your company is what it shares. At least make your interns read this chapter and then monitor every post and comment they make for a few weeks.

Addenda

Minichapter: How to Socialize Events

And I like large parties. They're so intimate. At small parties there isn't any privacy.

F. Scott Fitzgerald, *The Great Gatsby*

Events are a key tool in marketing, and social media can increase their impact. I speak at more than fifty events per year, and I've observed that most organizations do not use social media to increase their visibility and value. Instead, organizations focus on pre-event promotions to drive attendance and do little, if anything, with social media at the event itself.

In 2013 Peg Fitzpatrick and I worked the Motorola launch events for the Moto X phone in Mexico, Argentina, Brazil, Peru, Colombia, and Chile. I was the keynote speaker, and she was the social media ninja. On this road show we learned how to rock an event with social media:

• **PICK AN EVERGREEN HASHTAG.** We could have picked hashtags like "#MotoXBrasil2013," "#MotoXMexico2013," and "#MotoXPeru2013," but these hashtags would have lasted for three days, best case. Instead, we picked a short, generic, and evergreen hashtag: "#MotoX."

"Chutzpah counts in social media."

The goal is a hashtag that will trend and be in people's faces, whether it refers to an event in Brazil, Mexico, or Peru, or to new products. In our particular case uniqueness was a concern in using "#MotoX," because it's also used for motorcycle events. But if I had to choose between short and unique, I would (and did) choose short and deal with the confusion.

• **INTEGRATE THE HASHTAG INTO EVERYTHING.** Begin using the hashtag from the moment you start promoting the event. This means it should appear on your website and in your advertising and e-mail signature. The printed program should use it on the cover. The introductory slides should publicize it in sixty-point type; every subsequent slide should have it in the footer. Every employee, speaker, vendor, and guest should know what it is.

• **ASK EVERYONE TO USE IT.** It's not enough that you broadcast the hashtag; you also need to encourage other people to use it. Both the conference "voice of God" and the event host should ask people to share posts with the hashtag. Toward the end of the Moto X tour, I began my keynotes with a request that people tweet that they were at the event with the hashtag, and I waited until they did so.

Chutzpah counts in social media.

• **REACH BEYOND THE EVENT.** The audience for an event is anyone in the world who's interested in your product, not only the people at the event. A tweet such as "Not in Brazil? See what Mashable thinks of the #MotoX: http://mashable.com/2013/08/01/moto-x-hands-on/" is effective, and many people will reshare it.

• **DEDICATE A PERSON.** At least one person at the event should have the responsibility for focusing on social media:

- Before: share promotional posts to drive awareness and attendance.

- During: tweet what's happening and take pictures of speakers and guests. Upload these pictures during breaks and reshare other people's posts.

- After: share articles about the event as well as more pictures and videos. Encourage attendees to reshare their pictures.

Katie Clark, a market researcher from Portland, Maine, suggests hiring a social media personality to fill this role if you don't have your own internal expertise. This person will know what to do, amplify exposure with his or her own accounts, and call in favors from buddies who have followers. This is the role Peg filled for Motorola in South America.

• **STREAM LIVE COVERAGE.** Think of how much you're spending to make an event happen. Why wouldn't you broadcast live video coverage? Are you afraid that too many people will learn about your product? Get real. If you're announcing a product in Bogotá, you want a blogger in Moscow to write about it too. Also, you might as well record your live coverage and make it available for people to watch later.

Don't obsess about a broadcast's reducing event attendance—if watching a live stream is as good as attending in person, perhaps the bigger issue is that your event sucks.

- **PROVIDE REAL-TIME UPDATES.** If you're not live-streaming video, have your social media person provide blow-by-blow updates. You can use Twitter, Instagram, or your blog for this. Outfits like the *Verge* provide outstanding live-blogging of events, such as Apple announcements, so learn from what they do.

- **DISPLAY THE TWITTER STREAM.** Use services that display the tweets that contain your hashtag and beam it onto a screen at the conference. Displaying these tweets encourages more interaction and more use of your hashtag. For some people, seeing their tweet scroll by is like seeing their picture on display in Times Square. I'd use Twubs or Tchat to do this.

- **PROVIDE WIRELESS ACCESS.** Let me get this straight: you're spending thousands of dollars to put on the event. You're pounding your hashtag into everyone and asking them to use it. But you're restricting wireless access. Have you lost your mind?

When you're doing site selection, take a computer or a phone and run Speedtest at each facility. Tell the salesperson responsible for the venue that you anticipate several hundred people using the network simultaneously, so you'll take your business elsewhere if there's not sufficient Internet access. If all else fails, bring in mobile hotspots or turn some smartphones into tethering hotspots.

- **DON'T PASSWORD-PROTECT THE NETWORKS.** Password-protected networks are the enemy of social media buzz. If you must password-protect the network, then publish the password everywhere—which, of course, means security is an illusion, so you might as well not use passwords!

"Tell your executives to (wo)man up."

- **PROVIDE A PLACE TO TAKE PICTURES.** We set up an area for taking photos at the Moto X events. All that was necessary was good lighting and a backdrop with "Moto X" printed all over it. People saw the backdrop and thought it was fifteen-minutes-of-fame time: "Let's pretend we're Hollywood stars."

People will share roughly 100 percent of these photos—ideally with your hashtag.

• **TAKE AND SHARE CANDID PICTURES.** Hire a professional photographer to take candid pictures at your event. He or she will cost less than what you're spending on souvenir USB drives with your logo that people don't want.

At the Moto X events, I posed with anyone who asked (and asked anyone who didn't ask) in front of a backdrop with "Moto X." After the event, we sent e-mails to guests telling them where they could find the collection of photos, and we encouraged them to download the pictures and share them with the Moto X hashtag.

• **WORK YOUR EXECS.** At many events, company executives speak and then rush off to a limited-access press conference or to do interviews. They then make a short public appearance but are surrounded by their people to protect them from I-don't-know-what. This is a big mistake.

Tell your executives to (wo)man up. They should even go beyond the mere willingness to pose for photos and instead ask people to have a photo taken with them. No one will refuse this kind of request, and roughly 100 percent of those photos get shared too.

- **COVER THE EARTH.** Once you have pictures and video, share them on every platform. For Motorola we shared photos on Google+, Twitter, Facebook, and Instagram. The goal is to get everyone who was at the event to see his pictures and videos and reshare them too. With a little bit of social media effort and magic, you can make your event look like it was the place to be.

FAQ

Q: We're a small company, so should we use a corporate account or personal account?

A: You should use a corporate account because on Google+ and Facebook, corporate accounts have more features than personal ones. Also, with employee turnover, you won't want to deal with the trauma of deciding who owns the account.

Q: Should we curate the posts of our employees?

A: I assume that there is a corporate account for the business, and you're referring to people's personal accounts. Generally, what employees do on their own time and with their own accounts is not your business.

It becomes your business, though, when people position themselves as employees/representatives of your business and do things that harm the company's image. But then the solution is to address the root problem rather than censor the existence of the root problem.

Q: Should we have different content for different platforms?

A: Here's what I do: Google+ and Facebook: identical content that I find interesting, three to five sentences with a link to the source.

Pinterest: pretty pictures from websites. Instagram: pretty pictures that I took. Twitter: links to what I find interesting.

Q: What am I missing? Why do you like Google+ so much?

A: I like Google+ because of the design aesthetics, the lack of an EdgeRank approach where it decides who sees my posts, and the quality of comments. It's also from Google, and it's crazy to bet against Google.

Recommended Reading

Kawasaki, Guy and Peg Fitzpatrick. *The Art of Social Media—Power Tips for Power Users*. New York: Portfolio, 2014.

CHAPTER 10

The Art of Rainmaking

Pretend that every single person you meet has a sign around his or her neck that says, "Make me feel important." Not only will you succeed in sales, you will succeed in life.

—Mary Kay Ash

GIST

A rainmaker is a Native American medicine man who uses rituals and incantations to make it rain. In business a rainmaker is a person who generates large quantities of sales. Like medicine men, good salespeople have created rituals and incantations to make it rain. This chapter explains the art of rainmaking.

"Sometimes when it pours, it rains."

Two factors make rainmaking difficult for startups: First, entrepreneurs do not know who will buy their product and what it will be used for. Second, the products of startups are sold, not bought, because few people want to take a chance on a new product from a small, young company.

Before we begin, here's a story about how an entrepreneur overcame a retailer's resistance to stocking her product. When a Parisian store named Galleries Lafayette rejected the newest fragrance of Estée Lauder, <u>she spilled the perfume all over the floor</u>. Then so many customers asked about it that the store had to carry it. Sometimes when it pours, it rains.

Let One Hundred Flowers Blossom

I stole this concept from Mao Zedong although he implemented it during the Cultural Revolution to flush out dissidents. My application of the concept means sowing many products, seeing where they take root and blossom, and nurturing those markets.

> **"When flowers are blossoming, your task is to determine where and why they are blossoming and then adjust your business to reap your good fortune."**

Unfortunately, many companies freak out when unintended people use their product in unintended ways. They react by trying to reposition the product so that the intended customers use it in intended ways. This is dumb—first of all, on a tactical level, take the money!

When flowers are blossoming, your task is to determine where and why they are blossoming and then adjust your business to reap your good fortune. As a startup, you can't be picky or proud. Here are three eye-opening examples of blossoming flowers cited by the dean of entrepreneurship, Peter F. Drucker:

- The inventor of Novocain intended it as a replacement for general anesthesia. Doctors, however, refused to use it and continued to rely upon traditional methods. Dentists, by contrast, quickly adopted it, so the inventor focused on this unintended market.

- UNIVAC was the early leader in computers. However, it considered computers the tool of scientists, so it hesitated to sell its product to the business market. IBM, by contrast, wasn't fixated on scientists, and let its products blossom as business computers. This is why IBM is a household name and you can only read about UNIVAC in history books.

- An Indian company bought the license to manufacture a European bicycle with an auxiliary engine. The bicycle wasn't successful, but the company noticed many orders for only the engine. Investigating this strange development, the company found out that people were using the engine to replace hand-operated pumps to irrigate fields. The company went on to sell millions of irrigation pumps.*

See the Gorilla

Daniel J. Simons, a professor at the University of Illinois, and Christopher F. Chabris, a professor at Harvard University, ran an experiment with huge rainmaking implications. They asked students to watch a video of two teams of players throwing basketballs. The students' task was to count how many passes one team made to its teammates.

Thirty-five seconds into the video, an actor dressed as a gorilla entered the room, thumped his chest, and remained in the video for another nine seconds. When asked, 50 percent of the students did not notice the gorilla!† Apparently, they were focused on the assigned task of counting passes and were blind to an unrelated event.

The same phenomenon occurs in startups: everyone becomes so focused on a product's intended customers and uses that they fail to see flowers blossoming in unexpected ways. The lesson is to let a hundred flowers blossom and recognize the unexpected ones—the gorilla markets in your midst, so to speak.

Ignore Titles

"Database Administrator III" sounds like an unlikely title for a decision maker. It conjures an image of someone stuffed in a messy cubicle jammed full of technical manuals, eating Subway sandwiches for lunch.

"The higher you go in many big companies, the thinner the oxygen; and the thinner the oxygen, the more difficult it is to support intelligent life."

---

* Peter F. Drucker, *Innovation and Entrepreneurship: Practice and Principles* (New York: Harper & Row, 1985), 190–91.
† Michael Shermer, "None So Blind," *Scientific American* (March 2004).

When Lisa Nirell, author of <u>The Mindful Marketer: How to Stay Present and Profitable in a Data-Driven World</u>, was a rainmaker at BMC Software, one such Database Administrator III bought more than $400,000 worth of software from the company. Stuck in his cubicle with the phone constantly ringing, this employee had great influence over the major purchases his company made. When the executive vice president had questions about projects or vendors, it was Mr. Database Administrator that he visited.

The higher you go in many big companies, the thinner the oxygen; and the thinner the oxygen, the more difficult it is to support intelligent life. Thus, the middles and bottoms of organizations contain most of the intelligence, and intelligence is necessary to appreciate innovative products.

I've made dozens of decisions about companies and people by consulting three terrific key influencers: Carol Ballard, Holly Lory, and Gina Poss, all of whom were my assistants at some point. I'd ask, "What do you think of that guy?" or "What do you think of this idea?" If their answers were "He's rude," "He's an egomaniac," or "It's a dumb idea," the person never got to me.

This concept that people without lofty titles can affect sales means that you should ignore titles and work with anyone who is a key influencer, from secretaries, administrative aides, and personal assistants to product managers, support managers, and database administrators.

Learn to Suck Up, Down, and Across

Logically, the next questions are, "How do I figure out who the key influencers are?" and "How do I get to them?" Here are some ideas to use:

- **ASK FRIENDS AND COLLEAGUES**. Some acquaintance of yours must sell to the same organization. They'll help you because you have done, and will do, the same for them. Reciprocation is the ally of great entrepreneurs.

- **TWEET THE ORGANIZATION'S SOCIAL MEDIA ACCOUNT**. A public tweet asking for the right person's name is effective because brands are afraid to not respond to tweets. This beats the alternative of calling the corporate number and trying to get the right names.

- **SEARCH FOR PRESS COVERAGE OF THE ORGANIZATION.** Then try e-mailing, tweeting, and calling people who are mentioned in articles about the organization. Peruse the "About" and PR sections of its website. You never know. . . . You might get through, and you won't know unless you try.

- **TALK TO THE ASSISTANTS.** Ask for a pointer to the right person instead of the executive herself. Many secretaries, administrative aides, and personal assistants are happy to give you the right name in order to shield their boss from a sales call.

- **MILK LINKEDIN.** Maybe you worked with someone who works there now. Maybe you went to the same school as people at the organization. Maybe the contact of a contact can help. LinkedIn can produce marvelous results.

Many of these ideas involve influencing and persuading people whom you need more than they need you. This means you're going have to learn how to suck up, suck down, or suck across because they stand between you and decision makers. In the rainmaking context, think of them as umbrellas. This is how to work with umbrellas:

- **UNDERSTAND THEM.** You may suspect that someone's job is to prevent you from doing your own job. Don't flatter yourself; you're not that important. You're just one more e-mail or phone call, so don't take it personally when people don't jump up to help you.

- **DON'T TRY TO BUY THEM.** No one likes to be bought—or, more accurately, to be thought of as someone who could be bought—so don't send gifts as bribes. The way to get in is to have a credible introduction and a rock-solid proposition and then to treat people with respect and civility.

- **EMPATHIZE.** Many people you'll contact don't make much money— probably a pittance compared to the salaries of executives. Don't think this means that they are obligated to take your abuse. You should empathize with the difficulty of their jobs.

- **DON'T COMPLAIN**. Never go over the heads of lower-ranked people and complain about them. The first thing that will happen is that your complaint will get back to them, and then they may take an active role in ensuring you make no progress with the organization.

When you do reach the umbrellas, ask them these questions:

- Who is the decision maker?

- Who does the decision maker rely on?

- Who cannot be left out of the decision-making process?

These questions may seem redundant, but you're panning for gold here. You want to get the name of the key influencer, and this key influencer may be a son or daughter, college classmate, or investor—none of whom is on the org chart!

Educate People

One of the most effective ways to make it rain is to educate people about the use of your product. In the old days this meant getting people to physically come to a meeting place. Today you can do it easily and cheaply with webinars, using services such as Go to Webinar, WebEx, and Google Hangouts.

Allow me to explain how Canva uses this method. First, a little background: Canva provides an online design service to enable people to make beautiful graphics. People use it for social media posts, eBay stores, Etsy stores, Kindle e-book covers, real estate flyers, and presentations. In the past, creating these kinds of graphics necessitated buying a product like Photoshop and then learning how to use it.

We produced webinars for companies and associations in niche markets. For example, we created a Kindle-book-cover webinar for a book-industry publication called *Kirkus Reviews* and a real estate flyer webinar for a real estate firm called <u>Intero</u>. *Kirkus* promoted the webinar to its subscribers, and Intero promoted it to its agents and brokers.

Hundreds of people attended these webinars in order to learn how to use Canva. I taught the webinars from my home in California. The total incremental cost, in a sense, was zero dollars; since I am an employee, there was no travel involved, and *Kirkus* and Intero did most of the promotion (at little cost to them too).

Everybody was a winner: *Kirkus* and Intero provided a resource to their subscribers and employees; subscribers and employees received free training; and Canva attracted new users. Win-win-win.

To make a webinar work, you must make it 90 percent educational and 10 percent promotional. In our case, people weren't attending a "Canva webinar" as much as learning how to make book covers or real estate flyers.

EXERCISE

What can you educate your customers about that can also help your business?

Court Agnostics, Not Zealots

Jesus himself did not try to convert the two thieves on the cross; he waited until one of them turned to him.

—Dietrich Bonhoeffer

The hard people to convert to Macintosh were MS-DOS zealots. They worshipped an alternate (and false, in my opinion) god. The easy people to convert to Macintosh had never used a personal computer before.

Their unfamiliarity with what a computer should look like, what it's supposed to do, and where to buy it worked to Apple's advantage. In their case, Apple didn't have to undo established ways of thinking, much less violate corporate computing standards.

"Agnostics—people who don't deny the validity of your religion and who are at least willing to consider the existence of your god—are a much better market."

At first, however, we pursued the Fortune 500 information-technology market in order to supplant the IBM PC in these large organizations. We failed, and I learned to ignore zealots. Agnostics—people who don't deny the validity of your religion and are at least willing to consider the existence of your god—are a much better market.

They are easier to please than zealots because you're opening a brave new world for them—as opposed to displacing an entrenched one. Apple seldom got people to switch from Windows, but Macintosh was life changing and empowering for people who never used a computer before.

Make Prospects Talk

Nature, which gave us two eyes to see and two ears to hear, has given us but one tongue to speak.

—Jonathan Swift

My experience is that sales prospects who are willing to buy your product will often tell you what it will take to close a deal. All you have to do is shut up and listen. This sounds easy, but it's not because people who don't understand rainmaking are clueless (more on this shortly).

The process is simple: (a) create a comfortable environment by obtaining permission to ask questions, (b) ask questions, (c) listen to the answers, (d) take notes, (e) explain how your product can fill their needs—if it does. Many salespeople fail at this process, however, for the following reasons:

- They are not prepared to ask good questions. It takes research to understand prospects and how your product might benefit them. Furthermore, salespeople are afraid that asking questions will make it look as if they don't already know the answer.

- They can't shut up because they belong to the bludgeon school of sales: keep talking until the prospect submits and agrees to buy. Or, they may be able to shut up, but then they don't bother listening. (Hearing is involuntary; listening is not.)

- They don't take notes because they are lazy or don't consider the information important. Taking notes is a good idea, as mentioned in chapter 5, "The Art of Fund-Raising." First, it will help you remember things. Second, it will show prospects that you care enough about what they said to write it down.

- They don't know enough about their product to apply it to the needs of prospects. This is inexcusable.

Let's say that your product offers several different benefits (not features!), such as lowering costs, opening new markets, and reducing impact on the environment. Begin by mentioning all three benefits and let the prospects react. They will signal which of the benefits are the most relevant.

If nothing resonates, ask prospects what would. Pay attention to their body language, not only what they say. They will offer you a valuable tidbit: "This is how to sell to me." Remember: you're selling, but they aren't necessarily buying, so you need to do some detective work.

Enable Test-Drives

The most difficult barriers that startups face are inertia and a reliance on the status quo. People believe that current products are good enough: "I can do everything I want with what I have." Or, even worse, "My employees can do everything they need to with what they have."

This doesn't mean that every product in widespread use *is* good enough or optimal—only that customers have accepted them. Thus, an entrepreneur's job is often to show people why they need something new. The traditional way to do so is to bludgeon them with advertising and promotion.

However, many companies flood the market with similar claims: better, faster, cheaper! Also, as a startup, you don't have enough money to reach critical mass with advertising and promotion. Fortunately, a great way for a startup to attract customers is to enable them to test-drive the product. By doing so, you are saying:

- "We think you're smart." (This already sets you apart from most organizations.)

- "We won't try to bludgeon you into becoming a customer." (Again setting you apart)

- "Please test-drive our product."

- "Then you decide on your own. Or ask us if you have any questions."

Test-driving is different for every business. Here are some notable examples:

- H. J. Heinz gave away samples of his pickles at the 1893 Chicago World's Fair. His booth was stuck in a low-traffic location, so he hired kids to pass out tickets that promised a free souvenir for visiting his booth to taste a pickle.*

- Apple allowed people to test-drive a Macintosh for a weekend during the 1980s. The current policy of accepting returns or exchanges of Apple products with no questions asked is effectively a fourteen-day test-drive.

- Salesforce.com enables people to use its software for a thirty-day period at no charge. The beauty of this test-drive is that once you

---

* Maggie Overfelt, "A World (Fair) of Invention," *Fortune Small Business* (April 2003): 31.

have this kind of information about a company's product, you're less likely to switch because of the data entry you've already done.

Suspend your dependence on traditional and expensive methods of marketing your product and give test-driving a test-drive. It's a great way to overcome a potential customer's inertia.

Learn from Rejection

If you're not part of the solution, you're part of the precipitate.

—Henry J. Tillman

Rainmakers get rejected. In fact, the best rainmakers get rejected more often because they are making more pitches. However, good rainmakers learn two lessons from rejection: first, how to improve their rainmaking; second, what kind of prospects to avoid. Here is a list of the most common rejections and what to learn from them:

- **"YOU ARE ASKING US TO CHANGE, AND WE DON'T WANT TO HEAR THIS."** This is a common response when presenting to a successful group that is living the high life and sees no reason to change. What you're hearing is that you're in the right market but talking to the wrong customers, so look for customers who are feeling pain.

- **"YOU DON'T HAVE YOUR ACT TOGETHER."** One of two things happened: you or your startup either didn't have your act together or you offended someone. Force yourself to review your pitch and interpersonal skills to determine if it's the former. If you offended someone, figure out how to make amends.

- **"YOU ARE INCOMPREHENSIBLE."** You usually hear this when you are, in fact, incomprehensible. Go back to the basics: cut out the jargon, redo your pitch from scratch, and practice your pitch. The onus is upon you—if you need to find a customer who's "smart enough to understand" why they need your product, you're going to fail.

- **"YOU ARE A SOLUTION LOOKING FOR A PROBLEM."** This means that you are still inside your value proposition looking out. The appropriate response is to keep revising your value proposition until you are outside the value proposition (like customers) and looking in.

- **"WE'VE DECIDED TO STANDARDIZE ON ANOTHER PRODUCT (OR SERVICE)."** You're trying to sell to the wrong person if your product is truly, demonstrably better. Do your best to get an entrée to the key influencers. If your product isn't truly, demonstrably better, then make it so.

Manage the Rainmaking Process

You can't abdicate rainmaking to some "sales types" or to sheer luck. It's a process, not a one-time event or an act of God, and you should manage it like you manage other processes in your startup. Here are some tips for how to do so:

- **ENCOURAGE EVERYONE TO MAKE IT RAIN.** Someday you may reach the point where your engineers and inventors can toss a new product over the cubicle wall and salespeople will pick it up and sell it. But that day isn't here yet.

"It's easy to know where you've been—it's harder and more valuable to know where you're going."

- **SET GOALS FOR ACCOUNTS.** These goals include when you expect them to decide and how much each sale will yield on a weekly, monthly, and quarterly basis. Good rainmakers are of a different breed: they need goals, and they need to be measured. You don't tell them to "go out there and do the best you can."

- **TRACK LEADING INDICATORS.** Everyone has trailing indicators, such as the previous month's and quarter's sales. Leading indicators, such as the number of new product ideas, cold calls, or sales leads, are important too. It's easy to know where you've been—it's harder and more valuable to know where you're going.

- **RECOGNIZE AND REWARD ACHIEVEMENTS.** Don't allow rainmakers to submit low forecasts so that they can easily beat them. Certainly don't recognize and reward intentions—intentions are easy; rainmaking is hard. But do recognize and reward achievements.

If you don't manage the rainmaking process, you'll start with "Our projections are conservative" and six months later, you'll be saying, "Our sales are coming in slower than expected." There is nothing sadder and more disconcerting, and it can lead to your replacement by investors.

Addenda

FAQ

Q: Where should I find the early adopters and risk takers in large companies?

A: It's difficult to provide a general answer to this question. It's easier to tell you where you *won't* find these types of people: at the highest levels. So let a hundred flowers blossom within these companies—don't go in with preconceived notions of who the early adopters are. You can't afford to be picky.

Q: Should we go after the low-hanging fruit, or worry about more strategic sales?

A: First, from a biological perspective, the fruit at the top of a tree gets the most light and ripens first, so the low-hanging ones may be easier to pick but not as good.

My experience is that sales for a startup are so hard that this question is effectively rhetorical, and you are unlikely to encounter a choice between low-hanging and top-of-the-tree sales. You are more likely to have to try both in order to achieve your first sales successes.

Q: We have the opportunity to hire a rainmaker, but he wants significant stock options, plus $150,000 per year, plus another $75,000 in expense accounts. He's got a good reputation and accounted for $16 million per year in sales in his previous job and says this will be a big step down in terms of income. Why should we hire him rather than going with manufacturers' representatives?

A: Rainmakers are expensive, but if they can deliver, they're worth it. If he wants the world—and it sounds as if that's the case in this scenario—make him earn it with a compensation plan dependent upon results. I wouldn't give him everything he wants at the start. Let's see if he's Mr. Causation or Mr. Correlation.

Recommended Reading

Cialdini, Robert. *Influence: The Psychology of Persuasion.* New York: Morrow, 1993.

CHAPTER 11

The Art of Partnering

Alliance, n.: In international politics, the union of two thieves who have their hands so deeply in each other's pockets that they cannot separately plunder a third.

—Ambrose Bierce

GIST

Most companies that were part of the dot-com phenomenon in the 1990s formed partnerships. These included research partnerships, marketing partnerships, distribution partnerships, and sales partnerships. In hindsight, there were more partnerships than there were revenues.

Companies learned that making partnerships work is difficult. Both parties wanted two plus two to equal five, but most of the time they ended up with three instead. The problem was that the glamour of entering into partnerships seduced companies into nonsensical collaborations.

Good partnerships should accelerate cash flow, increase revenue, and reduce costs. Partnerships built on solid business benefits like these have a much greater likelihood of succeeding. This chapter explains how to create partnerships that matter and that last.

Partner for "Spreadsheet" Reasons

Effective partnerships can speed entry into a new geographic area or market segment, open additional channels of distribution, accelerate new product development, and reduce costs.

I call these "spreadsheet" reasons because they affect your financial forecast. Unfortunately, many companies form partnerships for reasons that aren't reflected in spreadsheets, such as doing it because everyone else is or just for the thrill of a deal.

"The lesson is clear: if your spreadsheet doesn't change, your partnership is worthless."

For example, Apple and Digital Equipment Corporation formed a partnership in the late 1980s in response to criticism of both organizations by the press: Apple did not have a data-communications story, and Digital did not have a personal-computer story.

Little came of this alliance—certainly no products that vaulted Apple into big-business legitimacy or DEC into personal-computer coolness. I doubt that spreadsheets at either company were affected, unless it was to increase costs. It was, at best, a PR ploy to get the press off the backs of both organizations.

I learned a valuable lesson from that experience: never partner for the PR.

Apple created a much more successful partnership with a startup called Aldus Corporation, the publisher of <u>PageMaker</u>. At the time Apple was floundering because big businesses perceived Macintosh as a cute little graphics toy, not a business computer.

Apple needed a killer application that would jump-start the sale of Macintoshes. Simultaneously, Aldus needed help selling its software by getting inventory into the distribution channel, educating retail salespeople, opening major accounts, and training end users.

Each organization needed the other to increase revenue. With its sales force, advertising, and marketing clout, Apple could help Aldus achieve critical mass. Aldus did its part by providing a compelling reason for people to buy Macintoshes instead of Windows computers. The Apple-Aldus partnership created a new market called desktop publishing, and desktop publishing saved Apple and made Aldus.

EXERCISE

Go back to the bottom-up revenue forecast that you made in chapter 4, "The Art of Bootstrapping." Does the partnership you're thinking about cause you to change any numbers?

Define Deliverables and Objectives

If you accept the idea that the foundation of good partnerships is spreadsheet results, you'll understand why the next step is to define deliverables and objectives, such as:

- Additional revenues

- Reduced costs

- New products

- New customers

- New geographic markets

- New support programs

- Training and marketing programs

There are two reasons few companies define deliverables and objectives: First, the partnership is built on hype, so it's difficult to come up with concrete deliverables and objectives. This is not a good sign.

Second, and less depressing, is that people don't have the discipline to establish deliverables and objectives because they are too busy, disorganized, or lazy—or they are afraid of measuring results.

Here is a checklist of areas that the members of a partnership should define:

- What will each organization deliver?

- When will they deliver it?

- What interim milestones must each organization meet?

You'll find that by basing a partnership on spreadsheet numbers and defining deliverables and objectives, you'll triple the probability of success.

Ensure That the Middles and Bottoms Like the Deal

A second fundamental flaw of the Apple-Digital partnership was that the middle- and bottom-level employees (that is, where the real work was done) of both organizations didn't believe in it.

> **"The best partnerships often begin when the middles and bottoms of organizations started working together before any executives got involved."**

As an Apple employee at the time, I remember thinking, *What would a bunch of East Coast, minicomputer people add to our story?* It's safe to assume that the DEC employees were thinking, *Why are we partnering with a flaky California company that makes a cute graphics toy?*

If you want to make a partnership work, don't focus on drafting a press release and getting CEOs to show up at a press conference. Ensure, instead, that the middles and bottoms understand the reasons for the partnership, want to make it work, and value each other's contributions.

An announcement, if any, should come after the partnership is working well. Indeed, the best partnerships often begin when the middles and bottoms of organizations started working together before any executives got involved.

Find Internal Champions

Partnerships need internal champions to make them work. CEOs are seldom effective in this role because most of them are too busy or are attention deficit—or both. Internal champions should ideally be a person or a small group who believes in the relationship and will live or die by it.

Many people have heard of <u>John Sculley</u>, the former CEO of Apple. Fewer people have heard of John Scull, the desktop-publishing champion inside Apple, who in 1985 was the point person for Apple's efforts in this nascent market.

It was John Sculley who persuaded the engineering, sales, training, marketing, and PR employees of Apple to help Aldus. Simultaneously, he worked with Aldus to fill Apple's needs for product information, copies of the software, and analysis of the hardware needs of corporate customers. Additionally, he proselytized desktop publishing to journalists and pundits. To both internal employees and external parties, John was Mr. Desktop Publishing.

If desktop publishing had failed, it would have been John's fault. Since it succeeded, it was many people's idea. (Such is the nature of a champion's life.) Here are the key takeaways from John's success with desktop publishing:

- **IDENTIFY A SINGLE POINT PERSON IN EACH ORGANIZATION.** The partnership's success can't be built on a matrix where everyone contributes a slice of his time. At least one person—and at most two people—in each organization should be designated as a champion of the partnership.

- **MAKE SUCCESS OF THE PARTNERSHIP THE SOLE GOAL OF THE CHAMPION.** For the point people, nothing but the partnership should matter. Thus, champions can seldom be executives because executives always have something else to do.

- **EMPOWER THE CHAMPION.** Making a partnership work involves cutting across internal departments, priorities, and turfs. It can require stepping on people's toes and getting them to do things they don't want to do. Thus, management must empower the champion with the authority to make things happen. It's also helpful to have a name that sounds similar to the CEO's.

Accentuate Strengths—Don't Cover Weaknesses

A third flaw in the Apple-DEC alliance was that it was built on weakness: both organizations were trying to alleviate fundamental gaps in their product offerings. The philosophy was "You cover up our weakness, and we'll cover up yours. Together, we'll fool everyone."

A far better philosophy is to accentuate the strengths of both partners, which was the foundation of the Apple-Aldus partnership. Aldus made killer software. Apple made killer hardware and had marketing resources, field salespeople, trainers, and national account connections.

Cut Win-Win Deals

Because many partnerships are formed between organizations of vastly different sizes, there is often a temptation for the larger organization to cut win-lose deals. To make the flow of products, customers, and money work in a partnership, though, both parties have to win.

In 1990 United Parcel Service (UPS) and Mail Boxes Etc. cut a win-win deal.* Mail Boxes Etc. provides packing, shipping, receiving, secretarial, faxing, and photocopying services via retail storefronts. UPS invested about $11 million in the company; here's how both sides won:

- UPS obtained an instant nationwide network of convenient sites for customers to drop off and pick up packages. It didn't have to invest the time and money to build and run its own offices.

- Mail Boxes Etc. locked in UPS's business, averted the competition that would have arisen had UPS decided to build its own offices, and gained new business from UPS customers driving to its stores.

The lopsidedness of many partnerships is not born of necessity but occurs because the larger entity can muscle the smaller one into accepting an unfavorable deal. This is a bad idea for both partners for three reasons:

- Win-lose deals won't last. Oppression has seldom proven to be a sustainable system.

- If you want the middles and bottoms of both parties to support the partnership, each side has to see the partnership as a win.

- It's bad karma, and karma is important in partnerships.

If you're in a startup, be wary of entering into a win-lose partnership,

---

* George Gendron, "A Sweet Deal," *Inc.* (March 1991).

no matter how attractive the terms may initially seem. They seldom work out. If you're in a big company, rein in your hormones and cut win-win partnerships. They are the only sustainable kind.

Wait to Legislate

For certain people, after fifty, litigation takes the place of sex.

—Gore Vidal

Here's a nontheoretical question. Which comes first: A meeting of the minds, or the draft of a legal document detailing the partnership?

Many organizations prepare a draft of a document to get the discussion rolling. The rationale is that whoever does the drafting has an inherent advantage. In practice, this is a high-risk approach for two reasons.

First, if you ask for legal advice or permission early in the process, you'll learn that the number of reasons not to do a deal exceeds the number of reasons to do it. Many lawyers view their role as the adults there to supervise and to prevent stupid deals from taking place. Their bias is that a deal is bad until proven good.

The better method is to agree on business terms before you bring in the lawyers. Then find a lawyer who wants to do deals, not prevent them, to create a legal framework. Having found the right lawyer, you need to establish the right perspective, which is, "This is what I want to do. Now keep me out of jail." This is the antithesis of asking, "Can I do this?"

The second reason not to ask for a document early in the process is that the document may take on a life of its own. It may, for example, be forwarded to an executive who wasn't informed that it was "just a starting point for our thinking." The unintended consequence is that the document raises premature red flags in management that derail the process.

Here's a better approach:

1. Get together face-to-face. Discuss the deal points. This may take multiple meetings.

2. When you start agreeing, write the points down on a whiteboard.

3. Follow up with a one-to-two-page e-mail outlining the framework for a partnership.

4. Reach closure on all details via e-mails, phone calls, and follow-up meetings.

5. Draft a legal document.

Many people try to go from step 1 directly to step 5—this is not a good idea. A document should follow a discussion, not lead it.

Put an "Out" Clause in the Deal

As the Japanese (*sic*) say, "Mazel tov"—you're close to getting the deal done. Because everybody should win, the last thing in the world you want is for your partner to be able to end the arrangement, right?

"[A] safety valve enables everyone to chill out and work harder to make the partnership function."

Counterintuitive as this may seem, you should include an out clause in the deal—something along the lines of "Either party can end this agreement upon thirty days' notice." The reason is that an easy out promotes the longevity of a deal because it assures both parties that they won't be trapped in an untenable predicament.

This safety valve enables everyone to chill out and work harder to make the partnership function. Also, people are more likely to take chances and be innovative when the partnership isn't permanent.

Don't misunderstand my point here: I am not advocating entering into partnerships that are easy to get out of. I am advocating that the reason partnerships should be hard to get out of is because they are valuable, not legalistically enforced.

Get out of the Belly

In the words of Heidi Mason, coauthor of <u>The Venture Imperative</u>, trying to form a partnership with a larger, established organization is like being "stuck in the belly of a snake." You may get it done, but in the end you'll wind up being just a pile of bones. Thus, it's important to recognize and interpret the top twelve lies of partnering (it was too hard to narrow down to ten).

I don't like to end a chapter on a downer, but before those jaws close around you and you are eaten alive, listen for these lies, spins, and exaggerations.

Big organization says	Big organization means
"We want to do this for strategic reasons."	They can't figure out why this partnership is important.
"Our management really wants to do this."	A vice president heard about the proposal for thirty seconds and didn't say no yet.
"We can move fast."	No one has talked to the legal department yet.
"Our legal department won't be a problem."	The legal department will be a huge problem.
"We want to time the announcement of our partnership with the release of a new version of our product."	We're way behind schedule.
"The engineering team really likes it."	The marketing team is going to kill it.
"The marketing team really likes it."	The engineering team is going to kill it.
"The engineering and marketing teams really like it."	The lawyers are going to kill it.
"The engineering, marketing, and legal teams really like it."	This is too good to be true.
"Our primary concern is whether you guys can scale."	You guys are smarter than we thought.
"We're forming a cross-functional team to ensure the success of this project."	No one is accountable for the success of this project.
"I'm leaving soon, but I've found a great person to take over my role in this project."	We're screwed.

Addenda

FAQ

Q: **Since partnerships are supposed to be fifty-fifty, win-win situations, shouldn't the other party meet halfway in setting up meetings, moving the process along, getting its employees to cooperate, and so on?**

A: "Should" and "will" are two different things. You're right that the other party should meet you halfway, but it won't. If you want a partnership, sale, or almost any transaction to happen, you've got to do what you have to do. The other party may owe you a phone call or response, but don't just wait for it. Call again. You'll have to make 80 percent of the effort to bring something about, so swallow your pride.

Q: **How do I avoid being bullied by my contractual partners if they are larger, more established, and better funded than I am?**

A: Never believe, or at least never act as if you believe, that might makes right. For all you know, the elephant needs your product as much as you need the elephant. Go in expecting to win but don't be afraid to walk if the deal isn't good for you.

Q: **We're in some partnerships that aren't going anywhere. Should we invest the time and money to make them work, or abandon them?**

A: There's an old medical proverb that says, "Nothing requires more heroic efforts than to keep a corpse from stinking, and yet nothing is quite so futile."* Focus your energies on partnerships that are working and new ones that have greater promise. But before you commit to new partnerships, figure out why the previous partnerships didn't work out.

---

* Peter F. Drucker, *Innovation and Entrepreneurship: Practice and Principles* (New York: Harper & Row, 1985), 152.

Recommended Reading

Rezac, Darcy. *The Frog and Prince: Secrets of Positive Networking to Change Your Life.* Vancouver: Frog and Prince Networking Corporation, 2003.

RoAne, Susan. *The Secrets of Savvy Networking: How to Make the Best Connections for Business and Personal Success.* New York: Warner Books, 1993.

CHAPTER 12

The Art of Enduring

Winning isn't everything, but the will to prepare
to win is everything.

—Vince Lombardi

GIST

Entrepreneurship is not a sprint because it takes years to win. It's not a marathon because there are multiple events. A decathlon is closer, but a decathlon is not a team sport. No sports analogy does entrepreneurship justice.

Entrepreneurship requires a team to do ten things at once. One aspect of a decathlon that does work as a metaphor is that it is a contest of endurance. In both cases, the winner is the one who has mastered the art of enduring. This chapter explains how to make your startup endure.

Strive for Internalization

Internalization means getting people to believe in your product and its way of doing things. For example, people who have internalized Macintosh believe in a transparent, what-you-see-is-what-you-get approach and the efficacy of individuals. The internalization of your product's way of doing things is a powerful way to make it endure.

The best way to illustrate this concept is with examples of companies with customers who have internalized their products. Here are six.

Company	Cause
Chez Panisse	Using local-farm, direct-to-table ingredients
Etsy	Celebrating crafts(wo)manship and entrepreneurship
Harley-Davidson	Rebelling and kicking ass
Maker Faire	Learning by doing
Philz Coffee	Bettering your day
Zappos	Trusting people by default

Internalization is difficult to achieve but it lasts a long time. I internalized Macintosh in 1983, and many years after working at Apple, I still evangelize it. (In thirty-two years of using computers, I've bought only one Windows machine, which I gave to Goodwill long ago.)

Push Implementation Down

Ensuring that people lower in the pyramid implement change is another way to foster endurance. For example, the traditional view of settling armed conflict involves bringing together the leaders of opposing forces. The assumption is that these leaders can deliver their people's support and agreement.

"The real work is done by the middles and bottoms."

Celia McKeon of Conciliation Resources, a charity organization that works to promote peace, disagrees:

Traditional diplomacy and conflict resolution approaches have largely focused on a narrow definition of a peace process—namely the crucial task of bringing the political and military leaders of opposing groups into a process of dialogue and negotiation with the aim of exploring, reaching agreement on and implementing measures to end violent conflict and create the conditions for peaceful co-existence. This approach is guided by the belief that the leaders have the power to reach decisions and bring along their constituencies in support of any resulting settlement.

However, modern civil wars present strong arguments for a more holistic understanding of a peace process. Negotiations between the leaders of opposing groups do not take place in a social or political vacuum. They may sometimes be unable to adequately address the complex and dynamic inter-relationships between these actors and other groups affected by and involved in the armed conflict, including the parties' constituencies, the wider public and even the broader regional or international forces. People's independent initiatives in their towns and villages, as well as at the regional, national and international level therefore have the potential to become key elements in a broader peace process that is capable of addressing these complexities.*

In other words achieving peace starts from the middle and bottom, not the top, of a population. For example, civilians helped bring about a lasting settlement in the border dispute between Peru and Ecuador in 1998. This development came out of a workshop at the University of Maryland called "Ecuador-Peru: Towards a Democratic and Cooperative Conflict Resolution Initiative."

The first workshop took place in 1997. Twenty members of the civilian populations of Ecuador and Peru formed the Grupo Maryland, and they worked together to find a common ground for the resolution of armed conflict. Its members were academics, businesspeople, educators, journalists, and environmentalists who shared similar characteristics—not political or military leaders.

To make your startup last, don't depend on the people at the top. They have their own agenda—such as power, money, and self-image—which doesn't necessarily reflect that of the entire population, much less the greater good. The middles and bottoms are the key constituencies to foster endurance.

---

* http://www.academia.edu/7855213/Hostilities_must_stop_democracy_and_respect_to_its_principles_must_be_anhenced_in_Mozambique_Annual_Report_2013.

Use Intrinsic Methods

Kathleen Vohs, a professor at the University of Minnesota, conducted a series of experiments that examined the effect of money on people's behavior. Here is a quick synopsis of three that provide insight into the effect of money on behavior:

- Researchers told subjects that they were going to play Monopoly. The researchers provided $4,000, $200, or zero dollars in Monopoly money. As they left the lab, a confederate dropped a bag of pencils, and the experimenters measured how many pencils the subjects picked up for the confederate. The subjects who received $4,000 were the least helpful, the ones given no money were the most helpful, and the $200 subjects were in the middle.

> **"If you started a great company, you won't need to use money, and bringing money into the picture may undermine your efforts."**

- Researchers gave subjects eight quarters for unscrambling phrases into sentences. Some phrases dealt with money, and some didn't. At the conclusion of the experiment, subjects were asked for a donation to a student fund. The subjects who unscrambled phrases mentioning money donated less than those who unscrambled phrases that had nothing to do with money.

- Researchers placed subjects in a room with a computer in three states: no screensaver, a screensaver showing money, or a screensaver showing fish. The researchers asked the subjects to set up two chairs for them to meet with other subjects. The ones who had seen the money screensaver set up chairs farther apart than the ones who had a blank screen or a fish screensaver.

You could dismiss these studies because they fall into the category of "these were college students in research projects, so this doesn't mean it's how the whole world works." This is true, but they may indicate that exposing people to money affects their attitudes and that extrinsic rewards are not effective to make your startup endure.

The most obvious example of this is Wikipedia. Volunteers and "amateurs" created the world's greatest information resource; no one contributed for money. By contrast, Microsoft threw millions of dollars at Encarta, and the project still failed.

Many organizations try to encourage its evangelists and customers to help by offering commissions and affiliate fees, but such enticements often raise suspicions among potential customers (*Are you spreading the word because you're getting paid?*) and alter the nature of company-client relationships (*Am I spreading the word because I'm getting paid?*).

If you started a lousy company, money won't help. If you started a great company, you won't need to use money, and bringing money into the picture may undermine your efforts.

Invoke Reciprocation

Invoking reciprocation is a powerful tool to help you endure. For example, in 1935 Italy invaded Ethiopia, and Mexico not only condemned its aggression but sent money to Ethiopia to help finance its defense. No other country supported Ethiopia like Mexico did.

In 1985 a major earthquake struck Mexico, and Ethiopia sent $5,000 to reciprocate for Mexico's help fifty years earlier. Five thousand dollars does not sound like a lot of money, but Ethiopia was then suffering the worst famine in its history. So a starving country gave money to people who helped them five decades earlier.

Another story of reciprocation: Kids from the White Knoll Middle School in West Columbia, South Carolina, presented a check for $447,265 to New York mayor Rudy Giuliani during the 2001 Macy's Thanksgiving Day parade. The students had collected this money to enable New York to replace one of the fire trucks lost during the 9/11 attack. (Admittedly, it included one huge donation from a rich individual.)

The kids from South Carolina reciprocated because 134 years earlier, New Yorkers collected money to buy Columbia a fire wagon after they learned that the city was using bucket brigades to fight fires. When the first wagon sank on the way to Columbia, New Yorkers raised more money and sent a second one.

A former Confederate colonel named Samuel Melton was overwhelmed by the generosity of the New Yorkers—many of whom were Union soldiers. On behalf of Columbia, he vowed to return the favor "should misfortune ever befall the Empire City."

"If you give a lot, you'll get a lot."

Here are the keys to invoking reciprocation for your product:

- **GIVE EARLY.** Do favors before you need favors back. It's obvious and less powerful when there's a clear link between what you're doing and what you want back—that's called a transaction. You want to do a favor.

- **GIVE WITH JOY.** The purest form of giving is to those who seemingly cannot help you (for example, Columbia immediately after the Civil War) and without the expectation of return. Ironically, giving in this manner often results in the greatest reciprocation.

- **GIVE OFTEN AND GENEROUSLY.** "As you sow, so shall you reap." If you give a lot, you get a lot. If you give high-quality favors, you get high-quality favors. Put aside the sales mantra of "always be closing" and think "always be giving."

- **GIVE UNEXPECTEDLY.** Richard Branson, the chairman of the Virgin Group, and I once spoke at the same conference in Moscow. He asked me if I ever flew on Virgin. I told him that I didn't, and at that point, he got on his knees and gave me a shoeshine with his coat. I've flown on Virgin America ever since. Years later I reciprocated too.

- **TELL PEOPLE HOW THEY CAN PAY YOU BACK**. Don't hesitate to ask for a favor in return when you need it. This is a good practice because it relieves pressure on the recipient—you're providing a way for him to repay the debt. This enables the recipient to ask for and receive more favors, and your relationship can deepen.

I learned these lessons from Robert Cialdini, the author of <u>Influence: The Psychology of Persuasion</u>, and it be would hypocritical and ironic if I did not tell you to read this awesome book if you want to be a successful entrepreneur.

Invoke Consistency

Forty young people who loved Hawaii's unique culture and lifestyle started an organization called <u>Kanu Hawaii</u>. They started it because changes in the environment, declining civility, the high cost of living, and declining job opportunities threatened what they loved.

Kanu Hawaii asks its members to make personal commitments such as buying locally made products and cleaning up beaches. Then it helps members publicly communicate these commitments to friends and family via Facebook, Twitter, and e-mail. This increases their follow-through because people want consistency between what they do and what they say they're going to do.

Invoking consistency can help make your startup endure because it provides a mental break from choosing between options and reconsidering past decisions. It also enables people to avoid the conflict between their beliefs and their actions: *I am an honorable person. If I don't do what I said I'd do, it means I'm not an honorable person.*

Invoking consistency is a powerful way to make your startup endure if you can encourage people to take these actions:

- **COMMIT IN CONCRETE WAYS.** When not-for-profits raise money, they try to get people to commit to a specific dollar-amount donation. This is much more effective than letting them off with "Sure, I'll give something." A written commitment is even stronger, so don't underestimate the power of a pledge!

- **COMMUNICATE THE COMMITMENT TO OTHERS.** When people let others know that they've made a commitment, they tend to complete that commitment. Not doing so makes them feel inconsistent with respect to qualities such as honesty and perseverance.

- **IDENTIFY WITH THE SAME VALUES AND GOALS.** When you help people identify with the values of your startup, their behavior is usually supportive. For example, if people identify with energy conservation, they are more likely to support your green products.

There is a creepy aspect to invoking consistency, though. It is a form of playing with people's minds, and consistency has made people do things that are against their best interests and, at an extreme, downright evil. So consult your moral compass when you use this technique because some ends do not justify the means.

Invoke Social Proof

One of the reasons that the iPod became popular is that it used white earbuds. At the time, the earphones of most devices were black if there were earphones at all, and people learned that white earbuds equaled iPod.

"Social proof doesn't work for crap—indeed, social proof can (and should) kill crap."

The presence of white earbuds served as social proof of iPod's goodness and made people comfortable with buying an iPod. Then the more they bought iPods, the more they added to the proof of iPod's acceptance. This encouraged even more people to buy iPods—a powerful upward spiral that should warm the heart of any entrepreneur.

Social proof is a powerful way to make your product endure. These are the key components necessary to make it work:

- **GREAT PRODUCT.** This is a recurring theme of this book. Social proof doesn't work for crap—indeed, social proof can (and should) kill crap.

- **FEAR OF MISSING OUT (FOMO).** An element of fear of missing out is helpful. *If I don't buy an iPod, I'll be missing out on a great music experience.* People don't want to be on the outside looking in when it comes to cool phenomena.

- **INVOLUNTARY BEHAVIOR**. The choice of earbud colors ran the spectrum from white to white. It was involuntary. You should try to make providing social proof a default—for example, e-mail from Apple phones contains the text "sent from my iPhone." People can remove this text but few do.

- **CRITICAL MASS**. There are several indices of social proof: experts (<u>Marques Brownlee</u>), influencers (<u>William Shatner</u>), users (<u>Yelp</u>), and crowds ("over one billion served"). So consider what kind of social proof registers most powerfully in your niche and use all the available tools. (Read "<u>Social Proof Is the New Marketing</u>" by Aileen Lee.)

EXERCISE:

How can you invoke social proof of your product?

Build an Ecosystem

A Sunnyvale, California, company called <u>Pley</u> provides a subscription service for LEGO sets. You create a wish list, and after you return one choice, Pley sends the next one. Its model is similar to Netflix in the old days when you received a new DVD after you returned the one you had.

Pley is part of the LEGO ecosystem and provides a cool service to people who like to build, but not keep, new sets. The presence of an ecosystem with players like Pley increases the satisfaction of using a product. Thousands of Android developers, for example, make owning an Android phone more satisfying.

Also, an ecosystem signals that your product is successful enough to *have* an ecosystem. Your product must be good if there are other companies building upon it. Anti-example: the lack of apps for the Microsoft Windows smartphone signals that it's not successful—and it won't be successful until there are more apps!

These are the major components of an ecosystem:

- **CONSULTANTS**. These folks have expertise in helping others install and use products. They increase the utility of your product, and they have a vested interest in your success because they can provide their services only as long as your product continues to sell.

- **DEVELOPERS**. Whether it's a gaming box like Xbox, a computer operating system like Macintosh, or an online service like Twitter, developers are a huge reason for a platform's success and survival. These people create games, applications, and services that increase the utility of the platform.

- **RESELLERS**. Stores and dealers provide a convenient way for people to try and to buy your product. They spread the word for you, and they provide credibility—"BestBuy isn't going to stock a piece of junk."

- **USER GROUPS**. During the darkest moments of Apple's struggle to make Macintosh a success in the 1980s and 1990s, there were hundreds of Macintosh fanatics who voluntarily ran user groups. These groups provided information, support, and enthusiasm when Apple could not or would not.

- **WEBSITES AND BLOGS**. Enthusiasts, often consultants and developers in their off hours, operate websites and blogs that are dedicated to a particular product. Try searching Google for "WordPress blog" to see how the WordPress ecosystem makes it a better tool. The existence of such sites assists and reassures both customers and potential customers.

- **ONLINE SPECIAL-INTEREST GROUPS AND COMMUNITIES**. Fans of companies and products form special-interest groups on the Internet—for example, the <u>Bluetooth Special Interest Group</u>. At these websites people exchange ideas, seek and provide support, and blow off steam. If your product is affecting many people, chances are good that they will form one of these about what you're doing.

- **CONFERENCES.** You know your product has arrived when you're big enough to hold a conference for it. And when you hold a conference for your product, it helps you grow big because people believe that only products that have achieved critical mass can pull off a conference.

Now that you understand the key players in ecosystems, here are the key principles of building an ecosystem. They are similar to the principles of creating a community discussed in chapter 8, "The Art of Evangelizing."

- **CREATE SOMETHING WORTHY OF AN ECOSYSTEM.** Once again, the key to evangelism, sales, presentations, and now ecosystems is a great product. In fact, if you create a great product, you may not be able to stop an ecosystem from forming. By contrast, it's hard to build an ecosystem around crap.

- **DESIGNATE A CHAMPION.** Many employees would like to help build an ecosystem, but who wakes up every day with this task at the top of her list of priorities? Another way to look at this is, "Who's going to get fired if an ecosystem doesn't happen?" Ecosystems need a champion—an identifiable hero—within the company to carry the flag for the community.

- **DON'T COMPETE WITH THE ECOSYSTEM.** If you want people or organizations to take part in your ecosystem, then you shouldn't compete with them. For example, if you want people to create apps for your product, then don't sell (or give away) apps that do the same thing. It was hard to convince companies to create a Macintosh word processor when Apple was giving away MacWrite.

- **CREATE AN OPEN SYSTEM.** An "open system" means that there are minimal requirements to participating and minimal controls on what you can do. A "closed system" means that you control who participates and what they can do. Either can work, but I recommend an open system because it appeals to my trusting, anarchic personality.

- This means that members of your ecosystem will be able to write apps, access data, and interact with your product. I'm using software terminology here, but the point is to enable people to customize and tweak your product.

- **PUBLISH INFORMATION**. The natural complement of an open system is publishing books and articles about the product. This spreads information to people on the periphery of a product. Publishing also communicates to the world that your startup is open and willing to help external parties.

- **FOSTER DISCOURSE**. The definition of "discourse" is "verbal exchange." The key word is "exchange." Any company that wants an ecosystem should foster the exchange of ideas and opinions. This means your website should provide a forum where people can engage with other members as well as your employees. This doesn't mean that you let the ecosystem run your company, but you should hear what members have to say.

- **WELCOME CRITICISM**. Most organizations feel warm and fuzzy toward their ecosystem as long as the ecosystem says nice things, buys their products, and never complains. The minute that the ecosystem says anything negative, however, many organizations freak out and get defensive. This is dumb. A healthy ecosystem is a long-term relationship, so an organization shouldn't file for divorce at the first sign of discord. Indeed, the more an organization welcomes—or even celebrates—criticism, the stronger its bonds to its ecosystem become.

- **CREATE A NONMONETARY REWARD SYSTEM**. You already know how I feel about paying people off to help you, but this doesn't mean you shouldn't reward people in other ways. Things as simple as public recognition, badges, points, and credits have more impact than a few bucks. Many people don't participate in an ecosystem for the money, so don't insult them by rewarding them with it.

The bottom line is that you should do everything you can to foster an ecosystem around your product. It is a powerful tool to increase the satisfaction of your believers and to attract new believers with greater ease—in short, making your product endure.

Diversify the Team

A diverse team helps make a startup endure, because people with different backgrounds, perspectives, and skills keep a startup fresh and relevant. By contrast, when an emperor runs a kingdom of sycophants and clones, the product will deteriorate.

> **"Populating your startup with a diversity of people and capabilities is a powerful way to make a startup endure."**

Ideally, you'd like people of different ages, genders, races, economic standing, religions, and educational backgrounds as part of your team. In addition to these obvious differences, you also want people to play different roles.

Populating your startup with a diversity of people and capabilities is a powerful way to make a startup endure. There's no such thing as too much diversity in a startup that's staffed to last.

Take Care of Your Friends

> *Everybody can be great . . . because anybody can serve. You don't have to have a college degree to serve. You don't have to make your subject and verb agree to serve. You only need a heart full of grace. A soul generated by love.*
>
> —Martin Luther King Jr.

Taking care of your friends by providing awesome customer support can make your startup endure, because people will stick by products that aren't the latest and greatest if they're well supported. For example, the reason

Derek Sivers believes that his company, CD Baby, succeeded is not because of its features, design, prices, or partnerships. He says the <u>number one reason was the quality of customer support</u>—especially that customers could talk to a real person at CD Baby.

Here are the key elements of awesome customer support:

• **BE GENEROUS AND TRUSTING**. Great customer support, according to Sivers, comes from a mind-set of generosity and abundance, and lousy customer support comes from a mind-set of scarcity. The ramification of a generosity and abundance mind-set is that you provide human telephone support, allow people to use your restroom without a purchase, and provide free Wi-Fi access.

No doubt a bean counter will tell you that if every customer called for technical support, if everyone used your bathroom, and if everyone with a broken product got a free replacement, you'd go out of business. This is probably true if, literally, everyone did, but everyone will not. So be generous with your customer support and see if the upside of an awesome reputation can exceed the downside of higher customer-support costs.

• **PUT THE CUSTOMER IN CONTROL**. Have you ever shopped at Nordstrom? If you want to learn how to provide great support, you should. When you shop at Nordstrom, you are in control: you can buy items at any department in the store and pay for them in any other department. When you want something gift wrapped, they don't send you to a line behind the men's room. They wrap it, always cheerfully, at the sales counter.

Most companies have rules against refunds and exchanges, sending out free samples, or accepting collect calls. The right way to treat customers is to do what's right for them, not adhere to rules, so put your customers in control and let your employees do the right thing.

Underpromise and overdeliver for great support.

• **TAKE RESPONSIBILITY FOR YOUR SHORTCOMINGS**. Bad support refuses to take responsibility for a company's shortcomings. Good support takes responsibility for a company's shortcomings. Fantastic support takes responsibility for the customer's shortcomings.

Let me tell you a story. While getting a tuxedo fitted at Nordstrom, I lost two pendants that I had purchased elsewhere. We searched for an hour and could not find them. The manager assured me that their tailor was a longtime, trusted employee.

After several weeks, when the pendants still didn't turn up, Nordstrom reimbursed me for the loss, even though I didn't purchase them there. The point is that Nordstrom had taken responsibility for the loss even when it wasn't its fault—a few months later I found both pendants. And I gave the money back to Nordstrom.

- **UNDERPROMISE AND OVERDELIVER.** If you get to a Disney park a few minutes before it officially opens, the employees let you in instead of making you wait. Disney's official age policy is that children over three years old must pay for admission, but they never ask how old your small children are.

There are signs that tell you how much longer it will take you to get to the ride, but the times are overestimated to make you feel that the wait wasn't so bad. Disney says it does not offer rain checks in the event of bad weather, but if you ask, they give them to you. Disney has policy and Disney has implementation. Implementation supersedes policy and delights the customer. Underpromise and overdeliver for great support.

- **HIRE THE RIGHT PEOPLE.** Though everyone in a company should be supportive of customers, the support function isn't the right role for everyone. The people on the firing line should embody three qualities:

- Empathy. Support people should feel pain when customers are not satisfied. Unresolved support issues should bother them. This is the most important quality of people for the job.

"The best Apple employees were people who already used Macintoshes before they started at the company."

- ENGROSSMENT. Some employees want to design products. Some employees want to sell. Some employees want to help customers. Support people should derive satisfaction from helping others.

People who view working in support as a goal, and not as a means to a goal, are the ones you want.

- **KNOWLEDGE**. Support people should know and love your product. Hence, one of the best sources for finding support people is your installed base of customers. The best Apple employees were people who already used Macintoshes before they started at the company.

- **EXPOSE EVERYONE TO CUSTOMER SUPPORT**. Many organizations put all employees on support lines to understand the issues that customers face. Instead of having employees review numbers and charts depicting the state of customer satisfaction, get them to spend a few hours in support—that drives the message home. For example, new-employee training for all positions at Go Daddy involves a course about the customer support function as well as a visit to the customer support area to listen to calls.

- **INTEGRATE SUPPORT INTO THE MAINSTREAM**. Support should not be the butt end or lowest tier of a business. Unfortunately many companies consider support a necessary evil and staff it that way. Support should be a heralded and celebrated group—not an unavoidable part of overhead. It influences sales as much as your packaging, advertising, and PR, and it's much cheaper to retain a current customer than to win a new one.

OBLIGATION

CHAPTER 13

The Art of Being a Mensch

The true measure of a man is how he treats someone
who can do him absolutely no good.

—Samuel Johnson

GIST

This chapter explains how to achieve menschhood. This is the state when the people who matter recognize you as someone who is ethical, graceful, and admirable. It is the highest form of praise and the pinnacle of a career.

"Right is right, and wrong is wrong."

I want you to aspire to a higher goal than making lots of money and building a large organization. This chapter explains how to be a mensch.

Help People Who Cannot Help You

Mensches help people who cannot reciprocate. They don't care if the recipient is poor or powerless. This doesn't mean that you shouldn't help rich, famous, or powerful people (indeed, they may need the most help), but you shouldn't help only rich, famous, and powerful people.

Help Without the Expectation of Return

Mensches help without the expectation of return—at least in this life. What's the payoff? Not that there has to be a payoff, but the payoff is the pure joy of helping others—nothing more, nothing less.

Help Many People

Menschdom is a numbers game, so mensches help many people. This is in their operating system. They almost cannot stop themselves from helping others. (Of course, not even a mensch can help everyone.)

Do What's Right

Mensches do what's right. This means taking the high and, sometimes, difficult road. For mensches, "situational ethics" is an oxymoron. Right is right, and wrong is wrong. A mensch does the right thing—not the easy thing, the expedient thing, the money-saving thing, or the I-can-get-away-with-it thing.

Repay Society

Mensches realize that they're blessed. These blessings come with the obligation to repay society. The baseline is that you *owe* society—you're not doing society a *favor* by paying it back.

EXERCISE

This is the last exercise of the book. Pretend it's the end of your life. What are the three things you want people to remember about you?

1.

2.

3.

Addenda

FAQ

Q: How can I prevent success from going to my head?

A: All the riches, fame, and power don't matter if you're sick or dead. So whenever you're feeling especially invincible, just remember that you could be gone in a split second, and "richest person in the hospital" and "richest person in the cemetery" are lousy positioning statements.

Q: How can I make sales calls and close business deals without always feeling as if I pulled one over on the customer?

A: If you're selling something that the customer needs, you should never feel this way. If you do feel this way, stop selling what you're selling—or sell it to people who genuinely need it.

Q: Won't a potential investor consider being charitable as a sign of softness, weakness, or otherwise unsuitability for entrepreneurship?

A: If a potential investor feels this way, it says more about the investor than it says about you. Doing good and making good are not mutually exclusive—nor are they identical. But don't think that an investor will fund you because you are doing good—investors mostly want to make money.

Q: What if otherwise helpful and positive me wants to lash out at someone?

A: This is what hockey is for—although I've been known to lash out off the ice a few times myself. (In every case it made the situations worse.) As I've gotten older, I've learned to shut up (or not send the e-mail) and walk away.

Q: People are always asking me for my expert advice, but it's interfering with my ability to get my job done. What should I do?

A: I face this challenge every day, and I've come up with two solutions. Sometimes I explain that I don't have the time to help because of my commitments (professional and family), and because most people are amazed that I responded at all, they are understanding.

Sometimes I tell them that I'll review their pitch or business plan (this is what most people ask about) if they will donate $500 to the UC Berkeley ice hockey team, for which my son plays. This works well: the entrepreneurs who are willing to pay are really serious, and the team gets donations.

Recommended Reading

Halberstam, Joshua. *Everyday Ethics: Inspired Solutions to Real-Life Dilemmas.* New York: Viking, 1993.

Afterword

Books are good enough in their own way,
but they are a mighty bloodless substitute for living.

—Robert Louis Stevenson

Thank you for reading my book—perhaps both editions! This took an investment of your time and your money. In return I hope that you have gained insight into how to make meaning and change the world.

There are many ways to describe the ebb and flow, yin and yang, bubble-blowing and bubble-bursting phases of business cycles. Here's another: microscopes and telescopes.

- In the microscope phase, there's a cry for levelheaded thinking, returning to fundamentals, and focusing on short-term financial results. Experts magnify details, line items, and expenditures, and then demand forecasts, market research, and competitive analysis.

- In the telescope phase, entrepreneurs bring the future closer. They dream up the next big thing, change the world, and make late adopters eat their dust. Money is wasted, but some crazy ideas stick, and the world moves forward.

When telescopes work, everyone is an astronomer, and the world is full of stars. When telescopes don't work, people whip out microscopes, and the world is full of flaws. The reality is that entrepreneurs need both microscopes and telescopes to achieve success. I hope this book helps you with your microscopic and telescopic tasks.

Lewis Pugh is the first person to swim across the North Pole—one kilometer to be exact. He did this in order to build awareness for climate change; one would have thought that the North Pole, of all places, would be frozen. After a few minutes in water that's minus 1.7 degrees C / 29 degrees F degrees cold, you'd be toast—not in the warm-and-toasty sense but in the comatoast (sic) sense. His swim lasted eighteen minutes, and he was in a Speedo, not a wetsuit.

He used a mental trick to achieve this task: placing a national flag of every member of his team every one hundred meters to break down a one-kilometer swim into ten more achievable segments. The second-to-the-last flag was Australian because, as a Brit, he wasn't going give up at the eleventh hour in front of Australia—Commonwealth rivalries being what they are.

In the dark, daunting, and depressing days (believe me, there will be some), remember Lewis's story and break the impossible into ten possibles. A billion-dollar business is ten one-hundred-million-dollar segments. A million-dollar business is ten one-hundred-thousand-dollar segments. Apple sells Macintoshes, iPhones, iPads, and iPods, but it started with a few hundred Apple Is.

Finally, I hope to meet you someday. If you have the book with you, you can show me how you took notes, dog-eared pages, and underlined text. Nothing is more gratifying to see than that you pounded my book into smithereens.

I've kept you too long. Now get going because the essence of entrepreneurship is doing, not learning to do.

Guy Kawasaki
Silicon Valley, California
GuyKawasaki@gmail.com

What Do Entrepreneurs Do?

I have four children, and I've found it difficult to explain exactly what I do. My kids' friends are doctors, lawyers, teachers, and real estate brokers. Those careers are easy to explain. But how do you explain to a kid what entrepreneurs do? This is an extra "gift with purchase" from me to help you explain what entrepreneurs do.

What Do Entrepreneurs Do?

by
Guy Kawasaki

Illustrated by
Lindsey Filby

Buy nice
stuff?

No.

Create cool stuff.

Sell it.

Hire people
to help.

To make the world
a better place.

To do something
they love.

To give you a good life.

After Afterword

Are you Jackie Chan?

—Anonymous teenage girl

Twenty-five years ago I owned a Porsche 911 Cabriolet. One day I stopped at a traffic light on El Camino Real in Menlo Park, California. I looked over and saw a car with four teenage girls in it. They were making eye contact, smiling, and laughing.

I thought that I had truly arrived: even teenage girls knew who I was. One girl motioned me to roll down the window—she was clearly not a 911 owner because 911s had power windows. I did so, expecting her to tell me how she loved my books or speeches or maybe my anonymous good looks.

Instead she asked, "Are you Jackie Chan?"

What does this have to do with startups? Not much, but the mark of a good author is the ability to stay on topic. However, the mark of a *great* author is that he can go off-topic and then return. I will show you how this works.

Getting this far in a book is like staying through the credits of a Jackie Chan movie to see the outtakes. I will reward your perseverance with, as Steve would say, "One more thing."

The Top Ten Mistakes of Entrepreneurs

These are the top ten mistakes that entrepreneurs make, compiled in one list to help you avoid as many as possible. If nothing else, please try to make new mistakes.

1. **MISTAKE: MULTIPLY BIG NUMBERS BY 1 PERCENT.** Entrepreneurs love to take an enormous potential market (such as the Internet-security market), calculate that even a 1 percent market share will be huge and easy to attain, and then imagine the revenues they'll achieve.

    FIX: CALCULATE FROM THE BOTTOM UP. Do a bottom-up calculation instead. You'll see how hard it is to attain even a 1 percent market share when you start from zero. Once you ship, you'll learn that your first-year results are closer to zero dollars than even 1 percent of the huge number.

2. **MISTAKE: SCALE TOO FAST.** A consequence of multiplying a big number by 1 percent is concluding that you need to scale your infrastructure and head count for huge, inevitable, impending success. So you increase your burn rate, which uses up your capital, which eventually gets you fired.

> **FIX: EAT WHAT YOU KILL.** Take the risk of foregoing sales and jeopardizing your service reputation by not scaling until sales are in hand. I've never seen a company fail because it couldn't scale fast enough, and I've never seen a company ship on time. You may be the first, but the trend is not your friend.

"One of my life goals is that someday a teenage girl asks Jackie Chan if he's Guy Kawasaki."

---

3. **MISTAKE: FORM PARTNERSHIPS.** Entrepreneurs love to use the *P* word—"partnership"—especially when they can't use the *S* word—"sales." Unless a partnership enables you to alter your spreadsheet, it's bullshiitake. Most partnerships are a PR exercise and a waste of time.

> **FIX: FOCUS ON SALES.** Instead of spinning your wheels with partnerships, focus on sales. Tattoo this on your forearm: "Sales fix everything." If a picture is worth a thousand words, a sale is worth a thousand partnerships. The longest you can stall using the *P* word is six to twelve months. Then you'll hear the *F* word: "fired."

4. **MISTAKE: FOCUS ON FUND-RAISING.** Success is not raising money. Success is building a great company. Many entrepreneurs forget that fund-raising is a means to an end, not the end, so they spend weeks working on their pitch and business plan and getting in front of any investor with a heartbeat.

FIX: FOCUS ON PROTOTYPING. Building a prototype is the most important goal in the early days of your startup. A prototype enables you to get real-world feedback and, heaven forbid, sales. Bootstrap, borrow, and crowdfund what you need to survive, and pour your energy into building a product.

5. **MISTAKE: USE TOO MANY SLIDES.** When you do have to pitch, don't use fifty to sixty slides. I know that you know in principle that less is more, but you will be tempted to think you are the exception to this rule. You are not. If you need fifty slides to pitch your idea, your idea is flawed.

   FIX: OBEY THE 10/20/30 RULE. The optimal number of slides is ten. You should be able to give your presentation in twenty minutes. The ideal font size is thirty points. Even better, try to get away from slides and do a demo . . . which is another reason you need a prototype.

6. **MISTAKE: PROCEED SERIALLY.** Entrepreneurs try to do things in a serial manner: raise money, then hire people, then create a product, then close deals, then raise more money. They want to do one thing at a time and do it well. This is not how startups work.

   FIX: PROCEED IN PARALLEL. Life for entrepreneurs is a parallel existence. Get used to it, understand it, and live it. You need to do many things at once, and good enough is good enough. You don't have enough time to do things one at a time.

7. **MISTAKE: RETAIN MATHEMATICAL CONTROL.** Founders love to retain control, so they try to maximize valuation and sell as little stock as possible. They think that as long as they control at least 51 percent of the votes, they run the company.

   FIX: MAKE A BIGGER PIE. The way to make money is to increase the size of the pie, not to hold on to as much of the pie as possible. It's better to own .01 percent of Google than 51 percent of a piece of Mediocre Technology, Inc. And control is an illusion—the moment you take outside money, you are working for the investors.

8. **MISTAKE: USE PATENTS FOR DEFENSIBILITY.** Entrepreneurs read stories about how patent infringers lose multimillion-dollar lawsuits, and they think that this means patents can protect their intellectual property. This is like reading that a burglar was arrested and therefore you don't need to lock your door.

> **FIX: USE SUCCESS FOR DEFENSIBILITY.** Patent protection is a game for big companies with lots of lawyers and money. Does that sound like your startup? The only thing that makes a startup defensible is that it's growing, succeeding, and sucking the oxygen out of the market. You won't have the time or money to out-litigate anyone who's worth suing.

9. **MISTAKE: HIRE IN YOUR IMAGE.** Many entrepreneurs hire employees who match the rest of the company. Engineers hire engineers. MBAs hire MBAs. Men hire men. Fitting in is one thing, but this is going too far when everyone is young or male or techie or anything, really.

> **FIX: HIRE TO COMPLEMENT.** A startup needs a variety of skills, perspectives, and backgrounds to succeed. Rather than hiring mirror images, you should hire people who complement one another. The two most important complementary skills are making and selling, so cover these two bases right away.

10. **MISTAKE: BEFRIEND YOUR INVESTORS.** During the honeymoon period, which is the ninety-day period after your first missed ship date, you may have an insane desire to befriend your investors. This is because you and your investors are simpatico, and they

will never fire you because they invested in the startup because of you. Hello, Tooth Fairy. . . .

> **FIX: EXCEED EXPECTATIONS.** If you want intimate relationships, use Tinder or eHarmony on the weekends. Your job is to raise money from investors, use it wisely, and then return ten times more than they invested. It doesn't matter if you end up hating one another as long as you meet your deadlines and exceed sales projections.

If you'd like to see me in action, I've given a speech about this topic for the Haas School of Business that's <u>on YouTube</u>. I'm a funny guy—not Jackie Chan funny, but funny enough. And one of my life goals is that someday a teenage girl asks Jackie Chan if he's Guy Kawasaki.

Index

The greatest enemy of knowledge is not ignorance;
it is the illusion of knowledge.

—Daniel J. Boorstin

INDEX